D0467029

1866-1991

125th

ANNIVERSARY

IN SEARCH OF THE
AMERICAN WILDERNESS

HENRY HOLT AND COMPANY
NEW YORK

GRIZZLY YEARS

Doug Peacock

Library of Congress Cataloging-in-Publication Data
Peacock, Doug.
Grizzly years : in search of the American wilderness / Doug Peacock.
—1st ed.
p.   cm.
ISBN 0-8050-0448-3
1. Grizzly bear.   2. Peacock, Doug.   I. Title.
QL737.C27P366   1990
599.74'446—dc20   89–24672
                                                              CIP

Henry Holt books are available at special discounts
for bulk purchases for sales promotions, premiums,
fund-raising, or educational use. Special editions
or book excerpts can also be created to specification.
For details contact: Special Sales Director,
Henry Holt and Company, Inc., 115 West 18th Street,
New York, New York 10011.

Book Design by Claire M. Naylon

Printed in the United States of America
Recognizing the importance of preserving
the written word, Henry Holt and Company, Inc.,
by policy, prints all of its first editions
on acid-free paper. ∞
3   5   7   9   10   8   6   4

*The events of this book are true. A number
of place names have been changed to
protect the untrammeled.*

IN MEMORIAM
L. D.

CONTENTS

The big bear stopped thirty feet in front of me. I slowly worked my hand into my bag and gradually pulled out the Magnum. I peered down the gun barrel into the dull red eyes of the huge grizzly. He gnashed his jaws and lowered his ears. The hair on his hump stood up. We stared at each other for what might have been seconds but felt like hours. I knew once again that I was not going to pull the trigger. My shooting days were over. I lowered the pistol. The giant bear flicked his ears and looked off to the side. I took a step backward and turned my head toward the trees. I felt something pass between us. The grizzly slowly turned away from me with grace and dignity and swung into the timber at the end of the meadow. I caught myself breathing heavily again, the flush of blood hot on my face. I felt my life had been touched by enormous power and mystery.

I did not know that the force of that encounter would shape my life for decades to come. Tracking griz would become full-time work for six months of many years, and it lingers yet at the heart of any annual story I tell of my life. I have never questioned the route this journey took: it seems a single trip, the sole option, driven by that same potency that drew me into grizzly country in the beginning.

GRIZZLY
YEARS

1

THE
BIG SNOW

NOVEMBER (1980s)

It was mid-November and a winter storm was coming to the mountains of northwest Wyoming. The wind was gentle, chinooklike, swaying the bare branches of an aspen grove against a gray sky. The trees' leaves, already drawn to the forest floor by the October frosts of the brief Rocky Mountain autumn, lay silent under crusted drifts of November snow. I struggled carrying a bulky rucksack up the open slope toward groves of mixed fir, spruce, and pine. I had a 9,000-foot ridge to climb, another valley to drop into and cross, then a steep north-facing mountainside to crawl up until I reached the 9,200-foot contour.

At that elevation, under the roots of a large, lightning-struck whitebark pine, was a five-foot-long tunnel dug into the side of the forty-degree mountain slope. The hole had been dug by a young grizzly bear. I knew because I had watched him dig it. He had started on the twentieth of September, removing hundreds of pounds of gravelly loam. He planned on sleeping out the winter in there. When he wasn't working on his den, he fed on the whitebark pine nut caches of red squirrels. In October he left the area. If he had not yet returned, this storm would, I thought, bring him back.

The upland country of the Yellowstone Plateau was open, pleasant country. I stepped across a tiny creek and saw, hidden behind a boulder, a layer of golden aspen leaves placered against the bottom of a dark pool. The tops of yellow grasses were still exposed in the meadows; under the shadows of the conifers, low banks of windblown snow awaited winter. The breeze drifted north of me on the lee side of the ridge, while a high wind ran over the rocky spine above.

Through my binoculars, far below me, a bull moose stood motionless in the bushy willow bottomland. The elk and a small herd of mountain sheep on the distant slope had bedded. My blood felt sluggish too. The barometric lows preceding major storms heralded lethargic times: the ungulates brushed up, the fish did not bite, and the grizzlies hightailed it to denning sites, where they moped around and waited for the big snow. Grizzlies could sense winter storms days in advance. My three-year-old bear was probably putting the finishing touches on his den just then, raking it out one last time before adding bedding—grass, moss, or boughs of young firs. He would then withdraw to his porch, a dish-shaped depression in the loam just in front of the three-foot-wide opening to the tunnel, and lie like a sleepy puppy watching the darkening skies for the whiteness that would seal him within his mountain.

I walked uphill under the canopy of mature whitebark pines. Under a large tree, next to the trunk where the snow had melted, was a small pile of pinecones. A bear, probably a grizzly, had dug up a number of squirrel caches and raked out the seeds with his claws. Red squirrels were the middlemen; bears did not harvest the cones directly but were dependent on the arboreal rodents. Even in years when there were lots of pine nuts, if the squirrel population was down, the bears would not get many nuts. These pine nuts were a major source of food for Yellowstone's grizzlies. The three-year-old grizzly had been feeding on mast when I had stumbled across him digging his den six weeks earlier.

I climbed over a string of mossy ledges and topped out the ridge. Before me, to the south, lay the gentle, rolling up-country of the Snowy Range: willow bottoms, sagebrush meadows, and undulating grassy hillsides patched with groves of aspen and stands of pine and fir. The den site of the three-year-old bear lay four miles away, up on the steep side of the next low mountain. I could have gotten there by dark if I had pushed. But I had not come out here to hurry. Instead, I would hole up for the night and wait for the snow to begin falling.

Grizzlies at their denning sites are extremely shy; if they are disturbed they may abandon the area altogether and be forced to dig another den somewhere else. Once the first major storm of the fall begins, undisturbed bears become sluggish and are much less likely to be bothered by my presence. But I didn't plan on letting this little grizzly know I was around.

The high wind had died. The air felt heavy, still warm under its blanket of monotonous blue-gray sky. The snowy front pushed before it a low-pressure trough of languid creatures, a chorus of yawns. I stumbled down the mountain slope, through the dead grasses and winter trees, toward a narrow creek that meandered through willow thickets. By the time I reached the valley, just at dark, the wind had stopped altogether. The air was still and snow had begun to fall. Nothing moved except the large white flakes and the small creek, whose dark currents gathered the silent snow.

I followed the tiny creek up into the trees where the waters pooled behind the roots of a giant spruce. An eerie calm settled in over the mountains as I located a spot to sit against the huge spruce. I gathered wood from a nearby whitebark and kindled it with dry twigs off the lee side of a smaller spruce. I dug a down parka and wool stocking cap out of my backpack and prepared for a long night of staring into the fire. The temperature was dropping. The snow would be dry, and the spruce boughs would keep most of it off me. I carried no tent or sleeping bag this trip. I planned on sitting up all night tending the fire.

I spread out a small groundcloth—raingear, actually—dug into the bottom of the pack, and pulled out a foot-long oblong bundle wrapped in a spare wool sweater. I unwrapped a skull and placed it next to me facing the fire, balancing the upper jaw carefully upon the mandible. It was the skull of an adult grizzly, a female. I had come by it in the White Swan Saloon in the town north of here. A local horn hunter, a friend of mine, had bought it for me from a rancher who had poached the bear three months earlier on a grazing allotment in the national forest a few miles from the border of Yellowstone National Park. The same sheepherder had also shot at, but missed, another grizzly who was hanging around the female. That much was common knowledge. What was not known was that the two bears were related, and the previous winter they had denned together up the hill a mile south of my fire.

I didn't know what to do with the skull at first. I just did not want the sheepherder to have it. He had already made enough money selling the bear's paws and gallbladder. The sow* grizzly had never killed any sheep that I knew about, though that didn't mean she would not have started at any time. At the time she was killed, the female grizzly was almost eight, fairly old by Yellowstone standards. She had successfully mated once, probably when she was four and a half. The following winter she had given birth to a single cub—at least there had been only one cub with her the next spring, when I had gotten to know her. She had emerged from the den in late April, dropped down to the valley I had crossed an hour earlier, and fed on an elk carcass. I had backtracked her to her winter denning site. She and her cub had made a highly distinctive family: the sow's fur had a slight golden hue with a darker stripe running down her back. The cub had been nearly black with a silver collar extending into a light-colored chest yoke, which had faded sometime during his second year. They had been back on these slopes feeding on pine nuts the same fall, and I found their den the following spring. Altogether I had found five dens on this same hillside within a few hundred yards of one another. All but the first could have been dug by the same female.

I consider the mountainside a special place, a place with power, as I do certain other valleys and basins there and up in northern Montana where grizzlies still roam. I return to these places year after year, to keep track of the bears and to log my life. The bears provided a calendar for me when I got back from Vietnam, when one year would fade into the next and I would lose great hunks of time to memory with no events or people to recall their passing. I had trouble with a world whose idea of vitality was anything other than the naked authenticity of living or dying. The

---

*I have retained the normal usage of "boar" and "sow" for male and female adult bears. A few experts object to this usage because of the association with domestic pigs. I agree with the spirit of this objection, but the term "boar" has been traced to the same origin as "bear" and its Icelandic cognate means "man."

world paled, as did all that my life had been before, and I found myself estranged from my own time. Wild places and grizzly bears solved this problem.

When I ran into the goldish mother bear and her dark cub on this mountainside I was more than a decade away from the war zone, and my seasonal migration to grizzly country had become a pattern. I had come to this place in the spring to greet the grizzlies as they emerged from their winter sleep and again late in the fall to see them into their dens. Since the female always denned in the same small area, it was easy. What I hadn't known was whether the young grizzly would return to den there after his mother was killed, or whether he knew how or where to dig a winter den. On September twentieth I had found my answer. Besides what he learned from his mother, this young grizzly had his own instincts.

The cub was now back on the family estate. I wondered what he would have done if the sow had still been alive—move off to another mountain? I was curious about these things, although I had come here this time for other reasons. I poked another stick into the flickering fire.

"Payback was a motherfucker," the grunts in Vietnam used to say. Meaning something about the difficulty of getting what you deserve—a sort of Stone Age notion of justice. Over there, believing nonsense in defiance of the blatant absence of any just distribution of earthly rewards and punishments helped you get through the night. After Vietnam, I caught myself saluting birds and tipping my watch cap to sunsets. I talked a lot when no one was around, especially to bears.

I tied a woolen scarf around my neck and held the skull up to the flames, staring beyond it where huge snowflakes glistened in the reflected light of the fire. Strings of connective tissue clung to the poorly scraped bone. The sheepherder had done a lousy job. I heard he had buried the grizzly's hide. He only dug up the skull 'cause someone offered a bundle of money. I should have gone back and blown a dozen of his stinking, bleating sheep into woolly heaven.

I felt the corrugated bark of the spruce tree pressing against my shoulders and looked back at the bear skull. "I wonder what you know, bear," I said to no one. Where had she spent her summers? Had she ever consorted with the great Bitter Creek Griz or fished the cutthroat spawning streams? I had never seen her play with her cub, although she had been a very protective mother. She had probably been pregnant when she was killed, having mated just subsequent to weaning her cub. Even in death, she was better off here on the mountain than mounted on some asshole's wall.

I set the skull down and threw a large deadfall on the coals. The log popped and sputtered, showering sparks that rose into the lower boughs of the spruce. I pulled my coat tighter around my shoulders, glad for the dead calm, which felt almost warm even though the night temperature had plunged far below freezing. I had a sense of urgency, even danger—the need to finish my business as soon as possible and get out. This was the storm that would begin winter. November blizzards had been known to dump over a foot of snow a day for several days. By the next evening, walking out would be difficult. All the roads on the plateau would be closed. In three days it would be all I could do to slide my pickup across the passes behind the snowplow. An accident or miscalculation could mean freezing, or wintering up here. But the predicament was familiar. Danger was part of what attracted me to grizzlies in the first place—danger married to great beauty.

My seasonal calendar was often tied to these blizzards: they told me when to leave the mountains. Big snows make winter. They send the grizzlies into their dens. At least, they do on this mountainside. Grizzlies do not all den at the same time; it all depends on sex, altitude, and how far south they live. For instance, the last Mexican grizzly in the Sierra Madre may not den at all if the winter is mild. South of Canada, females who are pregnant or living with young at higher elevations den first.

I nodded off briefly, leaning my head against the gnarled trunk of the spruce, thinking I could feel the weight of the snow piling up on it. I wrapped up the skull and packed it away, watching the big flakes filter through the branches like feathers of snow geese. Sitting in a major mountain storm in search of what some people regard as the fiercest animal on the continent instills a certain humility, an attitude that pries open in me a surprising receptiveness. My friend Gage, who was here with me when I stumbled on the first den on the mountainside, could find humility before nature in his backyard. I cannot: I need to confront several large, fierce animals who sometimes make meat of man to help recall the total concentration of the hunter. Then the old rusty senses, dulled by urban excesses, spring back to life, probing the shadows for shapes, sounds, and smells. Sometimes I am graced by a new insight into myself, a new combination of thoughts, a metaphor, that knocks on the door of mystery.

The fire's glow cast a halo of light in the falling snow, and I conjured an aura of reverence surrounding my mission.

◀ Vietnam Notebook ▶

We walked point for the 101st Airborne during the summer of 1967. The operation centered on the country just north of the village of Ba An on the Song Tra Na in Quang Ngai Province. I was the only American green beret with our point platoon of mixed Vietnamese and Montagnard troops out of our A-camp at Bato. Behind us were three platoons of U.S. paratroopers.

The operation was not going well. Each unit had taken casualties. We had lost our platoon leader the night before. He caught a carbine round through his head just under and behind his eyes, which paralyzed his respiratory system. While I was keeping him alive by giving him mouth-to-mouth, the Americans mistakenly called in gunships on our position. I was the only one in the point platoon who spoke English, and by the time I could call off the air strike we had two more wounded. The platoon leader died while I was screaming fucking stop on the radio.

The next morning we led out into the rice paddies, walking along the low dikes. There were half a dozen water buffalo near the far side but no people except one nine- or ten-year-old boy in shorts. The boy might have been tending the buffalo. We walked across the paddy without incident. The airborne troops followed close behind.

The boy stood in the rice paddy thirty meters away watching me and the twenty irregulars as we walked by. When the boy saw the Americans he ran. Why he decided to run I would never know, but when he did the Americans opened up on him, first one or two, then an entire platoon, tearing chunks off his small body with M-16 rounds. My people watched, silent and grim-faced.

' ' '

The truth was that any last vestige of religion had been choked out of me during the last two months in Vietnam by scenes of dead children. To this day, I cannot bear the image of a single dead child. In the years that followed, I had found it easier to talk to bears than priests. I had no talent for reentering society. Others of my generation marched and expanded their consciousness; I retreated to the woods and pushed my mind toward sleep with cheap wine.

By daylight I was cold and cramped, anxious to start moving up the hill. Five inches of fresh snow covered everything except the ground under the thickest trees. The air was still, no wind yet. Once it begins to blow, beware. This easy late-season stroll through the woods could quickly grow dangerous and I would have to get out fast.

The dry snow fell softly though harder now from the gray sky. I shuffled up through the pines in the morning gloom. Visibility was a couple hundred feet and decreasing. I figured the den lay half a mile directly upslope, and, although I thought I knew exactly how to approach it, it was possible to get turned around in this increasingly white landscape where every view looked the same. I pulled the thick wool cap down over my forehead to shield my eyes from the snowy glare, which even in low light could cause snow blindness.

At the base of a whitebark I saw the remains of a squirrel's nut cache scattered onto the fresh snow. I stepped over to the debris: ear-shaped flakes of whitebark cones, pieces of cones, and whole pinecones scattered over the snowdrifts. A frozen bear scat lay near the pinecone midden in the snowless crescent on the lee side of a tree. I poked at it with a stick, finding a couple of undigested red berries from a mountain ash tree. This sort of scat is common just before grizzlies den up, when they empty out their digestive tracts for the long sleep. The ash berries may act as a purgative, although I wondered where they came from, since I had not seen any *Sorbus* bushes for days.

The grizzly's carnivore gut, although elongated for a carnivore, is not made for digesting cellulose or the kinds of vegetable foods available in winter. Neither can he count on his skills as an opportunistic predator to keep him in food. So he must den up and hibernate. Some early springs I find the first scat a grizzly has dropped after emerging from the den: a cemented plug of hair. Bears don't eat, defecate, or urinate during their winter sleep. They slowly metabolize their own body fat. Their bodily functions slow, although bears may wake if disturbed or warmed by an unusually mild winter day. The sleep of bears is not the true hibernation of rodents, but it neatly solves the problem of winter survival.

The vertical fall of snow from invisible skies formed a gentle arc with the rising wind that blew in my face. About a foot of fluff had accumulated in the open and it continued to fall. The wind picked up and gusts blew bursts of powder snow off the tops of the pines.

I recognized a stark, dead fir with a double-pronged branching top. The den should be just uphill, across a rocky gully, maybe two hundred feet away. I stopped short to make sure my scent was not drifting in the direction of the den site. No problem, the wind was still in my face. I moved silently in the muffling snowfall directly downwind from the place where I thought the den was. I stood motionless for several minutes, sniffing the air. I could make out the faint but distinctive odor of the young grizzly. Until that moment I had not been certain I could relocate the spot or that the bear had not moved to another den.

Clark's nutcrackers cackled harshly just ahead, the first birdcalls all day. They were scolding, probably at the young bear, who may have lifted his head; the grizzly must have been moving. I waited for the jabbering to stop, then quietly crept uphill. I reached the trunk of a large whitebark pine and glimpsed a patch of bare dirt and stomped snow. I froze and slowly pulled my field glasses from under my outer sweater. A hundred feet up, I could see two brown ears protruding over a bench of loamy talus: the grizzly was asleep on the porch just outside his den. The bear raised his head and peered into the falling snow. His eyes closed; he yawned and dropped his muzzle again.

The last time I had seen this grizzly so lethargic was in the summer of his first year, when he and his mother had escaped the clouds of summer insects by bedding out the afternoon on a wedge of high snowfield. The cub had tired himself out by prancing up and down the angle of snow, suddenly folding his legs beneath him and rolling down to the icy edge of the snow patch, where he tried to bite off chunks without success. Finally he had turned inward in his frustration and bitten his rear paw. He had done this for a full third of an hour, once biting himself so hard he had bellowed in pain. His mother had watched him sympathetically and leaned back into the snow on her hind feet, offering her paps. The strange, rhythmic puttering sounds of nursing filled the air.

I thought about the days spent in the company of these two grizzlies, the one stretched out on the porch of his winter home, the other encapsulated in memory, her skull wrapped up in my pack. I needed to put this small part of the universe back in order.

The young grizzly stirred. He rose, shook off the snow, and turned, disappearing into his den. He may have known I was about but was too sluggish to do anything other than retreat within the mountain now. The season was very late. I crawled on up the slope using the trees as cover until I reached a tree across the gully almost opposite the den. I could clearly see the pile of excavated gravel and loam. In the crotch of the tree, at eye level, a crude scaffold of willow was tied to the branches. The platform faced eastward across the open ground in front of the den.

It was a child's idea. My little daughter had explained that bringing the skull back here would make a new bear.

The snow was blowing so hard I could barely make out the bear's porch forty feet away. I dug into my pack; my anger evaporated and all my attention focused on the present. Moving quickly, I set the skull on the framework of woven willow facing the den. I slipped a small bear paw of silver and turquoise off my neck and draped it over the skull; your fur against the cold, bear. When my skull lies with yours will you sing for me? The long sleep heals. We will find new life in the spring.

Only the black eye of the den entrance peered into the face of the blizzard. I shook the snow off my wool cap and shouldered my pack. I turned and half ran back down the slope, the soft snow tugging at the tops of my gaiters. In fifteen minutes I hit the valley bottom. The meadow was a whiteout. I turned east and walked with the storm as the wind slapped at my back. I checked my compass: a piece of cake. The big snow would lead me out.

2

BACK TO THE
SOUTHWEST

(LATE 1960s)

The road back had not always been as easy as walking out
with the snow. In March of 1968 I found it hard to come back,
difficult to return to the hills and canyons I had known as
home. Less than forty-eight hours after leaving the jungles of
Southeast Asia, I was standing outside a small airport in Michigan
staring across the cornfields where I spent my childhood hunting
arrowheads and pheasants.

All the worldly possessions that tied me to Vietnam were
stashed in my duffel. I alarmed my mother by tossing the military
paperwork into the garbage, then bent down and rescued my
journal from the wastepaper basket. I tried to crack it open but the
pages were mildewed together. Everything else was crammed
back into the duffel bag, which I drove downtown and deposited
in a Goodwill dumpster.

I was not able to talk to anyone. I felt like a voyeur, watching
myself from the outside; I sat, numb and speechless, all the time
knowing how hard my going to Vietnam was on my family. It had
almost killed my dad. My sister never expected me to come back.
My letters from the war zone caused my mom to support the
antiwar movement. These were the people who loved me most in
the world, and I could not talk to them.

✓ ✓ ✓

When I was training to become a green beret medic, I had a small road map of Wyoming and Montana I always carried with me. I kept it hidden in the notebook in which I was supposed to keep my military notes. I stared at it, especially at the blank spaces, for several hours of every day for over a year as I pulled duty on different military bases scattered over the deep South, where the soil was always the color of clotted blood.

With this map, I would travel in my mind over the ridges and peaks into hidden basins and high cirques of the Wind River Range and the Yellowstone Plateau, or explore the emptiness of the Bob Marshall Wilderness up north.

In those days the image of a single wild place—a great canyon of the Southwest, a cascading mountain stream, or a high ridge of tundra dropping off steeply into a hidden alpine basin—could bring on a bottomless homesickness.

In November of 1966 my orders for Vietnam arrived at Fort Bragg. I packed up the deeply creased map of the northern Rockies and made the ten-thousand-mile trip west to Nha Trang, headquarters of the 5th Special Forces, where I stayed a week or two until a slot on an A-team opened up. The A-team was at Thuong Duc up in I-Core. The senior medical sergeant at Thuong Duc had been on patrol with another green beret and a couple dozen CIDGs (Civilian Irregular Defense Groups). The two Americans were standing by the entrance to a bombed-out village when someone command-detonated a mine, which caused the hand grenades hanging from their web gear to explode, traumatically amputating adjacent limbs. Both died before serious help arrived.

I was the replacement.

The tattered map went with me to Thuong Duc. A month later I had it spread out on the table of the team house, poring over the wrinkles with a penlight. It was after chow, toward 2000 hours, and getting dark. Six U.S. green berets, a Vietnamese interpreter, and a Chinese Nung were sitting around the two tables, drinking beer and playing poker.

In my mind I was flying over the map again, over the huge

meadow complexes north of Yellowstone Lake. The map showed one creek draining from the north, and I imagined a narrow grassy defile through dense lodgepole thickets with tiny hot springs steaming away.

An explosion rocked the tin-roofed, half-sandbagged house. Gravel and debris rang off the roof and cut through the screen wire. Everybody hit the floor, then ran crouching out the door and through the trenches to defensive positions.

The mortar attack went on for less than five minutes, although we returned fire with mortars and 50-caliber machine guns for much longer. That's all there was to it. Nobody seemed to be hit, and we never even knew where the 82mm mortars were being fired from. I was new and could not make any sense out of the attack, which was too early in the night and too weak to constitute a serious probe.

Then the casualties from the adjacent civilian resettlement village started to trickle up to the camp. The settlement, which had taken the brunt of the attack, had been the target because there would still be a lot of people out on the street and kids playing.

I was waiting in the medical bunker when the casualties arrived. There was one local RF/PF soldier; the rest of the wounded were civilians, sixteen altogether. Most were children under twelve. The American medic, who was my new boss, Art, was sorting the wounded into different areas around the small underground bunker. The Vietnamese special forces medic was getting IVs started on a group of four children who looked to be in bad shape. I moved in beside him. He was working over a five-year-old boy with a broken shoulder who was in shock. I had first thought the Vietnamese medic a worthless shit, but then he reached over and helped me find an open vein on the little boy. All the wounds were the nasty kind caused by large hunks of shrapnel. This was my first experience with mass casualties in Vietnam away from any hospital facilities.

We started IVs on everyone except a woman and a small girl. They had head wounds and the woman was unconscious. Next to them, a single military stretcher held two small lumps under a bloodstained sheet. Art helped me make a wire-mesh splint for the boy's crushed shoulder blade. The kid's collarbone was also busted, so we elevated his little arm with a sling, then bandaged his upper arm to his chest. Art called the kid "ti ti," and the boy seemed to be responding well to the half-dose of morphine we had given him.

We sat the kid on the floor leaning against the wall and went on to the others. I stepped over to the girl with the head wound but Art called me back.

"Best just leave them there," he said. "We ain't going to save them all and those are the ones who aren't going to make it anyway."

I moved on and saw the boy with the mangled shoulder blade slumped against the wall. Art was already there.

"Shit, look what we missed," he said as he brushed the sticky, blood-clotted black hair out of the way, revealing a quarter-sized hole into the kid's brain.

I reached in for a pulse. Art stopped me: "Forget it. He's already gone."

By 2400 hours the marine helicopter had taken the seriously wounded to Da Nang. The dead had been carried back down the hill. I sat alone in the team house. The others were trying to get some sleep in case the Vietcong hit us again before morning.

I poured myself half a milk glass of bourbon and spread out the beat-up road map in front of me. I looked at Wyoming and found the drainage on the Yellowstone Plateau that I had been following before the attack. The smell of blood clung to my clothes. I gagged on the warm whiskey and watered it down with a Coke. It was hard getting back into the Yellowstone country. I sipped and peered into the map, waiting to be transported like when you sometimes stare at paired stereographic photographs until the third dimension suddenly springs out at you and mountains shoot up and canyons drop down.

Finally, just as I finished the milk glass of whiskey-Coke, I managed to ease myself back into the landscape again. I smelled the sage and could see around the corner of the timber into the next meadow. A warmth spread down my body as the whiskey did its

work. I sat back and looked out at the dark sky. At Thuong Duc I
knew I would be looking at something more than homesickness. I
had a year left to go in Vietnam. I would be needing the map.

                          ′ ′ ′

I bought a jeep, the only kind of vehicle I had ever owned, packed
up my gear, and headed west. I did not have much of a plan. I just
wanted to go somewhere in the Rocky Mountains where it was not
winter and see if I could get a handle on what had happened to me
during the previous two years. Since the mountains were still
buried in snow in late March, I aimed south, toward the big
canyons and desert playas of Arizona. It would be somewhere to
begin trying to get back into the country.

Something was wrong. On the outside I was calm, even
passive, but there was something frenzied on the inside. I drove
nonstop for two days at exactly forty-seven miles per hour, driving
with a head full of leftover combat-issue dextroamphetamine,
partially counteracted by a steady trickle of six-packs. Finally I
found myself asleep at the wheel in the middle of Kansas. I checked
into a run-down motel, not wanting to camp among crop-covered
fields, and jumped into a hot shower. Coming out, I flipped on the
tube to the evening news. There was the war I had just left, blaring
out over the TV, the entire catastrophe before my eyes in black and
white. Suddenly a close-up of a snow goose appeared on the
screen. "There are no easy answers." The camera panned the
swamp, revealing an oil refinery in the distance. ". . . Can oil and
wildlife mix?" Something snapped. I buried my fist in the face of
the smiling mustached man in the hard hat.

The next morning I bandaged my hand, paid for the television
set, and climbed back into the jeep. I had what to me was a lot
of money, blood money. Enough to keep me going for years. I
drove on.

The plains gave way to foothills in Colorado and the Front
Range rose out of the western horizon. Endless fields were replaced by piñon and juniper scrubland. A snowcapped volcanic
peak loomed to the south as I entered a broad, low pass.

The country was all familiar then as I reached the bottom of the San Luis Valley, climbed up through the Uncompahgre toward the San Juans and the great mesas of the Colorado Plateau beyond—all places I had lived. This was the land I had waited three years to wrap around me like a blanket.

It was dark when I dropped down from Four Corners toward Shiprock. I had a feeling I wouldn't find everything as I had left it, a feeling intensified by how badly I wanted to. I was, as always, armed to the teeth with a .22 Magnum derringer of Saturday night manufacture, .357 and .44 Magnum Ruger single-action handguns, plus a bolt-action 30.06 rifle and 12-gauge Ithaca Lefever double-barreled shotgun. I also had a complement of more primitive weapons next to my M-5 medical pack complete with human albumin and a wide range of injectable emergency drugs. The first thing I did was go cold turkey on the booze and amphetamines. I did not want trouble; not then, anyway.

An April storm forced me to drop south into Tucson. Urban sprawl development covered the valley and spilled over into the foothills like a giant cowpie from the sky; the city was going through a growth spurt, and the desert that had been my home was being steadily scraped away by D-7 bulldozers. I decided to push on. I needed something strong enough to pull me outside myself, a good dose of wild country maybe. The Navajo or the Wind rivers might do it.

The first place I tried was a miniature Grand Canyon located on the way to Indian country. It was a place I had found years ago while trout fishing, and I saw the biggest black bear I had ever seen there. This canyon, West Horse Camp, was where I had gone whenever I needed a wild yet gentle desert retreat.

I pulled the jeep off the highway and headed north on a local Forest Service road. Three miles up, a faint track led off to the east below a fallen rim of red sandstone and yellow volcanic rock. I jammed the transfer case into compound low and inched and jerked up the steep, rough road. It leveled off above the head of a secondary canyon feeding the distant purple haze of Horse Camp.

I drove the jeep off the main trail onto faint tracks made by cattlemen. Driving cross-country for the last hundred yards, I parked it in a dense clump of juniper where it would be out of sight. I filled my canteens from the five-gallon jug I carried in the jeep, packed my backpack, and stepped off, down over low cliffs of columnar basalt where ancient Anasazi, the prehistoric ancestors of the Pueblo Indians, had pecked the dark patina to produce stippled figures of deer, antelope, and sheep.

I stopped for a moment to admire the petroglyphs. The sheep and antelope were no longer there, having given way to what the Indians called "slow elk"—the domestic cow. The grizzly bear, who was also here before the turn of the century, had gone the same way, shot out by sodbusters making room for their dim-witted beasts. With overgrazing, the succulent grasses, which had made the bear and other animals fat, had disappeared.

The Anasazi, too, had misused their home ranges, killing off the game and using up the firewood. Their descendants, the Hopis and other Pueblo tribes, said the Anasazi were blown away by the Wind for abusing the Earth: they had disappeared suddenly toward the end of the thirteenth century, during a period of great droughts. All that remained of their culture were these lovely rock figures and lonely stone dwellings.

I picked up an old cow trail near the bottom of the side drainage off the main canyon and followed it down. Far below, the soft spring green of cottonwoods and sycamores traced the bottom of West Horse Camp Creek.

This hike was my first since leaving Vietnam. I had grown up in the jack pine and lake country of northern Michigan. My dad was the only one of eight brothers who had not gone to World War II, because he was the chief chemist in a sugar plant, a vital industry then. His favorite brother gave my father his Boy Scout troop to look after while he was gone. My uncle never came back. My father quit his job and went into professional Boy Scouting when I was five, too young to take part in organized scout activities. Instead, I was unleashed to run alone through the woods, exploring rivers and swamps, fishing for bass or catching turtles. My solitary expeditions into the woods became the focus of my early life. Later, the same instincts led me to the American West, all the way from the Arctic Ocean to central Mexico, but especially the Rocky Mountain section of the Cordillera.

I dropped through layer after layer of volcanic breccias inter-bedded with continental sandstone. I vaguely remembered that, before Vietnam, I had spent three months in the mountains of Colorado preparing a survey for a graduate degree in geology, a profession to which I was attracted because I had liked trout fishing and mountain climbing but had abandoned when I learned that a successful career in geology largely depended on joining forces with the oil and mining industries, whose rape of wild country repelled me.

I reached the bench, the narrow flat running parallel to the creek bed, above the main chasm of the inner canyon by late afternoon. I contoured along it upstream, heading for my old campsite. The terrace was cut by a steep gully. Just at the bottom I stopped above a dark tank of rainwater caught in a rock basin to examine a mark in the sand. There at my feet was the pug mark of an adult mountain lion. Remembering a tiger track in Vietnam, my heart raced at the thought of the big cougar.

The shadows had fallen. I found the last level spot of ground under a giant piñon pine just where the bench pinched out against a cliff. Stashing my pack, I grabbed my canteens and started picking my way down an ancient game trail to the inner gorge of West Horse Camp. There was a big pool below a slick of rapids between red sandstone banks. There would be trout in the tail of the rapids. Tomorrow I would try to catch some. But not tonight. It was already too late, and some dark association had been triggered. Tonight I would just fill my canteens and get out.

I started back up the game trail, forcing myself not to look back. The hair on my neck bristled. I resisted the urge to run, making myself climb steadily up the path. I gathered up some piñon twigs, grabbed a handful of dead grass, and kindled a small blaze. I added live juniper boughs, and the sweet, pungent aroma rose all around me. The Indians had used smoke and sweat lodges in cleansing rituals. How many smokes and sweats would it take to wash out the contamination of the past eighteen months?

The western sky darkened and I made out the faint glow of the evening star. Gradually other stars joined Venus and a cool breeze began to blow down canyon. I had not seen a sky alive with stars like this in three years. I crawled inside my sleeping bag and watched the constellations unfurl, checking the celestial clock as the Big Bear, Ursa Major, whirled counterclockwise around Po-

laris. Hercules rose into the northeastern sky and started kicking
ass on the Stymphalian birds—Lyra, Cygnus, and Aquila—one of
his dozen great labors. Gemini descended into the canyon and
Scorpio popped out over a ridge. I dropped off.

I woke with a start: somewhere in the Central Highlands it
was night under a jungle canopy. I was on a high narrow ridge. I
was sleeping in my hammock as I did during combat operations.
Suddenly the place exploded; they were blasting away at me from
ten feet off in the dark. In my dream, I must have fallen asleep,
allowing the Vietcong to sneak up. I rolled out of the hammock
and crawled toward the edge of the ridge. They knew I was there.
They started looking for me with flashlights, firing blindly into
the brush. I began to crawl off the top of the ridge. One burst
caught me in the ankle. I was afraid I'd cry out in pain. I had five
Syrettes of morphine. I took out one and plunged the needle into
my thigh. I was still afraid I might scream involuntarily, so I shot
up a second. I started climbing almost vertically down through the
vines and underbrush. I moved silently, slowly. The opiate turned
the vines I was hanging on to into writhing bamboo vipers. I was
climbing through a jungle of living serpents.

The next morning I waited for the sun to creep up over the
rimrock before I stirred from my bag. Today I would go back
down to the inner gorge and do some fishing. I climbed down to
the dark pool. It did not seem so ominous now.

I took the small pack rod out of the case, assembled the pieces,
and tied on a black woolly worm—knowing these were stone
fly waters. I walked upstream until I reached the foot of the small
waterfall. Below it a slick of bubbles disappeared into deeper
waters. I stripped out line, then roll-cast into the head of the
bubbles. As the fly drifted into the edge of the deeper water I
caught a flash of silver and struck at the fish, feeling the throb and
tug of a ten-inch rainbow pulling in the current. I played the trout
for a couple of moments, then flipped it back over my head onto
the bank.

A gentle breeze stirred the new green leaves of cottonwood

and sycamore, pushing back the thin cloud of tiny gnats buzzing around my head. I immediately whacked the fish on the back of the neck and cleaned it, examining its stomach for hints of flies to fish with. Giant stone fly nymphs—inch-and-a-half-long black bugs—*Plecoptera california*. I wrapped the trout in ferns and stuffed it in a small garbage bag.

Hopping from boulder to boulder, I hiked upstream. By midday I had caught four trout and was anxious to get out of the bottom of the canyon. Even in broad daylight, when there was nothing to confront, it was too dim for my taste. I topped off my canteens and climbed back up to the sunlit bench.

On my last trip in there before Vietnam, I had climbed high up the slope opposite me, glassed the rim country, and spotted what might have been a cliff dwelling high up on the two-thousand-foot slope just below an overhang of the rimrock. I had not had time then to scramble up the talus and have a look. I had thought of exploring the ruins a hundred times during the past eighteen months.

The climb up the treacherous scree took most of the afternoon. Once I almost walked over a sunning rattlesnake, and three times I stepped on pickup-sized rocks that started to roll. It was a little past midafternoon when I scrambled up the last slope and topped out under the great rim of windblown sandstone. I saw timbers sticking out of the rock and could make out the faint pattern of stone masonry across the face of the cliff. I stepped up under the rim and the entire front of a three-story Anasazi cliff dwelling opened up.

Large shards of broken pottery painted in red and brown polychrome lay underfoot. A few bones, unmistakably human, were mixed in with the pottery in the midden spilling down from the structure. A doorway opened into the main room, which still retained its ceiling of woven bear grass and mud. The timbers of ponderosa pine looked as if they had been logged but thirty years earlier. I stepped through the low doorway. Basalt metates for grinding corn and other seeds lay on either side. Dried corncobs were scattered against the bedrock wall. Everything was perfectly preserved, as if the people had departed suddenly a few decades ago. On the rock wall were paintings of deer and sheep in red ocher. Alongside one of the paintings was scrawled a name, "Ben Brown, 1929." So I wasn't the first.

It looked as if someone had been digging in the midden outside. Still, the fact that large, nearly whole pieces of pottery lay around meant not many white men had been there since the Wind blew the People away. I was careful not to disturb anything.

By the time I had skidded back down the scree the shadows had fallen into the canyon bottom. I quickly dropped into the inner gorge to refill my empty water bottles. I kindled a small fire on the bench and wove the four trout onto a three-pronged stick of green mesquite, which I held over the coals for a few minutes on each side. I took a small bottle of lemon juice and squeezed a few drops on each small rainbow. I wolfed down the trout and gathered more firewood in the rapidly fading light. I wanted to be prepared for a long night.

I dozed awhile, snapped awake out of another dream, then drifted off again. I threw cedar bark on the coals and fed the flames with mesquite twigs. I added a juniper log and sat up in my sleeping bag facing the blaze. The fire calmed the jitters, but I was shivering. I wished I had stuck in a flask of brandy for such emergencies.

The next morning, ten thousand miles from Asian vipers, I packed up my gear, filled my canteens, and climbed back down the bench, past the lion track, and up the winding game trail used by the cowboys. For all the space in this wild canyon, cattle had penetrated nearly every corner of it. Later this spring, after the snow had melted, I would wander up to the Wind Rivers of Wyoming and the Yellowstone Plateau, far from the tame hoofprints of slow elk.

The bright browns and yellows of the rock lichens reflected so intensely they seemed luminescent. In Alaska, caribou nibbled them off rocks as grizzlies and wolves watched from the tundra. I needed to encounter something—a spectacle on the magnitude of a sky blackened by a single flock of passenger pigeons flying over, or the sight of sixty million buffalo stomping through the High Plains; no chance for that. The best I could get might be a scene strong enough to pull me away from all that had been my world the past year and a half. I wanted some breathing room from that.

My canyon had not worked out. I had a friend up on the Indian reservation I wanted to look up.

3

INDIAN
COUNTRY

I went north and dropped down into the Painted Desert toward Indian country and the Colorado Plateau. I passed Gray Mountain, crossed the Little Colorado, and turned off east out of Tuba City. I had heard that Peabody Coal was going to strip-mine Black Mesa and ship the coal by rail to Page to fuel the new power plant there. The whole rim of the great canyons of the Colorado surrounded by power plants, the skies darkened, all to light southern California.

Off to the right a steel tower, the metal framing left behind by a drill rig, overlooked the upper end of a big canyon system. I decided to have a look. It was an old hole, drilled and capped sometime the year before. Enough equipment still lay around to indicate that someone was coming back. I picked up a wrench and fit the spanner around the hole cap and removed it. I wondered what they were looking for down there: oil shale, coal, or gas? Their endless greed drove them to probe the remotest corners of the last wild places. I dropped a piece of pipe down the hole. I got back no sound, only cool air whistling. I looked around the site and picked up anything that would fit into the hole, including a pile of used-up diamond drill bits. I dropped it in the hole: more wind whistling.

I recapped the hole. It should take them a while to drill

through all that junk. It was a token gesture; just so that the scumbags would know not everyone applauds.

I took the back way through the Navajo into Fort Defiance. My friend taught there at the Bureau of Indian Affairs school. I had left him my motorcycle in case I didn't make it back from Vietnam. He had given me, for luck, the brown chert arrowhead I carried in my medicine pouch throughout Vietnam. It protected me from enemy bullets. My friend had picked up this particular point on a gray winter afternoon on the banks of the Shiawassee River a dozen years earlier, when I was with him. He was my oldest buddy. If I couldn't talk to him I couldn't talk to anyone.

I pulled into his yard, walked up to the door, and knocked.

"Hello, Pfeif," I said.

He embraced me and I trembled. It was the closest I had come to anyone in years.

"Do you still have the spearpoint?" He grinned.

After his classes my friend and I got together. He introduced me to a young woman who also taught at the school, and told me they planned to marry in a few months. At that time marriage was still a big deal to us. We took a walk and he wanted to talk about it. But I could not; the words wouldn't come out. I was helplessly unresponsive though I tried hard not to be. If something wasn't a matter of life or death, I just wasn't there anymore.

I had already known something was wrong with me. Just two weeks after I had gotten back from Nam, Martin Luther King had been assassinated. I had known King slightly from my university days when I ran a speaker program and brought him in to speak. Although I had been associated with the beginnings of the New Left back then and my political leanings were known, I was still surprised at the phone threats and the glut of political hate mail I had received on Martin Luther King. That man had some real enemies. Six years later, I was not surprised when he was murdered. I knew they hated him and all he represented and now they had finally gotten him. In 1968, that was what I expected of the world.

This reaction bothered my friend. We had known each other for most of our lives and we shared gut feelings, registering similar emotional valences on matters of importance—until then at least.

———

I quietly passed the days until the snow melted in the higher mountains by exploring the canyons and mesas of the Navajo reservation. During the days I went into the hills with a hundred-twenty feet of climbing rope and rappeled into remote canyons. At the bottom I walked out, finding along the way evidence of the ancients: petroglyphs of deer and horned dancers and Kayenta black-on-white pottery.

I found a rare set of petroglyphs; it was one of only two examples of bear rock art I knew of among thousands of petroglyph panels in the Southwest. The bear was evidently part of a longer story told by stippled figures pecked into the dark patina of a slab of Navajo sandstone. The central bear figure was surrounded by representations of hunters throwing spears. Several stuck out of the bear's body, and below one wound, it looked as if pockmarks of blood flowed. More pockmarks in the stone covering the back and shoulders of the bear made me wonder if real spears had been thrust against the dark, blood-colored stone. Along the lower edge of the plaque were petroglyphs of bear paws next to ones of human hands. I knew from studies of cave art in Europe that paintings or petroglyphs of bears, uncommon in comparison to the number of representations of horses and buffalo, were seen as magical or symbolic. They placed the bear at the very beginnings of human spiritual life.

Friends of Pfeif's took off to Mexico for a long weekend and left me to look after their house, an agency dwelling several miles north of Fort Defiance surrounded by scrub forests and a few scattered hogans.

The second night that I was house-sitting, a spring storm blew in from the northwest. Six inches of wet snow fell on the juniper and sagebrush. About midnight, I was enjoying my solitude when I heard something stamping around outside in the snow and a knock came on the door. A young, slender Navajo, maybe thirty years old, was standing in the blowing snow, leaning on the doorway. He looked as if he had been drinking.

"Yahtahey," I muttered, pronouncing the only word I knew in Navajo: the traditional greeting.

"Yahtahey," he answered. He stared at me for a moment, then said something in Navajo. I gathered that he was looking for shelter from the storm. It is not uncommon for Navajo to freeze to death during the winter months, especially during a drinking spree.

I pushed open the door and motioned him inside by the wood-burning stove. My guest said something else to me in Navajo. I quickly explained that I did not know any Navajo. I had an open beer by my chair; the Navajo pointed at it by pursing and extending his lips toward the can. I offered him a beer. Every now and then my visitor would speak to me in his own tongue. I would nod and say a few words to indicate that I didn't know what the hell he was talking about. He spoke in longer sentences and finally began telling me what must have been a story. Every time I spoke to him in English he answered me in his Navajo. The next time the Indian addressed me in Navajo I answered him in Hre. He paused for a moment, then nodded and told me something in Navajo that took two minutes. I nodded back and went out for two more beers. When I returned I told the Indian a story in Montagnard. He listened attentively.

We talked on like this for two hours, drinking up all the beer. Outside the storm raged. I went into the bedroom and came back with two blankets. I stoked up the stove and we turned in.

The next morning we got up and I fixed Jimmy Begay a breakfast of bacon and eggs. Jimmy, who worked at the Greasewood trading post, spoke English just fine: he was only on a binge.

The days passed. The cottonwood leaves darkened toward a summer green and the last of the snow under the ponderosas had long since melted. I knew it was getting to be time to move on. I was too withdrawn to be much of a companion.

One night my new friend got hold of some peyote buttons, and I ate a fistful. I drove my jeep out to Blue Mesa and sat on the edge of the rimrock overlooking the valley. Images of war strangled out everything but side effects: nausea, insomnia, and unilateral muscular twitches. I sat on the lip of Blue Mesa for twelve hours, jerking uncontrollably, ready to puke, staring into space, unable to penetrate any benign secrets. Then I thought about the tiger.

* * *

The summer day began with the scolding of birds hidden in the jungle canopy, soon joined by the chatter of waking spider monkeys. It was July of 1967 and we were on a routine four-day patrol of the Nui Goi Rieng mountain country in Quang Ngai Province maybe eight kilometers southeast of Ba An, walking on a high, open ridge top along the crest of the dissected plateau separating the valley of the Song Hre from the coastal strip. Though it was still early morning, the day had already become hot and sticky. Far below, to the east, strings of thin fog lay over the narrow coastal plain stretching inland from the South China Sea. In every other direction were block fault mountains.

With me were the usual motley assortment of irregulars, a dozen Hre tribesmen and a handful of Vietnamese. The other American was a new lieutenant on his first combat patrol. The new *thieu uy* was watching my every move and letting me make all the decisions, which was about the best I could expect from green Special Forces officers who got moved around so much they seldom had their shit together.

Despite the rising heat, we were about as happy as we ever got on a combat patrol. Only the lieutenant did not know that we had picked this high ridge route because there was never any sign of enemy activity up there. In Nam we called enemy territory "Indian country." Everything below us as far as you could see was Indian country, but the ridge was no-man's-land. Unlike the Americans, the CIDGs did not rotate in twelve or thirteen months but were here for the duration. There was no point in looking for trouble. In the past six months, I had learned not to push it. We were just putting in our time.

On such days you noticed things you ordinarily overlooked. This was about as clear a day as you ever got in the highlands. I thought this had to be the most beautiful mountain country in all Vietnam. All around were timbered summits and impenetrable grassy slopes rising above the remnants of a deeply eroded plateau. To the west, from high on these slopes, you could see a half dozen thick ribbons of white water cascading down and disappearing into swift rivers.

We were strung out along a descending ridge. We had tall elephant grass on either side of us and could not see much below. Suddenly the point man, Dinh Hun, raised his arm and signaled us to stop. Hun squatted low with his weapon ready. Everyone froze. After a minute, the platoon leader, Dinh Ngai, and I worked our way past four CIDGs to the point. Hun pointed down the ridge and cupped his hand behind his ear. Somewhere downslope someone or something was coming up through the elephant grass. We could hear it making a lot of noise, maybe fifty meters away.

Whoever it was probably didn't know we were there. Intelligence had told us there were NVA in the area. It also could have been a larger force of VC. Since we were beyond the range of accurate support fire from the camp's 105mm howitzer, we wanted no part of a firefight with a unit whose size we didn't know. Small patrols like ours sometimes ran into NVA battalions and simply disappeared.

The three of us crept forward to the lip of a steep outcrop overlooking the elephant grass. We eased up to the cliff and peered over the edge. Hun grabbed me by the arm and pointed. I tensed up and squeezed the CAR-15, thumbing the selector to full automatic. But Hun was smiling. "*Bac Si, con nai,*" he whispered. Thirty meters below was the biggest deer I had ever seen. It had the body of an elk, except stockier and with shorter legs. The antlers were small, like an ordinary deer back home.

Dinh Ngai let out a little laugh and the giant deer bolted and ran into a timbered ravine draining the grassy slope. The troops relaxed again and I heard some joking. We continued down with me on point just behind Dinh Hun. We picked up the deer's trail and followed it into the thicket and down into the gorge. Below we could hear a trickle of water.

The steep jungle slope was wet, and we held on to vines and slid down the red mud to the bottom of the tiny creek. The rest of the patrol followed. I found a small pool of water and started filling my canteens. Ngai and some of the other CIDGs sat down and burned leeches off their ankles with cigarettes. The big deer with the little antlers had crashed on down the canyon. His hoofprints were as big as those of a Wyoming elk except the toes of the track were a bit more spread out at the tip.

Again, I heard Dinh Hun call me over: "*Bac Si, lai day.*" He was pointing down at something on the creekbed. He uttered a glottal word in Khmer, but I didn't know what it meant. I squatted next to the trickle of water. In the mud was the track of a round pad, five inches across. The back of my neck bristled. "*Con cop, Bac Si.*"

The air became charged with some kind of energy; the entire country was suddenly imbued with fresh potential.

A fucking tiger.

4

THE WIND
RIVERS

Maybe what I needed was a long infusion of solitary living. I didn't seem much good around people. The snows were melting in the high country. The bears had emerged from their winter dens. The geese had long ago flown north. If anything, I was behind schedule according to the timetable I felt in my bones. Something was drawing me north, back into the land of the road map. I packed all my gear and said good-bye. I piled into the blue jeep and headed toward the northern Rockies.

I traveled north slowly, killing time since there was still snow in the mountains. It was May 1968. I had been out of Vietnam for less than three months and could not see much change in either myself or the country. In the war zone, events unfolded with sudden violence, and from there you got pushed along by the instincts and the mechanics of survival. Except for the undeniable reality that someone or something was trying to kill your ass, you had no idea what was going on. You hardly ever knew who or where the enemy was. Sniper fire came out of the forest, automatic weapons fire from the tree line, and rockets and mortars invisibly out of the night.

This confusion followed me back home. From Arizona, I headed north toward the Wind River mountains of Wyoming. I made weekly forays into towns for gas and supplies but never lingered in "syphilization." For the next five months, my contact with the human race was limited to "Filler up" and "Gimme a beer." I avoided women without thinking about it. My primal instincts were intact, but there was no way I wanted to get close to anyone. Later, when I sat back and thought about it, I realized I had spent two and one-half years of unconscious celibacy in partial compensation for manslaughter. The applicable phrase, I read later, was "walking wounded."

Sometimes I ran out of money and had to call my dad, who kept my bucks for me. I was in rural Utah heading for the Wind River Range when the cash ran out. One daybreak I stopped at a phone booth by a deserted gas station to call Dad and have him wire me gas money. I got the operator, who told me to deposit $2.10, a quarter more than I had. She was not pleased. I asked her to wait while I went into my backpack where I carried change for such emergencies. By the time I got back, the line was dead. I dialed "O" and got the same operator, who was still put out. The phone did not return coins so I deposited $2.10 again, all the coins I had in the world just then. I heard the coins fall and then the phone went dead again. I redialed the operator, who said the phone did not return money but that I could have a check for four dollars mailed to my home.

I hung up. Outside the spring wind rattled the booth. Down the highway I could see the steeple of a Mormon church: definitely Indian country. I dug around in the back of the jeep and pulled out the 12-gauge and a box of double ought. The first double blast caught the telephone and tore it off the bracket on the wall of the booth. I reloaded, backed off, and fired another salvo; the force of the buckshot cut the metal corners and the phone booth slumped over onto the ground. I blasted the phone again from six feet. I grabbed the jerry can off the jeep and poured half the gas on what was left of the phone. I flipped a match onto it. Through my rearview mirror I could see the black smoke rise.

I reached Wyoming in late May and spent another month watching the snow line retreat up the mountains, fishing the Popo Agie and camping out in the foothills near the Wind River Reservation. Just as summer reached the valleys, spring came to the mountains. I got ready for a long expedition into the high country, carefully packing my backpack, sorting out food and cold weather gear.

I drove the jeep up a faint muddy track leading high into the range and left it parked in a grove of pines. I shouldered the big pack full of heavy, inexpensive gear, and headed up the trail.

The Wind River area of northwest Wyoming was considered one of the wildest spots left in the lower forty-eight. In 1968 the only topographical map I could find was the old Frémont version made in 1906. The area was so rugged that the surveyors had to guess at much of the country. They missed lakes and valleys and even had rivers running the wrong way, all of which let me imagine I was going somewhere unexplored and uncharted. It did not bother me that I did not know where I was going.

The first day out the weather held and I hiked about a dozen miles, not bad considering that I had been wading through miles of creek bottom flooded by beaver dams. I made camp on the shoulder of a plateau that overlooked a long glacial valley running north. Heavy clouds gathered on the southern horizon, but I guessed that the weather would hold through the night. Just in case, I tied an army poncho corner-to-corner across the top of the hammock in which I would throw my sleeping bag; it was an old jungle arrangement.

The next morning broke gray and cold. Clouds blocked the passes and the weather looked as if it would get worse. I shouldered the pack and started down the trail toward the head of a long glacial lake with a logjam across its outlet. I would cross the creek there.

By the time I got to the bottom, the clouds were rolling in and the temperature had dropped twenty degrees. I was in for a spring storm sometime that day or the next. I dug out my compass and took a reading. According to the map, that bearing should bring me to the foot of a large lake by nightfall.

By late afternoon, a wet snow had begun to fall. I slogged along through sparse timber and outcroppings of granite. By early evening a couple of inches of slush lay on the ground. I kept on the compass bearing, aiming for the large lake, which lay not more than a mile or two away. I was wet, tired of bushwhacking, and eager to set up for the night. Just at dark I stopped at an outcrop. Through the trees I could make out the slate gray surface of a large glacial lake. The wind had picked up and was blowing snowflakes into my face. It was snowing hard. I quickly put up a small mountain tent and unrolled my sleeping bag inside. I got out of my wet clothes and put on a pair of black pajama bottoms and a dry T-shirt and crawled into the sleeping bag, listening to the sound of the blizzard slapping against the tent.

I was thirsty and remembered that I had forgotten to fill my canteen. I looked out the tent flap. All I could see was the first ten feet of swirling snow. "What the hell, it will only take a minute." I stumbled down the rocky ledges toward the lake, which was probably a couple of hundred feet away. The cold wind and snow stung my arms. I pushed through a fringe of fir trees and stepped to the shore, watching the whirling snow disappear into the grayness of the mountain lake. I squatted and filled the canteen. I screwed the cap back on and turned toward my tent, shivering slightly in the cold air. I followed my tracks in the snow back through the trees. When I got to the first ledge the tracks disappeared; the blowing snow had covered them up. I could see for only a couple of feet. I did not know where my tent was.

I told myself to calm down. The tent had to be within a hundred yards or so; it was up on a bluff above the lake. Although I was almost naked, it was not dangerously cold. Dressed as I was, I might freeze if exposed to the elements for an entire night, but I still had lots of time. Methodically I began going back and forth across a series of gentle ledges, upon one of which my tent was pitched. It was so dark by then that I could barely see my feet through the falling snow. I forced myself to go ten more feet up the slope and started a new traverse.

I kept at it for about half an hour. By then I was truly cold and wanted to give up. Suddenly I tripped, falling flat on my face in the snow. I felt a guy line. I had fallen over my tent in the dark. My fingers were numb and I clawed at the tent flap. I crawled in the entrance and stripped off my wet, frozen clothing. I zipped the sleeping bag up over my ears and pulled a woolen cap out of my clothing bag. My mind emptied and the war marched in.

***

We stumbled across the tunnel complex an hour before dark. A five-hundred-pound bomb had landed almost on top of it and a twenty-meter section had caved in. Otherwise we never would have spotted it. Charlie dug these things all over the place. We knew there were a shitload of hidden trenches under every one of these bombed-out villages in the Song Cai Valley, but we never looked for them or messed with them except sometimes to toss a grenade into an open hole or bunker. This time was different. Apparently part of this collapsed tunnel ran on another fifty meters right into the grove of trees in which we had planned on bivouacking. We were going to set up a perimeter around that little palm-covered knoll and spend the night there. The tunnel made us nervous.

The marines had bombed the hell out of the place a week earlier. Our patrol of two Americans and twenty-three Vietnamese CIDG was attached to a grunt company from Da Nang, which was all that was left of a bigger operation that had swept through there four days earlier. There had been some intense fighting during the first two days. The point company took thirteen casualties in three firefights that lasted less than two minutes each. A day later, two grunts stepped on trip-wire mines, one of them big enough to blow the marine's foot off.

By the time we got there things had cooled down. The last marines had been airlifted back to Da Nang, leaving us behind. We were assigned to do a body count. There was me, Irwin the weapons sergeant, and a Vietnamese interpreter in addition to the twenty-three CIDGs. We were supposed to mop up but so far had not found any bodies and had not even been shot at. If things stayed quiet, we would walk back to our A-camp at Thuong Duc in the morning. All we had to do was make it through the night.

First, somebody had to check out the tunnel. I would have gotten out of the job if at all possible. But for a bunch of reasons, I could not: it was my turn. I was new there and I didn't want the CIDGs to think I was scared shitless of going down into that hole—which of course I was.

Unlike most GIs, I liked Vietnam—because I had gotten to

some of the countryside before the war did. The country was
beautiful. I loved the Central Highlands and the people who lived
there. But the war had always caught up. By the end, there were
places in Vietnam I hated like no other spot on earth. The tunnels
were at the top of this list. They were gateways to a special kind
of hell.

We dropped a concussion grenade into the collapsed tunnel to
clear away any booby traps in the immediate vicinity and open up
the hole enough so I could crawl in. I dumped my pack and web
gear and got out new batteries for the flashlight. Sam, the Vietnamese interpreter, took my M-16 and I pulled out a Colt .45. It
was too big and loud for tunnel work, but it was the only pistol we
had with us. I jacked a round into the chamber and stuffed two
extra clips in each breast pocket of my fatigues. We stood around
for a few minutes while the CIDGs used their bayonets to open up
the entrance to the complex. They held onto my feet while I
lowered myself headfirst into the hole, feeling with my arms for
the walls of the tunnel. It was about a meter wide. I worked my
way forward until my feet were in. I crawled a little farther, until
the darkness was complete.

I lay there motionless for about three minutes. All I could hear
was my own breathing. I carried two standard army flashlights but
had not turned them on because I wanted my eyes to adjust and I
did not know who or what was down here. One had a red plastic
disc covering the bulb for low illumination.

The tunnel reeked. I had to get the job over with quickly. The
tunnel was the narrowest one I had ever seen. My heart beat like a
generator engine. I crawled forward, feeling my way along in the
dark. The dirt shaft was wide enough for my shoulders but too
narrow for me to stretch out my elbows. There was no way I could
turn around. I couldn't even reach the K-bar knife that I had
forgotten to take off my belt and tie around my neck where I could
get at it.

I rolled on my side and worked my hand down to the sheath
knife and pulled it up to my face, stuffing the Colt into the
shoulder holster. With the K-bar in my right hand I swept the blade
along the tunnel, feeling for wires and probing the earthen floor for
mines. With my left hand I felt along the side and ceiling. Then I

shifted hands to feel along the other wall, listened, moved forward a couple of feet, and repeated the procedure.

After about a hundred feet, the tunnel got a little bigger and turned off thirty degrees to the right. I thought I could feel a little cold air blowing around the corner. It smelled of shit and rancid fish or something else unbelievably putrid. I stopped short of the bend and listened. Nothing. I grabbed the flashlight with the low-illumination red light in my left hand. I had the .45 in my right. I held the light as far away from my head as I could so that my head would not be a target. Then I flipped it on and shot the beam down the tunnel. I eased my head around the corner and looked into the darkness. The faint red light illuminated about fifteen feet of tunnel, and near the end there was a shaft leading down. The doors to shafts or subterranean chambers were often booby-trapped.

As I switched the flashlight off, I glanced at my wristwatch; I had been alone in the tunnel for less than fifteen minutes. It felt like hours.

I inched along the floor to the mouth of the shaft. It was wet and I slid through a pool of slime that smelled of fresh rat turds. I made it to the shaft. No door or lid covered the opening. I probed with the knife blade around the hole. The stink coming up from the tunnel complex below was so bad I gagged. I felt around. The shaft slanted down for a yard or two and then leveled off. Time was running out. Outside it was getting dark and we were deep in enemy country.

Below, in the absolute darkness of the tunnel, I started down the shaft. I didn't dare use a flashlight. The shaft bent up toward the level and I had to arch my back to feel around the bend. My fingertips brushed the earthen ceiling and I felt a pencil-sized twig poking out of the roof of the tunnel. I ran my fingers down the stick to a joint, then out to the end of the bamboo whip, which was sprung back and anchored in a wire hoop with a trip wire running up to the roof and back to the tunnel floor in front of me. I shaded the red light until I found the commo wire stretched across the tunnel. At the end of the bamboo whip just short of the wire hoop was a rusty fishhook, a large treble hook with the points straightened out: a primitive little device designed to impale your eye. I checked for some trick, then grabbed the sprung bamboo and lowered the hook. The booby trap was recent; the whip still had a lot of spring left in it.

I turned the light off. My heart raced and my stomach heaved. I could smell human shit and a trace of *nuoc mam,* the rotten fish sauce the Vietnamese used, but these foul stenches were overwhelmed by something far more powerful.

A couple of yards more and I reached the end of the shaft. It opened up into some kind of chamber. I listened and felt around the doorway for hidden grenades or wired Claymore mines. Nothing there. This was as far as I would be going. I was out of time. I listened some more and thought I could hear the faintest sound of breathing. For the first time since crawling into the tunnel, I felt there was someone else down there.

In the darkness I sensed I was in a tiny chamber. There was someone sitting in the far corner. I could feel him. A Vietcong. I thumbed the automatic's safety down to off. The Colt .45 felt inadequate. I was probably outgunned: if he had an AK-47 it would be all over. I froze and listened. There was no sound, but I knew he was there.

Then I was not so sure. Maybe I was hearing things. I started to creep forward across the floor of the chamber. I crawled with the Colt ready, groping for trip wires with my left hand. Suddenly I touched something cold and smooth. My left fingers closed around a bloated human hand.

The darkness exploded. I leaped backward, at the same time firing eight .45 caliber slugs in the direction of what I imagined was the corner. I threw the empty clip across the room and pushed a loaded one into the butt of the automatic. I chambered another round but did not squeeze it off. For a moment I was deaf from the discharge of the heavy pistol in the closed space. Then I could hear myself puking. There was no other sound in the room.

I held the bright flashlight high above my head with the .45 leveled. I slid the switch on and the light fell on the corner of a chamber high enough to stand in. The corner was right where I thought it was, right where I had emptied the pistol. I lowered the flashlight beam and looked into the face of a dead Vietnamese draped in shreds of what had been black pajamas. The man had been dead for some time.

I scanned the room. There were three more corpses falling out of the sides of the room. They looked as if they had been stuffed hurriedly in holes along the walls and maybe jarred loose by the shock waves from the bombing. The bodies looked small. The ones I could be sure of were men. They had been folded up into little fetal-like bundles, just like the prehistoric Indian burials I had found in Michigan as a teenager. The bodies had been there for several days, but it was hard to tell, since everything rotted quickly in this humid heat. I looked at the bloated hand I had held a minute earlier. It was attached to an arm that stuck out of the wall. The rest of the corpse was covered with dirt.

I felt faint and started to black out, so I flipped off the light, just in case. After a minute, I turned the flashlight back on. I looked across the chamber at the first body, which apparently had slid out of the corner I had imagined a man was sitting in. This corpse also was folded up, but I could still see that his intestines had been rended from a violent wound to his abdomen. I knew now what the smells were.

Off to the left of the dead man another tunnel ran off. That was where the smell of *nouc mam* seemed to be coming from.

I had to get out. I shook so violently I dropped the flashlight, which went out. I did not try to find it. Instead, I turned and squatted, ready to start back out the shaft. The stooping brought on another dizzy spell and I might have passed out for a few seconds.

When I got my senses back, I was lying at the entrance to the shaft with my feet still in the burial chamber. I was there long enough to get another strong whiff of fish sauce rising above the stench of death. It was coming from the direction of the other tunnel. Now I could hear the unmistakable sound of soft breathing. Someone was alive just across the room near the mouth of the tunnel. Fifteen feet away. Breathing in the darkness.

We sat there on opposite sides of the temporary burial chamber listening to each other's respiration for what seemed a long time. Whoever was there could have killed me or tried to at any time. But he did not. Maybe the dead were his friends or even his family. He might have been paralyzed by grief or mourning his dead. The war could have been over for him. All I could hear was the regular sound of breathing. He did not move. He just sat there with the dead, and so did I.

Finally I turned into the tunnel and retreated quietly in the dark. I moved as quickly as I could crawl the hundred and fifty feet or whatever it was back to the caved-in trench where my comrades waited. It was nearly dark and everyone was jumpy, anxious to move into a night position. I told them I had not found anything down there, that the tunnel was cold.

/ / /

In the mountains of the Wind River Range, I lay there in the tent a long time without thinking, letting the blood recirculate. It had been an altogether avoidable close call and uncharacteristically careless of me. What happened to my concentration, to my survival instincts? This little mishap was one of several times in the previous year that I had mindlessly nearly killed myself. During the last few months I was in Vietnam I had stopped taking careful cover during firefights—I waltzed around during gun battles like a Sioux ghost dancer, invincible against enemy bullets. I had blamed this more on weariness than on a conscious choice to take chances. But now I was forced to admit that I was truly a danger to myself. The capriciousness of survival, that random slice that separates the living from the dead, seemed like a bad joke.

"The hell with it," I said. "I've got too much to look forward to." No whacko death wish was going to get me. There were too many wild places left to explore. Besides, I liked fishing, wild mushrooms, my own cooking, Mozart, good wine, woods, and women.

I slept until the drip of water on the tent told me that the snow was melting. Around noon, I sat up and rolled out of the bag and into a gray spring day. I crammed my wet gear into the pack and broke camp. Above the lake on the far shore, timbered wedges and rotten talus swept up to unnamed peaks penetrating the glaciers that blanketed the east side of the divide. I followed the big lake to its head, where a creek dumped into the milky glacial waters. I would follow it up to a chain of small lakes, where I wanted to set up a base camp from which I could fish and explore.

The snow had melted by the time I began bushwhacking up the rocky creek bottom. I did not expect more snow, although it could have rained at any time; the weather in the Wind River Range was fickle at best. I picked up a game trail running up the drainage. In the mud there were tracks of deer, elk, and a moose. Overhanging branches slapped me in the face. No matter: I was not in a hurry.

About midafternoon I arrived at another large lake which, according to the map, stood at the junction of two more strings of glacial lakes. I decided to go up the longer chain, the one leading into the heart of the mountain range. I circled the shore of the lake and lost the game trail but found the going easy enough. A heavy cloud bank hung on the crest of the range and spilled east over into my chain of lakes. Somewhere off to the west thunder rolled. The sparse lodgepole forest gave way to stunted fir and spruce mixed with five-needle pines, limber, and whitebark, indicating that I was nearing the upper limit of the trees.

Again the rumble of thunder echoed throughout the peaks and basins. I ducked into a clump of trees to wait out the passing storm—a few drops of rain with a dozen cracks of lightning. I reached the end of the lake and climbed up the creek bottom alongside a series of waterfalls. There were signs of beaver along the creek. I circled the marshy area, stopping in the mud where the game trail ran. A fresh set of bear tracks was printed over the older hoof marks of deer and elk.

I dropped my pack and got down on my knees to look at the large pad marks. I had heard that there might be a few grizzlies left in the northern part of these mountains. I found a good front track. The marks of the front claws were close to the toe; the toe prints were separated from one another and on a curved line: a black bear. On a grizzly, the toes touch, in more of a straight line, and the front claws are huge. Just the same, it was a big black bear. I started up the wet trail, anxious to find the next lake before dark.

I came out to the edge of the big lake just at dusk. It was the wildest area I had seen since coming home. In the middle of the mile-long lake stood a tiny, rocky island decorated with a few scrawny trees. One of these trees was on fire. I tensed and looked around. Who had set the fire? No one had, of course. It had been hit by lightning during the afternoon thunderstorm. I took it as a sign: my burning bush.

The small tree smoked away as I dug out my tent and poncho, preparing a shelter next to a large rock where I could put my fire pit. I carefully picked out all the small rocks and pebbles from under the tent. This would be a good camp, my base camp for the next two or three weeks—until my food ran out or I got sick of trout.

I lit a fire of pine, which sputtered and threw sparks and debris into the darkness. I felt the best that I had felt in months. The light of the fire shimmered off the huge quartz monzonite boulder. It must have been stranded after the most recent advance of the glaciers.

I did not want to go to sleep. Instead, I stoked the fire and ran through the fishing I would do the next day. In my mind I fished up the creek I had hiked today, casting a fly into each deep eddy. I started halfway down to the next lake and fished up, roll casting to avoid the brush, exploring each tail-out and run with a number 12 Royal Coachman. I fished all the way back to camp in my imagination. An hour, maybe two, had passed and I was exhausted.

* * *

It was the wildest country in all of Quang Ngai Province, the long valley south of Song Ha. We left two days after Thanksgiving and marched thirty klicks in four slow days of small but endless skirmishes with local VC units. A giant, iridescent green serpent was sleeping snaked along a horizontal limb ten feet above a foot trail. This viper was fully three times longer than any snake I had ever seen and twice as long as any green reptile that was supposed to live in Vietnam. It had a bulge a third of the distance down its gullet big enough to be a large monkey or barking deer, or a small human. The local Montagnards of my mobile guerrilla team said the beautiful snake did not have a name in Vietnamese but if it bit you, you went to sleep. For good. We all had to walk underneath it.

* * *

The next morning a fine drizzle dripped through the trees. I kindled a small blaze with the help of a candle. The smoke rose to the lower branches of the lodgepole and hung there like a blanket in the heavy air. This was the day I had planned to look for the big black bear, following his tracks up the drainage maybe into the next basin. Instead, I tied the poncho above the fire and huddled underneath it. I left the fire only long enough to fill my canteens at the lake and catch a few trout for dinner at the outlet of the creek. At least I was where I wanted to be: in one of the blank spots on my map.

I poked at the fire with a stick, glancing up every so often at the game trail, vaguely hoping someone might show up: a beautiful mountaineer with a pack full of kinky hardware or a Shoshone maiden clad in wet doeskins. Come and dry by my fire. Let's build a sweat lodge. A two-hour fantasy of girl bums followed. The fire had burned out. It was what the grunts in Nam called an ass trance.

Five days later I was still waiting for the rain to stop. Each day I squatted around the campfire squinting into the smoke until midafternoon, when I walked to the creek to catch a dinner. I had no complaint with the diet or the solitude, only the lack of activity. I ached for a chance to explore the hidden lakes and basins. By the seventh day I was thoroughly bored. The drizzle continued, never really raining and never stopping for more than a few minutes. Far off to the east I could see the clouds breaking up. The weather there had to be part of a local pattern, with heavy clouds hanging around the crest of the range. At this rate, the rain might last all summer.

I did not have real rain gear, so I wrapped myself in a wool sweater and a windbreaker, stuck a bag of waterproof matches in my pocket, strapped on my Ruger .357, and stepped out into the light rain. A faint game trail led around the rocky edge of the lake. I followed it into a thicket of timber at the head of the glacial lake and along another creek that tumbled down from the lake above. According to the map it was only a mile to the big cirque at the head of the drainage. Above that, there would be impenetrable cliffs and narrow passes filled with snow.

The rocky game trail dropped down to the creek and paralleled a marshy strip of beaver meadow. In the mud were the day-old tracks of the black bear. I knelt on the trail and measured the bear's rear track with my fingers. The front print was there too, faint but unmistakable. The rain had washed most of the other tracks away; what was left looked as if a human had walked there barefoot. It seemed clear that the bear was headed up the drainage. Maybe he had not liked the smell of my campfire.

A black bear might raid your camp but otherwise presents little danger to human beings. It was too bad that no more grizzlies were left in there. They had been shot out decades ago or poisoned with the predacide 1080. Even a place as big and wild as this had proved too small for them. Grizzlies have enormous ranges: a male in country like this needs two or three hundred square miles; a female, half of that. In the spring, the big bears ranged from the mountains into ranch country and invariably got blown away.

I found a spruce tree tall enough that I could sit under it. It kept most of the rain off me. I waited, my thoughts drifting. Memories of the war came back, pushing other thoughts out of my mind. I sat with my back up against the tree listening to the rain and letting Vietnam sweep over me.

/ / /

During the Christmas truce of 1967 Dinh Hun caught four slugs from an AK-47 through his right thigh, fired into him by NVA walking down a foot trail as Hun lay at his listening post only two meters away. Nobody knew how it started. All of a sudden the NVA were running down the trail toward the coastal cities spraying the darkness with their submachine guns.

I was waiting for Hun at the medical bunker when they brought him back on a stretcher. Hun had become my best Yard friend, and for a minute I thought I was going to lose this big Hre with the quick smile and four gold teeth. The bullets had shattered Hun's femur, and I was afraid the bone fragments would chew up the femoral artery. I gave him a quarter grain of morphine and we worked him into a Striker frame. Hun cried out in pain when I started putting traction on the half-ring splint. I couldn't stand to see him in that kind of agony so I shot him up again with another half-dose of morphine—a bit more than I should have. That was about all we could do for him.

I called Duc Pho for a medevac, though the odds of getting a

Dust Off out here in the middle of the night with clouds all the way down to the ground were about nothing. The night was black, the ceiling zero, and visibility through the fog was the length of your arm.

But the helicopter crews came anyway, flying up the Tra Na river to Bato on Christmas Eve of 1967, a night as dark as they got. They flew up the middle of the river with the skids almost touching it, flying in slow motion with their landing lights shining through the gloom before them all the way to Bato. What a target they made! Every inch of the trip was Indian country. They didn't have to come. The WIA was only a Montagnard irregular. I couldn't imagine anyone being so goddamned brave, though I could tell the pilot did not think it was a big deal. Maybe it was just Christmas.

/ / /

Later, the wind picked up, driving rain through my light windbreaker. Chilled, I moved up the animal trail along the creek, finding more prints of the black bear. I struggled up a steep grade over a lip of bedrock and found myself looking out over a large lake filling a mountain cirque. Above me everything was in a cloud. The wind whipped the rain into squalls and froze it into sleet. I was cold but wanted to try the lake waters with my fly rod before I left.

I stuck the pack rod together with numb fingers, then quickly tied on a brown-hackled wet fly—one of my dad's experimental patterns—which I cast between gusts of wind. Immediately, I was struck by a fifteen-inch golden trout. I reeled it in fast, too cold to think of sport. I released the fish, a fat golden showing a trace of hybridization with rainbow. I tried another fly: nothing doing. I tied the scraggly brown hackle back onto the line and threw it out into the lake. Before I had time to retrieve the brown nymph, I was hit again by an even larger fish. I forgot about the cold and I played the pound-and-a-half fish for a few minutes before I let it go. This had been the best trout fishing I had yet seen up here. This high basin must have been loaded with game, I thought. In addition to the black bear, I had seen signs of lots of deer and elk on the way up. But that was for another day: I was cold and it was sleeting. I wanted to drop down out of this cloud and build a fire. My fingers were no longer functioning.

Several soggy days later I was on my way out, beaten down by the unceasing rain. Toward evening I stepped out into the meadow next to which my jeep was parked. I dumped my pack on the hood and inspected the damage that the curious range cattle had done. They had stomped a ring in the duff around it and chewed off its plastic directional signals. The jeep started right up and lurched down the rutted Forest Service trail, finally joining a graded ranch road. I hit U.S. 287 and turned back toward Lander to gas up and buy a few supplies—including a jug of tequila.

The sun had set behind the peaks and the wind was blasting the jeep with fifty-mile-an-hour gusts as I drove up a muddy logging road toward Union Pass. Just at dark, I pulled off a series of jeep trails and side roads left behind by the messy logging operation and parked in a grove of open timber. Using the far side of the jeep as a windbreak, I staked down the edge of the poncho and guyed it off against the wind. I unrolled the sleeping bag, pushing it under the poncho, and lit a fire a few feet downwind in a hole I dug with my entrenching tool. I sat by the fire and pulled heavily on the bottle. The sparks shot off into the night.

Sometime around 3:00 A.M. I sat bolt upright in the chilly silence. The wind had died down and the stars were out. I shivered and eased into the sleeping bag, hoping to warm up. My face felt as though someone had taken a hammer to it—that hangover peculiar to drinking half a bottle of tequila. I groped in my pack for some aspirin, took out two, then thought again and took four. I was restless and awake, ready to move on, another side effect of the tequila. Despite the headache, I was aware that I was after something—that this trip was part of a larger quest of some kind. I would move north.

My immediate problem was not to pull another lost tent act. I needed to quit pushing things. I wanted to find a place where the weather was better. What I had in mind was the Yellowstone Plateau and the Absaroka Range. That country had magic. Maybe I would even see a grizzly.

5
YEAR OF THE
GRIZZLIES

Before Vietnam, I had avoided Yellowstone because of all the tourists and the tame black bears begging along the roads. But a hundred yards from any of the roads or boardwalks, Yellowstone was still a wild place. The hot springs were an alternative to winter and the terrain there was forgiving. Compared to the east side of the Wind River Range, the topography was almost flat and the weather dry—a good place to regroup and rest up.

In addition to the tequila hangover, something else was wrong. I could feel a fever coming on. I had gotten pretty good at predicting it in Vietnam where, before a malaria attack, I would become lightheaded, feel a tingling all over, then come down with shaking chills. In the four months before I left Southeast Asia, I had contracted three species of internal parasites, amoebic dysentery, and malaria all at the same time. So, despite having gained back most of the sixty pounds of lost weight, I still felt a bit weak and vulnerable. In Nam we just called these fevers FUOs, fevers of unknown origin.

I passed Jackson Lake and started north, through lodgepole forests up a gentle grade onto the Yellowstone Plateau. What I had in mind was to hike into one of the backcountry thermal areas. I had visited the park during the early sixties and had a couple of areas in particular I wanted to visit. I found myself only mildly put out because of the tourist traffic, a tolerance born of spending three weeks alone in the sopping Wind River Range.

By the time I found a place to hide my jeep at the end of a seldom-traveled dirt road I was feeling shaky, shivering so much I put on my down jacket. I packed up my tent and sleeping bag and carried them as far as I could—less than a mile—through the lodgepole and down to the edge of a small river. I put up the tent and sat down to await the inevitable paroxysm. In my pack I carried chloroquine, aspirin, and a thermometer.

I filled my canteen and lay back on my sleeping bag racked with chills. Despite the relative sense of well-being one often has during a malaria attack, they are dangerous. You run an extremely high fever. And my malaria had never been properly diagnosed: it could be *falciparum*. I could never be sure the paroxysm would not lead to deadly black water fever, which had killed my best Australian friend in Vietnam.

The chills stopped abruptly. I could feel the heat on my forehead as my temperature began to rise. I knew from experience that the fever would spike in about two hours.

It never entered my mind to seek help. I felt I was on my own as I had always been. I had survived these things alone before. Besides, conventional American medicine was not used to this stuff. A couple of years later I was to stagger into a Boston emergency room with a temperature of 106 degrees, to the total bafflement of the Yankee staff doctors, who thought malaria had gone south with the witches.

I pulled the thermometer from my pack and stuck it under my tongue for a couple of minutes: 103.6 degrees. Twenty minutes later I took it again: 104.4. I knew my lucidity would give out somewhere above 105. I was worried about the loaded .357 Magnum lying next to my head. I emptied the chambers, pulled the pin, and removed the cylinder, stuffing the parts into a plastic bag that I jammed into the bottom of my pack.

I was burning up. In the past, these fevers had peaked in a couple of hours, lingered there for a few more hours, then slowly subsided over a period of several days. My symptoms were not classical malaria paroxysms; I never knew what to expect. I took my temperature one last time: it read 105.6. I was in for it.

I do not know how long I lay in that tent, but it was probably about three days. It could have been three hours or three weeks; I couldn't tell the difference. My mind drifted. I watched a long army of the dead march by in single file. I wanted to join them and felt lost when they marched away out of sight. Hallucinations came in waves and I could not shut them off.

I must have regained my senses a couple of times during those missing days because I woke up once and found myself freezing: I had sweated through my sleeping bag. I got up long enough to put on all my wool sweaters and then climb back in the wet bag for another day or so. When I came to I looked outside. The stars twinkled. Then I drifted off into another uncontrollable dream.

Some days later, I rolled out exhausted and stood in the sunlight. I limped down to the river and splashed water on my face. The day was crisp and a steady wind was blowing up from the south. I draped my sweat-drenched bag over an uprooted lodgepole to dry and started packing up my tent. I felt drained; I needed to go where I could slowly regain my strength. There was a place near there with boiling springs and azure pools and warm creeks which, earlier in the season, were fringed with yellow monkey flowers. I would try my luck there, recuperating in the healing mineral waters of the hot springs and the warm creeks.

I packed up enough gear for a week or so and hiked several miles to the head of a warm creek where I located a safe tent site in thick timber. On the way in I had crossed an alarming amount of bear sign, and I wanted to camp as far away from the bear trails as I could.

I felt wasted. The short hike had wiped me out. My brain was emptied out, brutalized by days of delirium and fever. I lay back on the pine needles, looking up at blue skies through the boughs of lodgepole. I turned in long before dusk. Several times during the night I woke to what I thought were animal sounds, but I did not have the strength to see what had made them. I didn't care what was happening to me; I wanted only to sleep.

I woke up cold and stiff, feeling as if I had been beaten up. I stepped out into the frigid air. A cold front must have slipped down from the north. I pulled out a couple of extra ratty wool sweaters, wolfed down a handful of granola, and started down the creek. The small creek flowed out of a huge hot spring not far from my tent and back to the river on which I had camped while I had the malaria attack. It was not more than a couple of miles in length, over which its temperature ranged from boiling to tepid.

I made my way downstream again amazed at the amount of bear sign. Stopping at a muddy wallow next to the creek, I traced the outline of a front paw: the claws left marks in the mud three inches from the toe prints. This was the track of a grizzly bear: the rear print was almost ten inches long, with the toes closer together and in a straighter line than the toe marks of a black bear. I immediately stepped back from the track and looked around.

Much more cautiously now, I eased along the shallow creek and arrived at a broad meadow. I tested the water with my finger: it was hot, but not too hot. From there I could survey the entire meadow. I moved back upstream until I located a bathtub-shaped pocket under a tiny waterfall. It was perfect. The waterfall dumped steaming water into the head of the hole. I dropped my bag on the bank and stripped off my filthy clothes. The cold wind hit me like a snowball. I put one foot in the creek; the water burned. Slowly I pushed one leg into the steaming creek while the rest of my body froze. I eased the other leg in. Finally I was sitting in the bathtub.

Hot water from the tiny waterfall splashed on my neck and poured over my shoulders, steam rose all around, and sweat dripped off my chin. I could feel my aching muscles relax, the knot in my back evaporate. It was an ancient arrangement: the purge of sweat, the purifying force of sacred waters. Through the steam I thought I saw something move out into the meadow. Three dark shapes lumbered out of the timber. Across the meadow, about a hundred and fifty feet away, a sow grizzly and her two cubs were walking straight toward me.

Although I had plenty of experience with most other species of big North American mammals, the only thing I knew about female grizzly bears with young was that you were supposed to avoid them.

The grizzly family ambled on, the sow nosing her way across the open grassland, the two cubs close behind. I stood up. Immediately, the world turned dark; I was passing out from the rush of oxygen away from my brain. I staggered toward the nearest tree, tripping over the bank, still blacking out from the whirlpool-like effect of the hot waters. I slammed into the tree like a fullback, knocking myself half silly and gashing my forehead. I clawed my way up the trunk of the small lodgepole, hugging the tree in a frantic embrace. Blood ran down my forehead into my eyes.

Reeling but driven by fear, I tore and scraped my way fifteen feet up the tree. I sat naked, cowering, perched in the uppermost branches of the pine tree like some large species of silly bird. The grizzlies paid me no attention whatsoever but went about digging up and eating coarse grass not a hundred feet from my tree. The wind howled through the forty-degree air. I clung, blue and bleeding, to the boughs as the wind swayed the lodgepole. The grizzlies wandered within forty-five feet of my tree, ignoring me. After what could have been an hour, they broke off feeding and walked away.

By now I was so cold I was worrying about hypothermia. The grizzly family disappeared into the trees. I counted to about fifty, then slowly slid back down the tree. I hit the ground but could not stand up; my legs had fallen asleep. I sank into the grass still hugging the trunk of the tree. After a few minutes the blood returned, and I waddled to the creek and plunged back into the hot water.

The restraint demonstrated by the mother grizzly, who by all rights should have charged me, was remarkable. I had not had a lot of choice; about the only alternatives were to call out or to stay in the creek. In either case, she might have been provoked into attacking by my shouting, or have wandered too close before she spotted me. I had heard that female grizzlies charge almost reflexively once something threatens their young.

The grizzly-generated adrenaline rush had effectively counteracted the malaria malaise. Now, however, the fatigue crept back into my burned-out body. I was tired far beyond the shell of my physical self. I felt my mind and soul had been drained: I was ready for a mending.

Now that I knew real grizzlies lurked in the shadows, my dreams were not so important. Something big was out there. For the first time since returning to the world, my thoughts chose themselves without Vietnam intruding.

That night I lay back awaiting dark, thinking about all the times I had lain awake listening to night sounds. When I was a teenager I had taken my first long solo backpack trip along the Big Two Hearted River near Lake Superior, in the upper peninsula of Michigan. I had a memorable time carrying a ninety-eight–pound army packboard complete with heavy canvas tent and an old Damascus-twist double-barrel 12-gauge shotgun because I was afraid of bears. At night I would lie in the tent, hand on the trigger, listening to the sound of mosquitoes, raccoons, skunk, and deer. I did not get a bit of sleep for days, slowly learning to identify the noises and see that they held no danger for me. Once I even saw a black bear track.

Of course, grizzly bears were a different matter. Grizzlies were more disdainful of men and their ways than black bears. Grizzlies tended to avoid everything human except garbage. They were less likely to approach a camp, especially a clean one, than black bears, who seem to learn about people quickly. On the other hand, if a grizzly did come around, he would be a lot bigger and more dangerous.

Black bears are forest creatures, evolved from Etruscan bears in the Old World. They crossed over into North America some 500,000 years ago. The grizzly bear is a much more recent product of evolution. The grizzly wandered over the Bering land bridge as recently as 40,000 to 12,000 years ago and encountered great open expanses of tundra, the rich periglacial of the Pleistocene. One of the consequences was that away from their ancestral forests in Asia and Europe, grizzlies became more aggressive in response to the treeless tundra, where mothers had to learn to protect their young from other bears, wolves, and several now-extinct Pleistocene carnivores. Defense became a good offense; this increased aggressiveness no doubt accounted for the bear's subspecies name, *horribilis*.

I got up feeling much stronger than I had the day before. I was ready to go look for grizzlies. I walked down the creek, picking up the game trail just above the wallow. There were at least three new sets of tracks, of big grizzlies. I slowly worked down to the meadow where the grizzly family had appeared the day before.

Across the flat, I could see four well-used trails in the morning dew. These trails were curious: they looked as if someone had run a double tire track, four inches apart, across the meadow, which merged as it entered the woods to the south. From reading sign in moist areas, I could tell these were grizzly bear trails. I explored two nearby meadows, finding a similar set of trails all leading to an area south of the creek. I remembered reading the Russian zoologist Middendorf—after whom the subspecies of grizzly living on the Alaskan coast is named—telling of brown bear trails in the Siberian forests. The bears walked in the same tracks year after year, and the thousands of superimposed paw prints cut narrow, deep trails so uncannily resembling human paths that the remote forests seemed haunted with invisible people.

In the afternoon I found a spot on a hillside where I could watch two of the networks of trails crossing the open areas. The sun came out and for a short time I dozed off on the hillside. When I woke it was with a start. Below me, strung out halfway across the meadow, a line of brown animals lumbered along one of the trails. For a moment I did not know what they were. I brought my binoculars to rest on the lead beast: a huge grizzly with an enormous head. Behind him were two smaller adults, a sow with two yearling-sized cubs, and four smaller grizzlies. Most of the bears were uniformly brown, except for the two big adults, who were darker. Three of the bears had light collars of fur around their ribs. The line moved across the meadow and disappeared into the trees. This group was several times the total number of grizzlies I had seen in my life. I wanted to follow them into the trees and see where they were going but decided I had better give them an hour or so head start.

I lay back in the shade of a lodgepole and watched for another half hour. Just as I was getting ready to leave, another grizzly popped up out of the trees and stepped into the meadow. Four bears of various sizes made their way at odd intervals across the opening and disappeared into the trees. Now I was really curious about where they were going.

I let the bears have a fifteen-minute lead, then cautiously climbed down my hill to the flat. I listened for a long time, then stepped onto the trail and followed them into the woods. I strained into the wind, seeing and smelling my way up the trail. Every half minute I stopped and listened. I could make out tracks in the duff under the trees; many of the bears walked in the same tracks over and over, leaving the curious double-tracked trails.

The trail led out of the timber and across a small open area. On the far side of the small meadow I heard a deep bellowing. I glassed the fringe of the timber. I saw bears moving over what appeared to be a pile of rubbish.

I had already guessed there was a garbage dump in the area. Many bits of human trash had blown into the trees and partway across the meadows. But I had no idea that the dump was so near or that it attracted so many grizzlies. I was disappointed at first: I wanted the bears who had startled me at my hot bath to be a portent or sign of some kind.

Despite the failure of the grizzlies to be the unspoiled creatures of my imagination, I was pleased to have them as companions. Their presence meant, of course, that I would have to be much more careful camping and wandering around the area. I watched as long as I dared in the lengthening shadows of the lodgepoles. I wanted to avoid traveling during the late hours when the grizzlies would be more active. I also wanted to travel off the bear trails at all times. I gathered up my things and made a long, cautious circle into the wind away from the path the animals had traveled. When I crossed the creek, the warm water was already steaming in the chill evening air. I kept to the center of the series of meadows which led upstream, not wanting to stumble across a bedded grizzly in the timber.

By the time I reached my camp I was breathing heavily, not so much from exertion, for I had moved up the creek slowly and warily, but from the exhilaration that comes of traveling through country occupied by something more powerful than you are. I was buzzed, as high as a hummingbird. In Vietnam you got that sensory intensity too, except the stench of human fear cut something off the high side of it. I remembered how Tet had worn me down.

/ / /

From Christmas on everybody around Bato knew something big was coming down. Only the American military missed that one.

The first indication of a general offensive came when a young NVA wandered into our A-camp late in 1967 thinking it was some kind of VC outpost. He was carrying advanced rocket-guiding technology. I bandaged him up after our Intelligence NCO beat the shit out of him during the routine interrogation. He was so young and naive I almost felt sorry for him. Despite all the loose talk by the military brass about NVA all over the south, this trooper was the first we had seen at Bato.

But we missed the significance of the NVA artillery expert. It was later—January 1968—during one of my weekly medical patrols to Ba Hiep, that I learned Tet would be a hard time for all. Ba Hiep was a Hre Montagnard resettlement hamlet on the extreme edge of our "Safe Area." I drove the two klicks out there by jeep every week along the old bombed-out highway to run weekly sick calls and hand out medicine. I looked forward to them because Long, my number one CIDG medic, and the nurses did all the work, and I got to drink rice wine with my friend, Dinh Rua, the village chief.

Drinking rice wine among Montagnard tribes was ceremonial and usually reserved for funerals, weddings, and other special times. Fortunately, the Hre notion of ceremonial occasion was flexible enough to include some of my medical visits. As it turned out, the occasion of this particular visit portended funerals. Many of them. But I didn't know this at the time.

Hre rice wine drinking included seven stages, beginning with the host's clearing out the long drinking straws, hollow reeds called *triengs,* by spitting out the contents to show they hadn't been packed with poison. The Hre were very big on that. You ended up drinking serially with the Hre, sucking large, measured cups of rice beer out of the meter-high earthen burial urn, taking turns until only the banana leaves covering the fermented rice remained. What constituted good manners differed among the various tribes of Yards. Just south of here, for instance, among Jarai Montagnards, it was polite to get slightly inebriated. But with the Hre, the highest compliment you could show your host was to get absolutely shit-faced.

I was the perfect guest. Long helped me into the jeep and drove back across the bridge toward Bato. At the edge of Tan An hamlet I told Long to pull over for a piss stop. We both walked behind some Vietnamese hootches into the trees. Some older men were building wooden boxes back there. Stacked against the back wall of the huts were thirty freshly constructed wooden coffins.

In all sizes.

/ / /

That night I lay in the tent listening to a mild wind, alert, thinking of the fourteen great bears I had seen who were now feeding just a couple of miles away. I wondered what natural foods they ate, where they bedded during the day, and to what mountain range they would trek when the snows came and it was time to den up.

I didn't know much about grizzly bears. I had caught a glimpse of my first one years before in Alaska and, believing all the stories I had read and heard, reached for my Magnum only to watch the big bear disappear into the tundra. I had known back then that I wasn't going to use the gun; I just watched the grizzly charge for about forty feet and then veer away without breaking stride. That youthful experience had not registered with full force.

Now I carried a gun only when I expected to live off the land or when I expected to run into people. Grizzlies seldom attacked people, and then it was usually only mothers protecting cubs. Still, I remembered with a chill at Bato reading in a sports magazine an account of two young women who were killed by two different grizzlies on the same night during 1967 in Glacier National Park. I had to remember that this animal was regarded as the most dangerous to man on the North American continent.

I dreamed of bears that night—a delicious, gentle journey with just a hint of danger—one of the first of hundreds of such dreams. All I can remember of the dream now is the quality of light, the clarity of air on those rare days spent watching grizzlies, the amber sunlight filtering through the tops of the pines and a mild breeze blowing across my forehead and the brown fur on the backs of bears.

I spent the next month on the Yellowstone soaking in the mineral hot waters and watching great bears. For hours every day I observed groups of grizzlies feeding, resting, traveling, and playing. The bears became the center of my world and all my activities were structured around their movements. The smell of danger floated on the mountain air. I felt I was part of a more ancient world where man no longer ruled. Each day I crept out of camp and cautiously walked the four miles to the hillside where I sat waiting for the parade to swing out of the woods. Some days I would sneak up and watch the bears feed. Occasionally, I would stumble across grizzlies playing in the meadows or digging along the creek. Once I watched a young bear mock-charge across a field, stampeding a herd of seven elk. Another time an adult grizzly circled three bull bison, closing to within thirty feet, until one of the buffalo lowered his head and thrust his horns toward the bear, who backed off thirty yards, then circled the bison again.

I was healing. The fever was gone. My strength was returning, conditioned by the dozen miles I walked every day. My physical senses were honed even sharper than they had been during my jungle days. I looked closely at bundles of pine needles disturbed on the forest floor. I heard the secrets passed by flapping ravens and smelled, when the wind blew right, the fetor of damp bear fur floating down the trails.

My spirits too were in better shape than they had been in the wet Wind Rivers. Living among grizzlies changed my way of looking at things. For the first time since I had left Vietnam, I dared think about the madness that had been my last two months over there. Until then, those memories had forced themselves upon me with random frequency and I was powerless to shut them out.

␣␣

When Tet arrived I was in all the wrong places, unconsciously swimming against the tides of battle. I could not have planned it any worse.

A week earlier, I had gotten medevacked to Da Nang for malaria, intestinal bleeding, and an ignominious foot wound I had received on my last patrol, when I had rolled out of a jungle hammock to take a leak and sleepily stepped in a *punji* pit. When the Tet Offensive hit the big cities, I was a patient in the Da Nang Naval Hospital. Bato was quiet while the offensive raged in the cities. I spent my hospital stay sleeping on the floor under my bed, unauthorized .45 automatic in hand, NVA sappers on the wire fifty meters away.

I went AWOL from the hospital and jumped the first chopper back to Bato. I had missed a strange sort of attack on our A-camp on February 1 by seven hundred Montagnards, half of them carrying spears and knives. By the time I got back the Vietcong had killed my friend Dinh Rua and cut his head off.

/ / /

I learned to distinguish the personalities of about fifteen individual grizzlies. The animals formed a social hierarchy with a huge brown grizzly, the alpha male, at the top. When he arrived at the feeding site, all the other bears scattered. Otherwise, the bears fed together without a great deal of conflict.

Another dominant grizzly, a female who was subordinate only to a couple of big males, showed up on the scene in August with four cubs. This group constituted the biggest family I had ever seen. Sow grizzlies usually have two cubs, sometimes one, and occasionally three, but hardly ever four. This mother bear was the most protective I encountered.

One day I decided to spend an afternoon watching this unusual grizzly. I circled the feeding flat downwind until I could approach to within a couple hundred feet of the open pit dump. An easily climbable snag made viewing bears relatively safe.

I pulled myself up into the limbs of the dead pine tree until I was about twenty feet above the ground. Two hundred feet away the sow fed with her four close-kept cubs in a corner of the dump away from the other eight bears. I had been sitting there for maybe twenty minutes when the wind changed directions. I looked at the family. The sow reared and spun slowly until she was facing my tree. I made an involuntary reach for a higher perch in the dead snag. The sow turned slightly, looking directly toward me. She had caught the movement. Grizzlies are not supposed to see well, though, as I would learn many times over in the years to come, they can pick up slight movement at a surprising distance, sometimes as much as a hundred yards.

Without hesitation the sow dropped to all fours and broke into a charge. In a heartbeat she covered half the distance to my tree, slid to a halt, turned, and loped back to her cubs, whom she nosed into a tight bundle. Leaving the alarmed but obedient knot of cubs behind, she charged me again, this time covering all but a third of the distance to the tree.

I clung to the upper branches of the snag, knowing that adult grizzlies were not supposed to be able to climb trees. If I did not fall out of the dead lodgepole, I was probably safe. The female kept her offspring balled close together. She picked up her head and, once again, charged across the open ground a hundred feet toward me. Over a period of about half an hour she charged in my direction sixteen more times, usually coming only thirty or so yards across the meadow.

I waited until the grizzly resumed feeding with her back turned toward me, then slid down the smooth trunk of the snag and retreated through the trees. I crossed the hot creek as the afternoon shadows reached out, and walked the timbered ridges, which were seldom used by bears, back to camp.

That was the last time I visited the dumps. The place depressed me. The fact that these beautiful beasts had been eating human garbage here for some eighty years gave me no historical consolation.

␣␣␣

We worked the south fork of the Nuoc Ong in September of 1967. A helicopter inserted us just at dark after making several false passes with four others flying in trail at treetop level. A six-man team jumped off into the elephant grass, then quickly regrouped and crawled off into the darkness.

We were moving by early morning, stopping every couple of minutes to listen for the VC. Within an hour they had a tracker on our backtrail. It was impossible for six men not to leave a visible trail in the jungles of the Central Highlands. Every fifteen minutes or so the tracker would fire his K-44 rifle in the air so all the other VC in the vicinity could get a fix on us. I guess these VC did not have radios for such things. The tracker appeared to be about a half hour behind us. No matter how fast we traveled, we never left him very far behind.

By noon, the crack of the Kalashnikov was less than twenty minutes behind. We had to stop to eat "indigenous rations"— freeze-dried fish and rice. Our four Asian teammates were inflexible on that one. The first time the little people insisted on stopping for lunch with the NVA in hot pursuit, I almost shit. I could not believe they would take a chance like that. What was worse, there on the Song Nuoc Ong they also wanted to take *poc* time— meaning they wanted to sack out for two hours—a kind of Vietnamese siesta. The four of them lay down in a tight circle facing out and went to sleep. Me and the other green beret watched as they slept, nervously fingering our CAR-15s and listening.

At 1400 hours, the rifle went off. The tracker was still twenty minutes away. We moved on and he kept up, never falling much more than a half hour behind, firing his weapon every fifteen minutes or so.

This went on for three days and I sort of got used to it. Nobody moved from 1200 to 1400 hours. Everybody observed *poc* time. The war stopped and the tracker never tried to catch up with us. The second day out, the VC could have set up an easy ambush for us if they had circled around us during *poc* time. But they did not. It was a kind of truce: as if by mutual consent we all agreed to grant the other side two hours of grace.

/ / /

By early morning crisp cold air settled into the draw in which my tent was pitched and I stepped out into the golden light of approaching autumn. I packed up a bag of gear, throwing in my .357 Magnum at the last minute. I still carried the gun out of habit although I had long known I would not need one in grizzly country.

I planned to spend the day exploring a long series of creek bottoms, finger meadows, and narrow defiles leading back into the heart of the plateau some fifteen miles away. The dew glistened on the grasses as I hiked up a tiny creek over a timbered divide into a long, narrow meadow. I looked for sign of bears along the way. There were old tracks along the bottoms. I found areas of digging along the strip of grass adjacent to the tree line, and anthills torn to pieces. Each time I crossed a reminder of the presence of grizzlies, I scanned the tree line, listened to the forest, and scented the air.

By midday the narrow finger meadows pinched out and the small creek bottoms gave way to a dense stand of timber. I did not want to go any farther and sat back against a tree. I rested for about an hour, figuring that was all the time I could spare if I wanted to get back to camp by dark. I had come maybe a dozen miles.

The finger meadows were in shadow as I approached the small creek I had followed that morning. I rounded a corner of trees and stepped onto a game trail leading down the defile. I took three steps down the meadow corridor and stopped dead. Thirty yards away on the opposite end of the clearing, walking toward me on the animal trail, was the huge brown grizzly, the alpha animal of all the bears I had watched.

I froze. The grizzly paused, catching my movement, then lowered his head slightly and, with a sort of stiff-legged gait, ambled toward me swinging his head from side to side. I knew from having watched this bear interact with other animals that the worst thing I could do was run.

The big bear stopped thirty feet in front of me. I slowly worked my hand into my bag and gradually pulled out the Magnum. I peered down the gun barrel into the dull red eyes of the huge grizzly. He gnashed his jaws and lowered his ears. The hair on his hump stood up. We stared at each other for what might have been seconds but felt like hours. I knew once again that I was not going to pull the trigger. My shooting days were over. I lowered the pistol. The giant bear flicked his ears and looked off to the side. I took a step backward and turned my head toward the trees. I felt something pass between us. The grizzly slowly turned away from me with grace and dignity and swung into the timber at the end of the meadow. I caught myself breathing heavily again, the flush of blood hot on my face. I felt my life had been touched by enormous power and mystery.

I did not know that the force of that encounter would shape my life for decades to come. Tracking griz would become full-time work for six months of many years, and it lingers yet at the heart of any annual story I tell of my life. I have never questioned the route this journey took: it seems a single trip, the sole option, driven by that same potency that drew me into grizzly country in the beginning.

I returned to camp and kindled a fire, tending it into the night. I threw a pile of lodgepole twigs on the embers and poked at it with a stick. I thought about my old road map and the huge brown grizzly. In Vietnam the primary predator was man. If I had salvaged a grain of wisdom from the agonies of combat, it had nothing to do with knowledge of killing or of waging war. There was no enlightenment in homicide. What was burned deepest into my consciousness was the little acts of grace, lessons that had lain dormant in memory and now were retrieving themselves from anesthetized corners of my brain. It never mattered why. The granting of quarter itself was a transcendence.

The grizzly radiated potency. He carried the physical strength and thorniness of disposition that allowed him to attack or kill most any time he cared. But, almost always, he chose not to. That was power beyond a bully's swaggering. It was the kind of restraint that commands awe—a muscular act of grace.

* * *

The days after Tet hit the cities were perilous for everyone at Bato. I held together long enough to see that period through. That part was easy. It was after it was all over that I began to lose it. Before I unraveled completely, I had learned that more trouble was coming. The NVA and Vietcong had pulled back from the cities and were massing outside Duc Pho. They were on their way to Bato. The spear throwing had been symbolic: Hre civilians driven by a few armed VC. The VC in this case were also Hre, whose political loyalties tended to be tribal. They were fiercely independent people who wanted their own government separate from the Vietnamese. It defied the simplicities of our-side their-side, which was what the American Command filed as military gospel.

I immediately set out after the VC who had cut off Rua's head. Enemy sappers blew up the district building. We pulled all our patrols back to Bato. The Hre resettlements were burned to the ground. Every night the sky was on fire.

On my last night there, Ba Hiep was burning, the inhabitants fleeing into the night. The VC herded the refugees across the river, back out into Indian country.

I watched helplessly across the river from the A-camp, from the porch of the Montagnard commander, as my A-team called in air strikes and artillery. An AC-47 Spooky arrived and hosed down the refugees with the vulcan miniguns—fiery snakes of tracers illuminated by ghostly pale flares. Over 180 civilians, mostly women and children, were caught in the crossfire. The VC drove them out there; we mowed them down. There were no clean hands.

Then it was all over. There was just "mop up"—meaning the dead and wounded, which was my job. At daylight I walked over to the old Colonial dispensary, which was where they would bring the wounded. No one was out on the main street yet, and the building was empty. A grass hut still smoldered behind the dispensary building. I sat down and dug into my small jungle pack and took out the PRC-25 radio and two packages of LRRP patrol rations. In the bottom, along with insect repellent and a smoke grenade, was a stained leather pouch, partially wrapped in a skimpy nylon hammock, that contained my little medicine bundle of all that was decent and sane. Inside was an arrowhead and a Bible-sized bound notebook.

I opened the journal, which held the folded-up road map. It had rotted into squares. I found two pieces where the mildew had not obliterated the print: they made up part of the Rocky Mountain front where the China Wall runs north toward Glacier National Park in northern Montana. I tried to imagine what was up there. I tried to figure out how many days it would take me to bushwhack in there and see what kinds of animals lived in those lonely morrainal basins.

"*Bac Si*," someone cried behind me. I turned and saw Ong Le, the village nurse. In the street behind him were a line of refugees carrying makeshift stretchers. I crammed the radio into the pack and walked down toward the smoking remains of the bamboo hut. I crumbled up the map and threw it on the embers of the house. It took a long time before it started to burn.

Inside the heavy walls of the colonial building I lit a cigarette and waited. Then the dead and wounded began arriving. The last casualties to come in were two little boys and an old woman. The boys both had shrapnel wounds in their legs. The flesh had been torn from their tiny thighs and buttocks, leaving the femur and sciatic nerve exposed. The woman was in worse condition; her left foot hung by a thread of flesh. During the night she had nearly bled to death. Because the old woman was in the most serious condition, I had to work on her first. My junior medic could not get an IV started on her; the woman's veins had collapsed. I did a quick cutdown. The IV solution began flowing. Then the eighty-year-old woman shuddered. Her heart had given out. Just like that, she was dead.

I was glad the old woman had died so I could begin working on the little boys. I had never felt that way before. Even in Vietnam, I had always fought and resisted death. Now I knew I couldn't take it anymore. I had had enough. It was the sign that told me I had to get out. I patched up the boys as best I could. The next day I packed my bags. I got on a chopper for Da Nang and never returned to Bato. Headquarters was glad to get me out of there. I had extended and was overdue anyway. I had been out in the boonies too long and everyone knew it but me. Four days later I left Vietnam. Twenty-four hours after that I was out of the army.

/ / /

That night I slept soundly. A deep tolerance and appreciation had crept into my dreams, born of living with the most dangerous animal on the continent and embracing the inherent risk. It lifted the burden of dominion, leaving me strangely open and vulnerable.

The trees creaked and groaned against one another in the evening wind. One last time, coming from the branches, I thought I heard the death rattle of the old woman. My journey had ended here in grizzly country, the empty space on the map I thought I'd never find. I was a traveler in an older, more complete world. The Indians thought that these bears were gods sent down to earth to make men humble. It was no accident I had arrived.

6

MISSING
SEASONS

(1970s)

After Vietnam I saw the world changing with amazing rapidity, with a violent tempo I had not noticed before 1968. The pace I had heard as a slow drumbeat in the fifties was now a rapid staccato. Resources once considered infinite were clearly diminishing. The entire culture's attitude toward the land grew confused and obsolete. Everywhere you looked, you saw a microcosm of the entire buzzing globe—even in the woods, in grizzly country. The entire concept of wilderness as a place beyond the constraints of culture and human society was itself up for grabs.

The decade of the Vietnam war was lost to me. Even today, I remember those years only as seasons, unable to separate with certainty the events of an autumn in the late sixties from one ten years later. I recollect late April of '69 in the backcountry of Yellowstone much as I do early May of '75 or April in '73. Those springs run together like rivulets of melted snow and converge into a single season. In my mind, these Aprils were the green-up of spring, sedges bending according to the angle of the sun, responding to the length of days, impervious to the dictates of eras.

This method of accounting does not tell much about the changes taking place from year to year, and through almost two decades, beyond making small adjustments for the annual depth of snow in a corner of my brain, about the only constant in my life all those years was that I kept an eye on the grizzly situation. Mostly, what I did was go out into the field and hang out with grizzlies. Things were changing even there.

In the beginning, I went into the wilderness to regroup and pull my life together. But it was soon clear that there would be no hiding. Any image of grizzly country as an Eden walled off from a troubled world was a distortion of truth. Not every journey felt primordial, and no trip unfolded as a simple natural idyll in a vacuum. Although I found moments dominated by wild beauty, cultural distractions—the sound of distant aircraft or scraps of human debris—intruded on every day. I might not have seen these forces at work, but I was always aware they were shading what I saw and influencing how I acted.

Meanwhile, I got what I could from these landscapes. There were times of course when only a big, wild expanse of hundreds of miles of tundra, forest, or desert gave me what I wanted. But usually I could get what I needed in a place like Yellowstone. Though only a quarter of a mile from any road or development, the lodgepole forest felt a light-year away—if you put some effort into it.

While the war in Vietnam raged, the grizzlies were having problems of their own. Even a stunned war veteran walking the backcountry of the Yellowstone Plateau during the early and mid-seventies could tell something was wrong. For one thing, I did not see many grizzly bears. Later, I heard that the government was killing them. I never found out whether the National Park Service at Yellowstone was guilty of the coverups—the animal equivalent of Watergate—of which they were accused.

Having just returned from a place where things like paranoia and schizophrenia yielded perfectly valid versions of reality, I had a hard time buying the official line. I had developed the habit of paying attention to the things people bothered to lie about. The same kind of skepticism I learned from the military at Tet carried over into my reading of the welfare of grizzly bears. Vietnam had hardened my doubts.

These considerations naturally colored how I saw things. The past was never far behind in those days. I had lost trust in the powers that ran the war rooms—regardless of whether they were the generals who ran the Big War in Vietnam or the politicians and bureaucrats who ran the smaller one against the grizzly. You could not miss the corrupting potential of power, the gravity toward self-serving lies, the means-over-ends thinking that cemented my lowbrow alliances.

I have never considered it coincidental that I became mixed up in the problems of the grizzly bear. My little quest into the wilderness to lick my war wounds was never imagined without difficulty. I might have been numb but I was not indifferent. Once I came to know grizzlies and committed myself to trying to keep a few of them around, all traces of complacency vanished.

The idea of anybody killing off the grizzlies of Yellowstone drove me crazy. These bears had saved my life. The grizzly was the living embodiment of wild nature, the original landscape that was once our home. The fact that they had not been hounded into extinction here told me America still had a chance to turn things around. I believed this despite the evidence of Vietnam. I believed it because I had to. A world capable of self-destruction, armed with the mentality that put us in Vietnam, would show no restraint next time.

Meanwhile, my life unfolded as a chain of seasons undifferentiated except by sporadic events: little things sometimes, like a sunset over the great bosque of the Rio Grande and a late November thunderstorm gathering on the western horizon.

* * *

Thousands of blackbirds—red-winged, Brewer's, yellow-headed, and cowbirds—smashed into the cattails, landing for the night. A bolt of lightning cracked in the cottonwoods; blackbirds exploded, darkening the sky; and beyond, ten thousand snow geese startled, rising simultaneously off the gray surface of the wetland, the water frothing, pink in reflection before the approaching storm.

* * *

This was my Wintercount, the way the Plains Indians named an annual cycle after events of great power or magic. October was the

bugle of a bull elk, whose passage was first marked by a trip in
Yellowstone I took with my friend Gage, one of the two or three
people who got me interested in making a film record to help
grizzlies. It was the early seventies and we were looking for bears.

′′′

An autumn storm brought low, blowing clouds, freezing rain, and
finally three or four inches of coarse snow. We struck out along a
fringe of timber into a great valley where hundreds of Yellowstone's grizzlies had summered during the past four decades. Low
clouds hung over the sagebrush hills, and pellets of sleet stung our
faces as we trudged along a sluggish creek fished by mergansers
and headed upwind toward a distant cluster of thermal springs a
few hours into the valley.

We passed a bull herd of four shaggy monarchs standing into
the wind, watching as we passed on the trail fifty feet away. From a
bluff we could see more bison grazing on the creek flats in the
blowing fog. Ahead we could see a blanket of steam hanging
about the hot creek, which drained a hillside with many hot
springs. All this was grizzly country. We turned upslope toward
the timber, hoping to ease up over a gentle divide and look into the
basin into which the hot creek ran. From off the wall of lodgepole
pine echoed the rising bugle and glottal coughing of a bull elk.
Another answered. The sound floated down across the valley and
disappeared into the wind.

We crested the hill and looked down into the narrow valley
filled with steam. Between the clouds of steam and fog animals
moved. More bugling drifted up, coming from both the basin and
timber above. The steam rose and rolled off the bottom to unveil
more animals. The valley was filled with milling elk, perhaps two
or three hundred of them. Some of the elk spotted us and began to
move away. A dozen massive bull elk blew their mating bugles
into the steam, each trying to maintain some residual control over
his harem. The rut was over, although this large herd appeared to
be the coalescence of a number of harem herds. About thirty bulls,
among them ten of the largest I had ever seen, were scattered
among milling masses of cows and yearlings.

The billowing steam surged and pulsed, opening pockets of high-stepping, ghostly silhouettes in the fog. The herd sensed alarm now and churned in confusion; though agitated, they couldn't get our scent. Bugles and barks bounced into the hollowness of the weather.

An hour later, after the elk had retreated to the security of the timber, we dropped down to try out the hot pools of the cascading creek. The October wind and driving sleet had chilled us. The bleached skull of a bull bison overlooked the steaming miniature waterfall. We soaked in the scalding waters till we turned lobster red, then stood cooling in the blowing snow. We dressed and walked down the creek out into the open valley. Down across the flat from out of a buffalo wallow, a pair of coyotes darted away into the sage, their tails held low to the ground. A second later four ravens lifted off the same piece of ground. The ground here was warm; even in winter the snow did not accumulate. The wind shifted and the smell hit us like a freight train.

The bull elk had been dead for about two weeks, probably a casualty of the rut. The coyotes and ravens had worked the carcass over pretty good, though plenty of rancid meat remained. It was significant that no bears had visited the carcass.

* * *

I had two friends back then; both were named Ed. Ed Abbey and Ed Gage. Gage I had met through a mutual acquaintance in a college bar a couple of years after I got out of Vietnam. We talked briefly and hit it off well. Though I doubted I would hear from him again, we exchanged phone numbers. The next morning I was out at my desert place when the phone rang. It was Gage. He apologized for calling, saying that although he did not know me well, he hadn't been able to get hold of anyone else and he needed to talk to someone. His house had burned to the ground that very morning, and Gage spent the next half hour telling me what that meant to him, how it had been a relief to be unburdened of his material possessions, and how the only real loss was his girl-friend's cat.

I was taken aback. His openness and intensity were unfamiliar to me; it seemed something out of Dostoyevski. I was moved: I had not had a close friend in a long time.

During the winters I retreated back to Arizona, where I had first run into Gage and Abbey. I was and am a total wipe-out as a mountain man. I do not like trapping and my feet get cold. I spent about seven months each year in grizzly country. Only once was I silly enough to endure a brutal Montana winter. Other years I fled south.

More winters passed. When I ran out of money, I took part-time jobs or worked as a mailman. Abbey and I split a full-time job as caretaker of a large private wildlife preserve and working cattle ranch in Arizona because neither of us wanted to be tied down all the time. In 1972 I caught a glimpse of one of the last Mexican white wolves out in one of those canyons. I stared eyeball to eyeball through binoculars at him for thirty seconds. We knew the wolf was there because of his considerable local notoriety as an expert ham-stringer of beef calves. I was told a decade later my chance encounter—enshrined within my memory alongside my grizzly bear dreams—was considered the last "reliable" sighting of a wolf in Arizona. At that time I did not consider myself reliable at anything.

Despite the surge of imagination a wolf or cougar track conjured up, I found the country tame and so did Abbey. Cows and cattledom had penetrated every last niche of the huge estate, as they had nearly everywhere else in the Southwest. I had no complaint against the few cows my good cowboy buddies ran in these hills. Rather, I was appalled by the intolerance of frontier pastoralism, which believed, in its endless quest to domesticate the planet, that it had to shoot, kill, blow away, trap, or poison every wild dog, cat, bear, eagle, skunk, badger, or weasel—all to protect frail and slow-witted livestock.

The passage of winter was marked by desert trips. One February I took Gage out into the vast Piedras Negras desert on the Mexican border. Winter gave way to spring early that year. Purple lupine and yellow brittlebush decorated the Growler Range. We moved west across the playa and camped at the foot of the Sierra Pinta along a wedge of granite. A Costa's hummingbird buzzed the flowers.

By the fire we mapped out the routes our expeditions would

take. We would be put ashore on a deserted island in the Sea of Cortés, where ospreys nested on every rock promontory and the barking of sea lions troubled our sleep, to live off the land for a month. We planned a trip into the last stronghold of the Mexican grizzly in the Sierra Madre. It was only a rumor but we had heard there was one left down there.

Back in Tucson, the saguaro cactus budded. Then it was April and time to think about moving up north. Each day I looked up at the Catalina Mountains, at the dark gray line marking the zone of timber at seven thousand feet, and felt an ache in my heart. The geese had flown north and the snow had begun to melt.

I had a new plan. I had accepted my third job with the federal government: first green beret sergeant, then hippie mailman, and now backcountry ranger with the National Park Service. Actually, it was Abbey's idea. "They give you a quitting date to look forward to," he said. I would be stationed in North Cascades National Park in northern Washington, living in a tent in a subalpine basin below the roar of waterfalls dumping off hanging glaciers. I would be paid almost four bucks an hour, more money than I had ever been worth in my life.

Having accumulated too much gear, I sold the jeep and bought an old pickup, which I outfitted with a small camper shell Abbey's girlfriend had been using as part of a chicken coop. I said good-bye to Gage and Abbey, popped a beer, and drove off into the night. Four days and seven six-packs later I arrived in the clearcut forests of the Skagit Valley.

Thus I began my career with the National Park Service. I was downwardly mobile within the governmental service: I tended to be demoted a GS grade every year or so, applying for and accepting lower-paying jobs with fewer responsibilities. Finally, I bottomed out as a GS-0, working as a fire lookout in Glacier National Park.

Anarchists make lousy law enforcement officers and I was no exception. The closest I came to the policeman's joy of busting was to write a ticket on an illegally parked Winnebago. By the end of the summer of 1975, I would wreck a government pickup under

dubious circumstances, pick a fight with a Watcom County dep-
uty sheriff, and leave forever, driving east into grizzly country—to
the great relief of North Cascade National Park.

But all that came later. In the meantime I logged another Wintercount and started counting the years again. One day I was reading
by myself when a young woman, dressed in hiking boots, a
summer blouse, and cutoffs, stepped over my sleeping dog, normally a wary animal, and into the government dormitory. I took
off for another five-day stint in the backcountry. When I returned
there was a fancy distributor cap with eight spark plug leads and its
coil wire cut off sitting on the table. I had missed something.

Lisa had befriended my dog, and the two of them went off to
the Pasayten Wilderness camping. On the way out she ran into a
party of horsemen who told her that if they ever saw her in there
again they would first kill her dog and then shoot her. Rednecks of
the worst kind from the east side. The macho hunters rode in and
Lisa walked out, finding their Ford Bronco and horse trailer at the
trailhead. She waited a little while, then opened the hood and went
to work with her Swiss army knife on the distributor cap, cutting
the leads and pulling it off. I could imagine the look on their faces
when they opened the hood after trying to start their rig.

I was impressed. After Vietnam, I did not want to see more
victims. I admired her spunk for believing, as I did, that debts
were cumulative and that it was better to get even than mad.

Much later, I'd look back on that summer—the same year I
began my full-time grizzly bear project—and remember the fullness of days, the perfume of ripe blackberries and the pungency of
shelf fungus on dead logs, the sweet, lush smells of harvest and the
bracken fern dripping with the rains of September. The time
lingers yet as a fragrance, the memory of olfaction. The sensate
days of late summer. We camped in the old orchard, where steel-
head splashed in the creek. I lay awake in the tent tracing the path of
the full moon, smelling the musk of wet dog, her scent, the
sweetness of berries, and the fruit of apples rotting on the ground.
And I remember the distributor cap.

7
THE BITTER
CREEK GRIZ

APRIL (1980s)

The deeper snows of the meadow melted away to gray volcanic sinter as I reached a large thermal area. I kicked off my
snowshoes and crossed a small, swampy creek on a log stained
white by carbonate groundwater. Ravens hovered over the nearby
slope of a timbered knob with steam pouring out from fissures
along its edges. I circled downwind, trying to pick up the scent.
There are winterkills here every spring, usually old bull bison.
There's no mistaking the fetor of a carcass in the area.

I moved cautiously upwind through deadfalls and timber.
Rounding a corner of the tiny hill, I saw white bones and dark hide
lying amid downfalls smoking from the sulfuric acid produced by
thermal sulfur and melting snow. No bears were in sight, though
they could have been bedded in nearby timber.

Ravens burst from a tree, startling me. Easy now, Peacock. I
am always a bit clumsy around bears early in the spring after a
winter of casual attentiveness. Take lots of time. Just do not walk
up on a grizzly bedded near a carcass. Half the time they will
defend their food cache and charge.

Having completed a cautious circle of the buffalo carcass, I
eased up to have a look. Grizzly sign: tracks and a scat about five
days old, the dish-shaped depression of an older day bed, not much

left of the carcass. There was plenty of recent coyote sign. The
grizzlies were done with this one.

I looked back at the sprawling, snow-filled valley I had crossed on
snowshoes. Long terraces and alluvial benches rose gently from
the narrow bottom toward a distant treeline. A monotonous blanket of snow was broken only by the dark waters of a sluggish
creek. April in Yellowstone is sufficiently wintry to allow me to
imagine how February might feel without risking the unmistakable hazards of six feet of snow at fifty below zero. Down below,
April was a soggy month, unlike this high plateau where snow
lingers into May. I liked this season in Yellowstone because of the
lack of people; the sloppy going discouraged both skiers and
hikers.

The second carcass lay on the edge of a thermal swamp, three
hundred yards away and crosswind from where I was. I circled into
the wind, following the course of a warm creek that sliced a
narrow swath through the snow-blanketed meadow. Through my
heavy binoculars I saw a raven perched on top of a dead lodgepole
pine. A coyote lurked in the shadow of the treeline. I edged over
the rise and froze: a huge dark grizzly shook the remains of a
buffalo carcass in the air, much as a dog might play with a stick.
From a hundred feet away I watched, motionless in the fading
light.

The bear slammed the carcass to the ground and circled,
stamping his forepaws on the bones and hide. I waited until his
back was turned, then retreated a hundred yards and climbed a
steep timbered hillside. I could see the flash of his claws as he
turned over the dead buffalo. These were much longer than a black
bear's, maybe four inches long. The grizzly looked almost black in
the dim light. His shoulders, nearly as high as mine, were separated by a mound of muscle, which rippled as the bear pawed and
slid the heavy carcass along the ground. His head was massive,
scooped out below the eyes, and he must have weighed well over
six hundred pounds.

After a few minutes I saw the bear pass below me, cross my
tracks, then pick up and follow my snowshoe tracks away from the

thermal swamp and out onto the snow. If he knew I was up here, he did not show it.

I sat nervously for ten minutes, maybe more, then dropped down and stared at the tracks leading into the timber. I followed, but the light was dim. I could barely see the bear tracks over the crosshatched marks of my snowshoes. I followed the trail for twenty feet into the trees. Something made me stop short; I sensed the chill of premonition. I hurried back to the hill and looked for a safe place to set up for the night. It was much too dark to be stumbling around in grizzly country.

At dawn I slipped over the hilltop and looked down on the scene from the evening before. No sign of bears. The bison carcass lay in a warm pocket heated by steam vents. I glassed the white thermal flat and spotted two dish-shaped depressions near trees, where bears had bedded near the carcass. Not much was left of it. A line of tracks led out across the flats.

Moving cautiously, I climbed down to study the bear prints. The rear pads were more than ten inches long on hard ground; the left track was asymmetrical and toed in. I checked more tracks to confirm the pattern. It's him all right, I had thought so—the Bitter Creek Griz, my favorite Yellowstone bear.

I first got to know this unusual bear in 1977 and have seen him almost every year since. Even back then, he was a huge grizzly with a grayish muzzle—probably a survivor of the purges of the early seventies, when almost a hundred grizzlies were known killed or removed from the Yellowstone ecosystem in a single two-year period. He also appeared to be an effective predator, killing yearling bison and an occasional moose. His pigeon-toed spoor, perhaps the result of an old injury, was distinctive.

I followed the prints out onto the crusted snow. The grizzly tracks followed my snowshoe trail for nearly a hundred yards, then veered off to the right in a tight circle to an icy depression behind a large deadfall ten feet off my trail. More tracks led away.

The story was clear: last night the Bitter Creek Griz had backtracked me, then circled around and bedded, waiting for me behind a log ten feet from where I would walk. Had I gone farther into the timber that night he would have been right there. The icy bed told me he lay in wait a long time.

This was the second time this had happened to me—a grizzly setting up what looked like a deliberate ambush. I do not know what it means. Maybe it is only curiosity. Still, there were moments when I imagined a malevolent intelligence lurking behind that log.

Stalking or ambushing humans during the day is exceedingly rare although not unknown in the literature of grizzly lore. There was one report from British Columbia that during the winter of 1970, a Doig River Indian tracked a grizzly that circled back behind a mossy hummock and killed and partially devoured him. So I don't know what to think. I do not think every grizzly lying in ambush intends to do me harm, but I do not think the bears are joking either.

This kind of unsettling behavior by grizzly bears resists easy categorization. It is one of the things that attracted me to them in the first place. Living with grizzlies is an eternal freshness: you can never be sure exactly what you are dealing with, and your curiosity transcends bafflement because you are bargaining with an animal who can kill and eat you.

I squatted and traced the outline of the grizzly's rear foot in the crusted mud. How humanlike it was. The first time I saw a skinned black bear carcass I was shocked by its eerie resemblance to a human corpse. Bears stand upright and, like us, have frontal, binocular vision. They are dexterous and can rotate their forepaws. They snore when they sleep and cuff their cubs when the youngsters mess up. The bear is an omnivore, the only one much larger than we are. In North America, a continent without primates, grizzlies are the most manlike animals. They are, like us, generalists who pioneer diverse habitats. They prefer their own company much of the time, and know both the joys and risks of solitude. Bears remind us of what we might have become if we had not left the wilderness to live in villages, towns, and suburbs.

Not knowing if the Bitter Creek Griz would return, I waited out the day watching from the hilltop. I avoided approaching the carcass, since a grizzly can detect a man's scent in the track of a Vibram sole, not to mention the stench we leave behind on the trees and bushes. I'll sit here, I thought, for a few days waiting for bears. If none show, I'll pack up and make the trip to Bitter Creek.

I moved about three-quarters of a mile downwind, to the end of the thermal basin. Snow lingered in the timber. I found an open patch of ground on the south side of a large lodgepole pine that was surrounded by downfalls. I pitched my green tent, then relocated a miniature forest of beetle-killed lodgepole saplings around it, making it invisible from twenty feet away or from the air. When I finished, I picked up a pine bough and backtracked, brushing away my tracks back to the small creek. This is the way I camp and live in grizzly country: invisibly—or as inconspicuously as possible. As long as I can remember, I have felt this way.

I leaned back against a tree and stoked the tiny fire, watching the purple sky darken. The silence was pervasive, broken only by the call of a sandhill crane gliding to an evening roost and the cries of snipe zigzagging in the fading light.

My strategy in Yellowstone is to greet bears soon after they leave their winter dens. Grizzlies here dig them in high, remote areas, go in about November, and sleep until mid-March or April. Then they drop down to wintering grounds of deer and elk or thermal areas, where they nose out carrion, rodents or their caches of seeds, and the first grasses and sedges. I look for bears here when the first ground melts out sometime in April.

It had been fifteen years since I first ran into bears here. This time I was in Yellowstone to film grizzly bears—a project I began in the mid-seventies. Since that time I had spent every spring here, usually arriving in April and leaving in early June. When the backcountry opens up and the people begin showing up, I head for more remote country in northern Montana around Glacier Park. When the crowds thin out, in October or early November, I go back to Yellowstone to check on a female grizzly I know, to see when she goes into her den.

In seven seasons of shooting with a movie camera, I have filmed some two hundred grizzlies up in northern Montana and only about fifty grizzlies—about a quarter, maybe more, no one knows exactly—of the total number surviving in Yellowstone.

I wanted to shoot 16-mm movie film of wild grizzlies far from roads and people. I wanted to see how they would behave

apart from man and his tools. I limited myself to bears living south
of Canada: grizzlies, who were listed as "threatened" since 1975
under the Endangered Species Act. It was not that the grizzlies of
Canada or Alaska were not as important or did not have plenty of
troubles of their own; I just thought the battle to save the grizzly
was down here.

I inherited the project from my friend Gage, who gave me an
old but functional Bolex movie camera. Back in 1973 we came to
believe that the grizzlies in Yellowstone were in trouble. Gage had
traveled up from Arizona to visit me in Yellowstone. I picked him
up at the Idaho Falls airport in late October of 1973, just as the
cottonwoods had turned yellow in the river bottoms. Gage
wanted to talk to a bunch of people up here and find out what had
happened to Yellowstone's grizzlies. We both had heard tales about
the bear situation in Yellowstone Park, mostly stories that the road
bears, the little blacks, had disappeared. Less had been heard about
the grizzlies, although there were lots of rumors they were being
killed off.

Gage's visit to Yellowstone in 1973 turned out to be a pivotal
event in my life. On one trip we encountered the ghostly herd of
elk churning in the fog and steam—which became my Wintercount. On another long hike, we dropped off the top of a 9,400-
foot ridge and descended into a gully, a deep flute lined with huge
whitebark pines, running down the north side of the mountain.
We stopped under a dead snag, a huge fir with a striking two-
pronged top, and stared at a pile of fresh talus and loam spilling
down the steep hillside. Creeping closer, we stared into a yard-
wide hole dug into the mountainside at the top of the alluvium. It
was a grizzly den.

Between trips, Gage had done his interviewing, talking with
over fifty people, mostly lower-level park and concession employees, about where the bears had gone. The story he received
was a rather consistent account of park personnel shooting the
begging black bears that frequented roads and campgrounds. It
was less clear what had happened to the grizzlies, though hardly
anyone had seen any. Gage was enraged. I had trouble buying the
commonly expressed argument that the National Park Service was
purposefully decimating the grizzly population. But it did seem

clear that an atmosphere was created wherein a spectrum of employees could dispose of "problem" bears without too many questions being asked. Park employees had told us repeatedly of one high-ranking ranger on the east side who personally killed over two hundred bears. I never knew what to make of such reports.

So Gage enlisted me to fight on the side of the bears, and gave me a camera. Filming grizzlies was also an excuse for learning about grizzlies—certainly about their chances of survival—but also little things about what individual bears do in early spring, when they leave their dens, where they travel, what they eat, and anything else I could infer about their age, sex, and reproduction. I do not always believe government agencies entrusted with protecting endangered species when they tell me the animals are doing just swell back in the deep woods where no one else goes, so I wanted to see for myself.

Besides, there simply wasn't a lot of information about what grizzlies do when there is four feet of soft spring snow on the ground. Before Yellowstone Park was established, grizzlies may have dropped off the plateau altogether in spring, following the ungulate herds, leaving the park area for the big river bottoms that green up first. Now those valleys are settled and grizzlies do not last long there. The remaining bears are mostly up on the plateau. Even within the national park's boundaries, bears have a tough time finding uninhabited areas. There are little centers of industrial tourism strung every fifteen miles or so along a network of highways—places like Fishing Bridge or Grant Village. For instance, some of the best spring habitat for bears should be in the Firehole River valley, but commercial development at Old Faithful and accompanying road travel have driven most grizzlies elsewhere. As late as 1975 you could find bears there. Of course, the road had been closed to snowmobiles and the three grizzlies there left within a few days after the road was reopened.

Back in the 1970s the Firehole was a special place full of animal herds and thermal areas, some of the best winter ground for ungulates. I lived with a big brown grizzly who, about every fourth day, would run down and kill a winter-weakened elk and drag it back into the timber, where he would cache and feed on it for about three days. Most of the time he ambushed them from

close distances within sparse timber. The one time I saw him work
the open meadows, he loped behind eight cow elk for two hundred
feet, then put on a burst of speed and caught the cow closest to him
by grabbing her flanks with his paws and throwing his chest on her
rump and collapsing her with his weight. He seized the dead elk
by the shoulder and dragged her into the timber before he fed.
Since then winters have been milder and the park has accommo-
dated the concessionaires by keeping the road open most of the
time. Grizzlies are denied the few weeks of hunting and undisturbed poking around they need after the winter.

After a couple of days of fruitless sitting and waiting for the Bitter
Creek Griz, I began wondering what was wrong. I decided to take
a closer look. I edged up on the old bull. He had been dead much
longer than I originally thought—since early March or so. Only
the hide remained. The grizzlies might be finished with that area
for the season. It was probably time to move on to Bitter Creek.
    I decided to explore the thermal basin, looking for the one
soakable drainage in the area, the others being too hot or shallow.
The light faded and a snow squall rolled in from the west, bringing
gusts of wind and flurries of snow. I stripped off my smoky,
muddy clothes and eased into the hot pool. The tub was big
enough across for one stroke and deep enough to boil you like a
poached trout by morning. I watched my step; I would hate to
black out and float up in this one. Yet this was the quintessence of
my Yellowstone experience: sitting naked in the pungent waters,
snowflakes melting on my sweaty, balding head, listening to
cranes and snipe, coyotes howling in the gathering shadows.
    The trek to Bitter Creek required crossing a major river—a
dangerous ford during high waters—waiting until early the next
morning for the snow to crust over to allow for snowshoe travel,
and then following game trails for a dozen more miles through
timber interspersed with meadows.
    I spent the morning repacking my backpack, an old Trailwise
I have used for two decades. It has a single huge compartment with
four side pockets and another on the flap. Accessibility is a problem, so I keep all my emergency and survival items in one side

pocket, medicine in another, and repair materials and commonly used stuff in the other two. The bigger pocket on the flap I use for camera equipment; light meter, cable release, lens cleaner, and the like. The big compartment holds all my cold weather gear. That leaves room for a little food in the pack, usually a large bag of granola, some protein powder mixed with dried milk, and a few sticks of jerky. The remainder of the compartment is taken up by the camera, lenses, and film.

Most of my gear is inexpensive. I use Korean War surplus Marine K rubber boots. The snowshoes are hand-me-downs. My sleeping bag is handmade and warm only to temperatures above freezing. I augment it with an army poncho liner. I also carry one of those thin space-age things, and when it really gets cold I wear all my wool clothing to bed—socks, hat, everything. Below five or ten degrees I tend to freeze my ass off. The tent is a cheap alpine-style arrangement with poles and guy lines. Since you cannot drive stakes that hold in snow, I tie each line from the tent to two-foot lengths of flat logs, which I bury perpendicular to the guy lines under a foot of snow. I stomp it to keep the lines taut. I don't bother with stoves. I don't cook out here and there is no need to melt snow in a thermal area. I tie the tent, sleeping bag, and pad to the outside of the pack. The twenty-two-pound wooden tripod, a fluid head, is secured to the pack frame. When I'm not wearing them, the snowshoes are tied on top of that. The entire package weighs close to a hundred pounds.

Before leaving for Bitter Creek, I had one more job to do: hide the head of the bull bison, which died in the open. If the Park Service discovers the head, rangers with sledgehammers are sent to smash the skull to pieces. They say this is to protect the bones from horn and head hunters, who spot the skull—perhaps from a helicopter—swoop down, pluck it up, and sell it to buyers who grind up every last piece of bone and antler for sale on the Asian market as an aphrodisiac.

Late in the morning, I packed up for Bitter Creek wondering where I should hide the bull buffalo head. He should have stayed where he was forever. Barring that, I thought he should rejoin the bull herd of about a dozen bison with which he spent his adult life. I had been looking after this herd for years, and stashed other skulls when bulls died during hard winters. He would join his buddies in a semicircle of four bison skulls facing the rising sun. A mile away, hidden where they would never be discovered, below trees and under the snow, I brought together a ghost herd of bison skulls, decorated with the feathers of crane and eagle, the recipients of bundles of sage and handfuls of earth carried in from sacred mountains and offered up in private ceremonies. In 1850, the bison numbered in the millions and were the center of the spiritual life of the people who lived around them. By 1883, they were virtually extinct and the bones sold at twelve dollars a ton as fertilizer. What had taken place was no hunt but a bloodbath. My little gesture was partial payment on a long-lived insult.

It was afternoon by the time I reached the river. The snow was soft and deep. I wallowed in the drifts, on toward the ford, making only two hundred yards the last hour, and arrived at the testicle-deep crossing as planned, during the warmest part of the day. I took off my pants and socks and stepped back into my rubber boots. Hitching up my pack, I waded out into the current, using my cross-country snowshoes as crutches. The danger lay in losing my footing and getting swept downstream into deeper water. I took my time, slipping once but catching myself with a long snowshoe.

The next morning I was gliding across the frozen snow in the middle of a mile-wide meadow when I heard the droning of an airplane engine. Instinctively, I raced for a small clump of sagebrush, kicked off my snowshoes, threw down the pack, and covered everything up with a white sheet I had at the top of my pack, hoping my tracks would not be visible from a thousand feet up. I never feel so naked or vulnerable as when I am hiding in the open from aircraft.

′ ′ ′

In October we found a giant Montagnard crossbow up the Gia Vuc valley armed with a six-foot spear aimed at the sky. An anti-helicopter crossbow. These Hre Yards didn't even have a word in their language for airplane.

A month later Graves's six-man reconnaissance team was

extracted out of A Shau, and on the way out they flew low and slow over a full company of NVA eating chow on an open hilltop. To a man, the entire well-armed enemy unit stuck their middle fingers up into the sky, flipping off the helicopter. Nobody fired or even reached for a weapon; they just gave the slick the bird. Giving the finger was not supposed to be a Vietnamese gesture.

*   *   *

The small plane passed. Although I probably knew who was in the plane—a biologist, a man I like and admire—my initial reaction persisted. There ought to be a few places out of which we keep aircraft, or keep them high enough so as not to be intrusive. What is the point of designating a two-dimensional wilderness and permitting the buzzing or hovering of a helicopter at treetop level? This place, so wild and big this time of year on foot, can be shrunk to a small, tame landscape by machines.

I arrived at Cimarron Basin, a small thermal area on Goose Creek and a good place to look for bear tracks. I found the fresh, chewed bones of a yearling bison, and, near the closest tree, a dish-shaped grizzly bed clawed out of the rhyolitic soil. Although the evidence in this case was quite circumstantial, I thought that the buffalo was probably a grizzly kill because of the position of the bones and a drag mark across the thermal mud. Leading to the buffalo skeleton was a faint set of tracks—the unmistakable pigeon-toed print of the Bitter Creek Griz.

To me the Bitter Creek Griz was the archetypal Yellowstone grizzly. He was what you could expect of a big male allowed to grow old and bold. Adult females are fully grown by the time they have their first litter; nutrition from then on serves cub growth. Male grizzlies, by contrast, continue to grow each year of their life, suggesting that greater size, and therefore dominance, serve some evolutionary function and that the social life of the bear may be more complex than is generally thought.

Far out in the meadow, huge white birds circled and dropped into Goose Creek, the only ice-free water for miles, disappearing below the river terrace. I took shelter under a solitary pine forty feet above the creek and waited, motionless, for the giant birds to

float below me, as I knew they would. These birds were white
pelicans with wingspans over a hundred inches. They regularly
float down Goose Creek during spring in great rafts—there were
two dozen in this case—dipping their huge heads in synchronous
motion, fishing for native cutthroat and suckers. The pelican flo-
tilla passed below and disappeared downstream.

I shouldered the big pack, made awkward by the heavy camera equipment packed at the top where it was handy, and moved to
the end of the valley where open ground radiated heat beneath the
trees. I set up another guerrilla camp.

The way I feel about camping and about grizzlies—I seem to
approach these things like warfare—has its origins back in Southeast Asia in 1968 and, a few years later, in Yellowstone National
Park, especially 1973, the year Gage visited. Gage had decided to
investigate the rumors that rangers were killing bears. When he
walked into park headquarters and demanded an answer, he was
received with some paranoia and considerable patronization, and
told that the animals he had been looking for were doing well, all
350 of them, hiding out in the backcountry being natural bears.
This was the stock answer handed out for a decade.

We knew something was wrong. It wasn't that park rangers
were killing off the grizzlies without reporting it—that was never
clear. But it was transparent that an insulated environment had
been created by the Park Service—which heard who it wanted to
hear. I witnessed a larger such system in Asia: just close ranks and
keep a stiff upper lip; this too will pass.

Our republic, Gage thought, was troubled; we had lies in
Vietnam, during Watergate, and in our oldest national park: the
Park Service was lying to us, and maybe themselves, about the
number of bears in and around Yellowstone, the living representa-
tion of paradise in the national mind. The Yellowstone region was a
microcosm, about as generous as a culture such as ours was likely to
get in granting land and other concessions to creatures like bears.

We thought we should do something. Back then, I considered
myself better prepared as a demolition specialist than an educator.
Still, I thought we should try. In the mid-1970s, the grizzlies of the
lower forty-eight had few friends. Only a handful of people

worked in the field, and virtually all of these were biologists tied to government agencies. Because grizzlies were controversial, scientists were discouraged from speaking out. Then Gage came up with the Bolex.

Gage's gift of the camera gave me a chance to publicize the grizzlies' situation and to make a record of their lives. I dragged the camera out into the hills and collected movie footage, feeling not unlike an early nineteenth-century ethnographer heading up the Missouri in the spring of 1837, when smallpox hit the Mandan villages, to record the vanishing ceremonies of a dying culture. From a Montana biologist friend, we knew that extant footage consisted of bears at the dumps or along roads and salmon streams in Alaska and that no one had much film of grizzlies in the wild. Maybe I could fill in here. I liked bears and didn't have anything else to do. So, after years of wandering, I acquired a project: to attempt to assemble a collective portrait, perhaps the last, of the grizzlies south of Canada. I began my work in the Yellowstone backcountry on April 17, 1975. Later, I realized that that was the day the Khmer Rouge rolled into Phnom Penh and began the killing. From my slightly twisted point of view, preserving grizzlies was a radical idea; it meant putting the brakes on a world gone mad.

* * *

I remembered Tet and the last time I went to Ba An. I waited on the hill above his house for the Vietcong who I had been told had cut off the head of my Montagnard friend, Dinh Rua. Bato District was that kind of small war back then, so I knew. At 1715 a VC in black pj's carrying a Swedish K left the house. I hosed down, firing on semiautomatic over seven hundred meters, arching the M16 tracer rounds down from a hill, shooting off half a magazine until he disappeared.

This was early 1968, the time of the Tet Offensive, a time of random murders and blind vengeance, and I wanted to find a scapegoat sufficiently monstrous to explain the necessity of all the corpses.

The next day some villagers from Bato saw the body; I had

drilled him dead-center. Later I learned the details and found I had killed the wrong man. What the hell, I told myself, he was a Vietcong and was carrying a rifle; so what if he wasn't the assassin?

But something happened to me after that. It was the beginning of my end over there, and I came apart quickly. The rationalization returned to horrify me. I quit killing strangers forever. It never had been my war anyway.

_/ / /_

By morning my snowshoes were gliding over the crusted snows of the huge meadow, leaving no visible tracks. I stuck to the north edge of the valley, paralleling the tree line, and arrived at the mouth of Bitter Creek just as the snow began to soften up and travel slowed down.

I sat out the middle of the day, as I usually did in late April and early May in Yellowstone. Traveling long or regular distances to preplanned objectives was simply impossible. Most of the time the snow was too soft for snowshoeing and too deep for walking. Thus, spring dictates Zen-like days: for hours you don't move at all, and you become more contemplative because you have to stay in one place, sometimes for days, running your senses repeatedly over the same scenes, finding subtle details you missed before. Moreover, my business was finding and bagging grizzlies with a movie camera which, in April, meant setting up in a good place and waiting for a bear to pass through. I have waited as long as three weeks at a single site without seeing a griz. Under such circumstances, vision tends to become myopic and the mind, meditative. The waking hours are spent on calcite crystals decorating the fringes of thermal drainage, the breeding of insects, the alarm cries of Clark's nutcrackers, and the skewed tracks left by a crippled bison.

Just before nightfall I began following the pigeon-toed tracks up Bitter Creek. There was snow-free ground there and grizzly sign everywhere. In addition to the Bitter Creek Griz, I could see that a sow and her single offspring had been excavating rodent burrows and tunnels. The valley was narrow and bordered with thick forests of pine and spruce. I slid off to the leeward side and looked for a good place to camp.

Where you choose to sleep in bear country is critical: of the nine people killed by grizzlies south of Canada in the past two decades, seven were in or on their sleeping bags. The grizzly that kills people during the night is not the same as the bear you surprise at close range who reflexively mauls you. The grizzly in your camp at night is looking for food, maybe prey. Once a marauding grizzly makes the transition from investigative curiosity to predation, you are in a world of trouble. Of course, these circumstances were exceedingly rare; more people die of bad egg salad in a year than from grizzly attacks in a century.

It is impossible to predict with certainty the temperament of the bear with whom you are dealing. Hence, the most important consideration in picking a safe campsite is finding a place that bears are not likely to visit: a spot that is not on or near a bear trail, a potential feeding site, or a place where bears bed or travel to or from beds. This means don't camp in a meadow, along a drainage, a saddle or ridge gentle enough to encourage bear travel, or hiking trails, since bears also use these corridors, especially at night. Anytime in doubt, bushwhack into the timber or brush for at least a hundred yards. In a defile, such as a coastal beach in Alaska, you will have to crawl deep into the miserable alder thickets if you want safe sleeping.

I moved across the shallow, bitter-tasting creek, far away from any sign of grizzly activity, and climbed the bank. Two hundred yards into the timber I dumped off my pack and kicked the snow off a tiny clearing in which I pitched my tent. Even during good weather I use the tent. I am not sure why. Perhaps it provides a visual screen, giving me one more chance to talk to the grizzly. I also sleep in the middle of the tent. I keep this tent and the rest of my bear-country gear as odor-free as possible; I never cook or use smelly foods around this gear, even when camping far from bear country.

Twenty minutes before first light, the snipe woke me with their hollow winnowing. Two inches of fresh snow covered my tent and the ground. I grabbed the camera and crept toward the edge of the valley. Far up the narrow meadow I saw a dark shape moving in the shadows. If it's the Bitter Creek Griz, I thought, this will be the first time I've caught him in full daylight. A cautious survivor, he prefers nocturnal roaming.

I made out a second shape at the edge of the trees. A medium-size silver-tipped grizzly stepped into the sunlight, joined by a second, smaller brown bear. At first I thought this was a mating pair, though it was a month early for such coupling. The pair was more likely a sow and her huge yearling or two-year-old. The bears swung out into the meadow opposite me and began excavating pocket gopher burrows, probably looking for seed caches— little piles of chocolate-chip-shaped onion bulbs. The young bear tried to nuzzle his mother and drew a growl; she was weaning him. "She'll probably come into estrus and mate again this June," I thought, "maybe with the Bitter Creek Griz." The cub sat back on his haunches, looking a little puzzled, and watched. They dug throughout the crisp morning. The sunlight warmed the temperature to almost fifty degrees, and the family moved off up the valley across the creek and into the trees. I watched them disappear, glad to have filmed without disturbing them.

This grizzly family was the sixth I had seen using the Bitter Creek area from 1975 to 1981. Five of the sows had a single cub, the other one had two. This was too small a sample to draw any conclusions, but I could not help thinking about all the talk of big male grizzlies killing cubs and yearlings. The average litter size here should have been two (actually 1.9; it was 2.24 cubs per litter during the period when bears ate garbage, which was more nutritious). I had never seen a male grizzly succeed in killing a young bear, although I have seen a half-dozen seemingly serious attempts during which the sow fought off the boar.

I broke camp and moved out, keeping to the trees lining the narrow meadows along the creek. I reached a larger meadow with hot springs and steam vents. Tracks of the Bitter Creek Griz and the sow and two-year-old were all over the open ground. Following the pigeon-toed tracks, I discovered a week-old moose kill.

The Bitter Creek Grizzly was the only bear I knew of in Yellowstone that regularly killed moose and bison. He attacked younger animals—ambushed them from nearby timber, then

dragged them back into the trees, sometimes covering the carcasses with dirt and sticks. I had seen this too many times to
believe that these animals had all conveniently died during the
winter. His was not the usual pattern of predation for grizzlies. In
1977, when I first crossed paths with the Bitter Creek Griz, a
biologist had found another grizzly who had passed up many
carcasses for live elk: The bear liked to kill what he ate. A few bears
learn to kill healthy adult elk during all seasons, and cow-struck
bulls during the rut were especially stupid and approachable. Yellowstone grizzlies also prey on elk calves, as they do caribou calves
in Alaska, and moose calves in both places. Adult moose were
generally a match for a grizzly except when snows were deep and
lightly crusted: grizzlies can walk lightly over a thin crust, distrib-
uting their weight evenly on their plantigrade feet, and they glide
over the top of deep drifts in which moose wallow.

I thought that grizzly predation was not as common here as it
had been a decade or more ago. The predatory segment of the
population had probably been killed off selectively, and continues
to be culled as they were born into it, because predatory bears are
bolder and more visible. The Bitter Creek Griz was a holdover
from the days when bears could afford to be bold and aggressive.
Which served, as it always had, an important ecological function
vital to survival of the species.

In the late 1970s, researchers found an unusually high proportion of young bears in Yellowstone's grizzly population: 43 percent
were less than five years old. Bears as old as the Bitter Creek Griz
were rare. An unhunted grizzly population should have about 40
percent solitary adults, 19 percent females with young, 11 percent
subadults, 13 percent yearlings, and 17 percent cubs. A decrease in
older individuals and an increase in subadults—which is the case in
Yellowstone—is generally the result of heavy hunting, poaching,
or managing.

The Yellowstone population is isolated from other ecosystems. Removals, legal or illegal, tend to be of bears who are more
mobile and visible, including those who are predatory, dominant
animals, bears who for some reason have less fear of man, and
those preferring open areas—such as sows with young, whose
nutritional needs make longer foraging necessary. With time, the

genetic composition of the population will shift and we will be left with an animal who looks like a grizzly, albeit a small one, but whose behavior will more closely resemble that of the meeker black bear. It will certainly be a more manageable animal, which will please some people, but this bear will have little affinity for the Bitter Creek Grizzly, whose crooked track made me tremble on that spring morning.

The tracks of the sow and two-year-old came out of a dead-end thermal drainage, which led up into the deep snow of the high country. Although it was a bit late, they may have just emerged from their winter den. I stashed my heavy pack and followed their trail, hoping to backtrack them and see where they had come from. The tiny creek followed a wild fissure in the earth, lined with steam vents and hot springs. Some of them were large—deep azure at the bottomless middles, turning sequentially turquoise, cream, yellow, and red as the waters cooled at the edges and supported the different algaes that refracted the various colors. A pair of ravens accompanied me out of this crack in the planet's crust and onto the deep, soft snow. The bear family had walked out the morning before. I gave up and turned back. Even if they had just left their den, it was probably miles away; grizzlies liked more rugged terrain for den building.

I headed back, exploring all the little thermals seldom if ever visited in an average year, sticking my fingers in the bubbling hot springs and rhyolite mud pots. I decided to take a last serious stab at finding the Bitter Creek Griz this year by following his most recent tracks. His prints led up out of the meadow along the open creek and through the timber to another meadow beyond.

Just as I was about to leave the area and strap on my snow-shoes, I rounded a timbered corner and spotted the sow and her two-year-old digging at the edge of the open ground. There was no way I could get around the bears without spooking them. I sat back and watched until dusk, when I retreated a mile and set up for the night. I went back to fill my canteen, but before I could get to the creek I saw the sow and cub grazing and digging their way downstream. I backtracked again, giving them room, and filled my canteen at a muddy rivulet back in the trees. It was their valley, not mine.

By daylight the bears had foraged down the creek well below me. I waited until they had reached the timber, then skirted the trees back up the creek and onto the snow. The going was slow; the night had not been cold enough to freeze the snow, and my snow-shoes kept breaking through the crust. By late morning, staying on top of the snow was impossible. The creek was open, though, so I shed my trousers and socks, pulled back on my rubber Korean War surplus boots and stepped into the thigh-deep water. Despite the frigid temperature, the boots kept my feet warm and I fol-lowed the four-foot snowbanks, walking the edge of the creek for two hours. I reached the arm of a shallow lake. Barrow's golden-eyes and a pair of mergansers spooked and flew off, but seven loons, more than twice the number I had previously seen together, remained behind. I wondered why these normally skittish birds seemed so unafraid.

There used to be a bald eagle's nest here. I climbed the bluff and found the remains of an enormous donut-shaped pile of sticks. The nest was abandoned, the eagle gone.

I trudged along the shore of the lake watching the loons. Just at the tip of the lake, I found the tracks of another sow grizzly and her single yearling-sized cub coming from the opposite direction. This spot was a crossroads for animals, grizzlies included. I en-tered the timber north of the lake and again saw the crooked print. It was getting late and I needed to find a campsite. But not here. I saw evidence that other people had camped here.

Whenever possible, one should never camp in old camp-grounds that have bear sign around them. If you do, you will inherit all the mistakes made by previous campers, especially if they left food out, which teaches bears to associate people and their camps with something to eat. Bears learn through their stom-achs. Food and feeding is their most important activity. They will put up with a good deal of discomfort and even pain if they are rewarded with something good to eat. Wild bears are usually shy around people but this changes in a hurry if they get into human food.

Of course most national parks require you to camp in estab-lished campgrounds. That could be a problem, since these grizzly-country camps are usually located where they are because of their scenic views and proximity to lakes, streams, and meadows—all prime grizzly habitats.

But something else was wrong here. The place simply did not feel safe. I could not quite put my finger on it, although the signals were coming so frequently I knew I had to move on. I stumbled on in the fading light, away from this disquieting place with its tame loons and network of trails and bear tracks. Two hours later I crawled deep into a thicket of spruce and erected my tent on three feet of snow. It was a place without a view, though no doubt safer and probably illegal as hell.

It was another cold, fireless camp. The waxing moon was full enough to trouble my sleep. By midnight the moon slipped behind the lodgepoles and I fell into a restless slumber until awakened by the calls of snipe. The day would be full, I thought, three miles to hike through the dense timber to the big valley with the complex of hot springs on the far edge, and the rest of the day to explore and return. During severe winters, bison sometimes use the area as a last stand because the warm ground keeps the snowpack from entirely covering the grasses. If the hard weather does not break, the deep snows trap the bison in the valley, who then run out of food. Later, the Bitter Creek Griz and others come to feed on the carcasses. The bear had passed through here two or three days earlier. With luck, he would still be around.

At daylight I packed up the camera gear, leaving the camping equipment behind since I would have to return by this same route. I moved rapidly through the trees on a hard crust with only a fifty-pound pack. Coming to the edge of the trees I saw hot springs steaming across the rolling valley. The creek, free of ice, cut the terraced bottomlands. Not a single tree decorated the lacustrine benches. I headed straight for the thermal area across the creek. Ravens circled above, but since the only open ground was on the bank of the creek, I assumed they were after grubs. I approached the creek, removed my snowshoes, and walked silently on the crust over a small rise—where I stopped dead. Sixty feet below, on the melted-out bank of the creek, dark fur rippled in the stiff breeze.

The wind blew at twenty miles an hour across my face and I

could not get a scent. A bedded buffalo, maybe, but the fur wasn't right.

I edged a few steps closer and stared down at the biggest grizzly I had ever seen, fifty feet away, lying alongside the creek. He was on a carcass. It was the Bitter Creek Grizzly, the first time I had ever seen him in broad daylight. If he heard, smelled, or saw me, it would be all over. Fifty feet is much too close to a dominant bear who is almost certain to be aggressive in defending a food cache.

Slowly I stooped, pivoted, and silently padded back over the snow out of sight, up the hillside, one step at a time. It took me an entire hour to withdraw. The wind held and the bear never got my scent. I circled as quickly as I dared; I wanted to get this griz on film from a safer vantage point. I waded the creek and traversed up to a hilltop directly opposite the great bear. He lounged and slept, waking intermittently to feed. Now and then he shook his head or made short lunges at a flock of ravens also feeding on the carcass. He watched a coyote pass, curious but wary. Finally he rolled over on the bank and went back to sleep. I studied all this through the viewfinder of Gage's camera. I had finally filmed the most elusive of my Yellowstone bears.

I watched from the hilltop across the creek most of the day. Sometime in the late afternoon he moved off, dipping his nose to the ground and swinging across the snowy meadow to the far end of the valley into the trees. The huge grizzly lumbered, seemingly oblivious of everything. His face looked relaxed and peaceful, an impression contradicted by a long scar below his left eye. The Bitter Creek Griz moved across the open valley as you might expect a dominant male grizzly to move even when other grizzlies were present. While such a bear looks taciturn to us, his body language sends a message of warning to other bears.

Before the Bitter Creek Griz disappeared, I filmed him with snow on his nose. He had a striking narrow silver-tipped collar around his ribs that I had not noticed earlier. Grizzlies look different as the intensity or angle of light changes.

I sat spellbound at my good luck for an hour, then loaded up the cameras and tried following his tracks over the snow. The crust

that held up a seven-hundred-pound bear was incapable of supporting me.

Feeling a bit cocky, I started snowshoeing the four miles back
to my waiting camp. I floundered in the deep snow under the trees
but did not mind much, since I was basking in the success of
having bagged my favorite Yellowstone grizzly. It was almost
dusk and I was pushing hard when I broke through a mound of
snow-covered downfalls, ending up in a hollow pocket of branches
six feet down.

I checked myself for broken bones and injuries and surveyed
my equipment. The old Bolex, wrapped in a down jacket, seemed
okay. Using my snowshoes, I started to claw myself out of the
hole. Then I saw the damage: the right shoe had broken cleanly in
two. The darkness was closing in and my repair kit was in the tent
two miles away. I dug out the snow with my one good snowshoe,
prepared a little cavelike opening to sit in, gathered some of the
downfall for firewood, and got ready to spend another cold, wet,
dismal night. I looked up an old entry in my notebooks.

,,*

The most serious health problem in the district was tigers. Every
dark, rainy night a half dozen tigers came into Ba Hiep and ate
water buffalo. The tigers came in groups of four to seven, the Yards
said, and killed the buffalo in their pens. Water buffalo were normally tethered outside the village limits. But these Montagnards
were an animistic people and the buffalo was their noblest animal.
The Hre were quite naturally terrified of tigers coming down from
the hills on black nights, and they huddled by their cooking fires in
bamboo houses on stilts while the roars and bellows of dying
buffalo filled the darkness all around. The Ba Hiep Yards became so
afraid of losing their animals, they brought the buffalo right into
the village and tied them to their front porches.

The health problem was that the entire village was five inches
deep in buffalo crap. It contaminated the village well and gave
everybody the shits. Hookworm and other parasites were epidemic. The Yard kids all walked around on stilts. I got my jeep
stuck in it once. The medical solution might have been to ambush a

tiger or two, though tigers and Charlie tended to be out on the same nights.

* * *

Tired and sleepy, I fell into a cold slumber for a few minutes, waking as the fire burned down. I was too cramped and wet to get any real rest. I tried to gain some distance on my current predicament. Every year I have to jump-start my life with something significant to get it going. After Vietnam, it was no longer sufficient merely to watch the changing of seasons; I had to mark their passage. Now I log the seasons by journeys into grizzly country, visiting five particular grizzly bears who show up at the same places, during the same months, year after year. My year begins when I see the Bitter Creek Griz in April; then I see Happy Bear at Glacier in the summer, the great Black Grizzly at the Grizzly Hilton, also in Glacier, in autumn, and then the strange Blond Grizzly I first saw the same day a woman was fatally mauled ten miles east at Many Glacier. In late October I drop back down from the Glacier Park area into Yellowstone and check in on the sow grizzly who digs her den fifteen air miles northwest of where I now sat.

These reflections gave me a handle on my predicament—it became an inconvenience, nothing more. I wrapped my camouflaged bandanna around my neck to soak up the melting snow. Wilderness camping, for me, resembles combat: treading lightly and staying invisible. I threw another stick on the fire. My stomach growled. I would have given up a whole lot of invisibility for a stick of jerky about then.

Much later, I threw the rest of my firewood onto the fire, which had melted its way down through the snow into a deep pit, and warmed my fingers. It had been a bloody long night. I splinted the snowshoe using an extra pair of shoestrings and two small planks of pine. Anxious to leave the snowy pit, I dug myself topside, buried the fire, and shouldered my pack.

A miserable though memorable night spent in an altogether avoidable bivouac. Should have taken more time; hindsight again.

8

DEMISE OF
THE GRIZZLY

The idea of saving an animal like the grizzly bear is shockingly new. Except for lip service to ecological diversity and talk about managing a few populations for sport hunting, no convincing reason could be found for keeping them around. Big bears were not essential to the functioning of ecosystems. There was a breeding remnant in zoos and there were still lots of bears in Canada and Alaska.

Prior to the last decade or two, the American brown bear was summarily dispatched on virtually every occasion over every inch of the hard and rapid conquest of the West. He was a varmint, a giant pest, the devil incarnate. He was poisoned in the wilderness and shot out on the trail. He was trapped, dynamited, blown away by set guns, and run down by dog packs. His rapid demise was facilitated by large bounties and boosted by government trappers.

In this history of extermination the grizzly had plenty of company. The wolf, for example, got it first, but then, old *Canis lupus* brought to America a history of centuries of persecution from the Old World. The grizzlies were a distinctly American problem and their fate was sealed by American know-how and other notions distinctly American.

The Spaniards were the first Europeans to see grizzly bears in the New World. Cabeza de Vaca may have run across one during his long slow trip home through the Southwest from 1527 to 1536 after shipwrecking off Florida. But he and his two companions were too busy staying alive to leave behind a pile of notes. It is also possible that Coronado, a decade later up in west-central New Mexico, might have come across them while stumbling about the pueblos with gold and lost cities on his mind. In 1602, at Monterey, California, Vizcaino saw a group of bears feeding on a whale carcass. These were certainly California grizzlies, since black bears were not native to that part of the northern coast.

California grizzlies, possibly a subspecies and the largest of inland bears, numbered in the thousands—ten thousand is what you hear, though it could have been many more or less—and occupied the best bear habitat in North America. The combination of chaparral, fertile grasslands, and marine resources made the place bear Eden. The Spaniards settled in the same habitat, conflicts arose, and the bears began falling before Christian firearms.

This steady genocide was sometimes interrupted for sport and punctuated by games. Lassoing a bear was the boldest of these pastimes, though the bull-against-bear fights were by far the most popular. The bullfights required live grizzlies, which meant lassoing them over moonlit bait. The meanest bulls were brought into the arena and tied by a leather rope fifty feet long from their front feet to the grizzly's rear paw. The bears usually won, of course. But the demands of the cheering, ticket-buying crowd made it necessary for the grizzly to continue fighting additional bulls— sometimes a dozen or more—until, as folklore has it, his "great heart gushed blood." Americans—as distinct from the colonial Spaniards—got a slower start in the grizzly war since we had not met any bears prior to the Lewis and Clark expedition in 1804, during which the crew shot and killed some forty-three grizzlies, mostly for sport.

Imagine going upriver in the spring of 1805, past the Mandan villages, into the great sweep of wild country of which one had only heard stories, the cottonwood bottoms and backwater marshes of the Missouri teeming with waterfowl, millions of buffalo, clouds of migrating birds, deer, elk, antelope, and, most impressive of all, the animal they called the white bear after his often pale yellow or tan coat—the grizzly.

The high plains grizzlies, never having experienced firearms, were not afraid of the men who shot them, of course. The expedition ran into its first grizzly on October 20, 1804, near the mouth of the Heart River in North Dakota. Later, Clark wrote: "It was verry large and a turrible looking animal, which we found verry hard to kill."

Up river they found the wildest scene imaginable, in a place of power and mystery, the great falls of the Missouri. There, in present-day Montana, Lewis and Clark encountered animal spectacle. The plains were stained black with bison, a bald eagle nested on the island below the falls, everywhere there were fat wolves and fearless white bears feeding on the carcasses of drowned bison that had washed over the falls. There were so many grizzlies here, the captains forbade the crew to leave the safety of the campfire at night. By the end of June, the men were sleeping with one eye open and finding the white bears "exceedingly troublesome, they constantly infest our camp during the night." On their way through, moving around the five falls of the Missouri, the expedition killed ten grizzlies. As Lewis recorded:

It was a most tremendous looking animal, and extremely hard to kill notwithstanding he had five balls through his lungs and five other in various parts he swam more than half of the distance across the river to a sandbar, & it was at least twenty minutes before he died; he did not attempt to attack, but fled and made the most tremendous roaring from the moment he was shot.

The century that followed saw the introduction of the repeating rifle and the rapid decline of the bears. The high plains grizzly went first and the California grizzly followed. Both were distinctive types of grizzlies and were once identified as subspecies, as were other regional ecotypes of grizzly bears. Virtually all these races disappeared, and today, probably only the "Kodiak" bear—living on three islands off Alaska—remains as a distinct subspecies, *Ursus arctos middendorffi*.

Survivors lingered in the more remote or rugged mountains. Everywhere the great bear was hunted, hounded, and harassed. Trappers and miners were replaced by homesteaders and stock-

men, who all shot bears on sight. Many went far out of their way
to track down and kill—with every deadly tool at their disposal—
the last grizzly in each remote mountain retreat, returning to nail
its hide with pride to the barn. These last stages in the decline of
the grizzly are well documented. In nearly every case, there is a
familiar air of casual irresponsibility and misplaced enthusiasm.

It was the livestock industry that finished off the grizzly in the
more arid states. Too many outfits ran too many cows into every
last niche until, shortly after 1900, no ungrazed sanctuary for bears
remained. For smaller ranches, the loss of a single cow or sheep
was seen as an economic disaster and all conflicts were resolved
against the bears. The primary predator of the Southwest was not
the wolf or bear but domestic livestock—they ate the succulent
grasses that constituted the bulk of the grizzly's diet.

At the end of the game there were the hunters, the specialists,
both self-appointed and government types. Some had vendettas
against grizzlies and tormented bears caught in steel-jawed traps
before killing them. Their pay came from the meat market and
depredation complaints. The galls of bears were sold to Chinese
apothecaries even before the turn of the century. One hunter made
a living by hunting down bears in northern Arizona for revenge
and for the gallbladders, which he sold for whiskey. A century
later, bear galls are still selling on the Asian market at $700 per
dried ounce.

More common were the government hunters, such men as
Ben Lilly, who worked sporadically for the Forest Service and U.S.
Biological Survey, killing grizzlies and other vermin in Arizona
and New Mexico. These hunters were skilled in the ways of the
wilderness but had not the slightest vision of the future. It was the
sad, familiar story of men who hastened the demise of the only life
they knew—recorded in cracked and yellowed photos of the last
mountain men posing with the carcasses of the last grizzlies.

The end of the killing in each region resulted in extinction of
discrete grizzly populations. It began with the Spaniards in California and continues today in Montana and Idaho, a sweep of
killing that goes back and forth across time for nearly a hundred
years, depending on when the local bears were blown into eter-
nity. The fewer the bears, the rougher the technique: a pipeline

worker wrapped a sandwich around a primed stick of dynamite, and a grizzly lost his head. From a town dump came a report of a bear caught in a culvert trap, then doused with gasoline and set on fire.

The last surviving grizzlies in each region were the stuff of which legends were made, and great tales were told about the passing of these old outlaws. The last grizzly of record in California was killed in 1922. In Oregon, 1931. In Arizona, 1935. In Colorado, one lasted until 1979. And so on.

The wildlife agents who paid the hunters stood by watching until it was too late. By the time anyone questioned whether we should keep a few grizzlies around, the big bear was already on his way out. Invariably, the last estimates of bear populations were overstated, and the grizzly was gone before the agencies could believe it.

The European and Asian brown bears, of which the grizzly is a subspecies, may have fared better. Although the bears have almost vanished from western Europe in the last three hundred years, there are small populations in the Pyrenees and Italian Alps, hundreds in the Slavic and Nordic countries, and a couple of thousand in Rumania and Yugoslavia. The great reserve of brown bears, however, is the USSR, where there are said to be 100,000.

In Europe, humans and bears reached an accommodation over the span of many centuries. Habitat encroachment came about more slowly than it did in the New World, and the European brown bear became smaller, more nocturnal, and forest-dwelling. Moreover, Europeans appear to be more tolerant of bears than Americans. In eastern Europe, grains and fruits were planted for the bears, who learned from this not to raid crops or livestock.

In the U.S.A. we managed the wilderness altogether more efficiently, tidying up those little pockets of resistance and taming the entire West in record time. As a culture, we saw ourselves as hard-pressed warriors, beleaguered frontier heroes righteously running over anything that was in our way. In little more than a century, we killed 100,000 grizzly bears with our rifles and westward expansionism.

Our dealings with the grizzly were not unique; grizzlies pro-

vide only one example of a native American species that did not
bend to our purposes. There were others: the graphs showing the
decline of native tribes and the one depicting the disappearing
grizzly are nearly identical. This could be coincidental, although it
is clear that the decimation of the American bison played a key role
in the final solution to both the Indian and the grizzly problem. On
the plains, plowing under the rich sod and the westward spread of
the livestock industry irreversibly sealed the fate of both. The cost
of Manifest Destiny was smallpox sweeping upstream among the
Missouri River tribes and the rotting carcasses of sixty million
buffalo.

The way we handled the bison, Indian, wolf, and grizzly was
the way we wrote our history, the convergent, blood-flecked roads
that carried us here. Despite a bit of latter-day remorse about the
way we treated the Indian, there are not many apologies.

The principal reason given for killing grizzlies was protection
of livestock. But few bears actually preyed on domestic animals,
though the reprisals were always unrelenting and unforgiving.
Bears were shot on sight out of ignorance, irrational hatred, and
because of illusions about what constituted duty or sport. But the
killing went well beyond these notions. The magnitude of the
pogroms, the unremitting persecution long after there was any
real justification for the mindless cruelty against grizzlies, were all
hard to account for; the cause-and-effect columns didn't add up.
The way we treat pacified Indians or Vietnamese villagers and the
way we manage wildlife draws from the same well.

Now we are suddenly in a period of relative enlightenment
and hope to arrest the effects of countless waves of brutal treachery
that have traced our relationship to the natural world. Despite the
odds against this, perhaps this is a good time to start again.
Something bottomed out in Vietnam. The technology of remote-
button warfare made the frontier gunslinger a thing of the past and
rendered our notions of pacifying nature forever obsolete.

Today the last remnants of the hundred thousand grizzlies that
roamed the continental United States are holding out in the wilder
parts of the northern Rocky Mountains and number less than a
thousand. Most of the few areas of real wilderness south of Canada
consist of isolated pockets and basins linked by networks of heavily

used trails. Whatever wilderness is, it is also a place where animals
live out their existence separate from a human agenda. Everywhere else the economic and social systems of man have priority.

There are only half a dozen places where these animals have
been permitted to range unfettered—grizzly bear ecosystems—
south of Canada. The great bear is extinct south of Canada in all
but three or four states and is found only in these six enclaves.
Only two of these contain viable and self-perpetuating populations: the Yellowstone Ecosystem and the Glacier Park area, or
Northern Continental Divide Grizzly Bear Ecosystem (NCDE).

The Yellowstone population may be in trouble. It is estimated
at less than two hundred. Grizzly mortality is high and deaths
exceed births in many years. Virtually all bears die as a result of
contact with people. Grizzly bear "management," both inside and
outside park boundaries, accounts for an alarming proportion of
known mortality. Of course, this is lower now than during the late
sixties and seventies, when an average of eighteen grizzlies per
year were removed from the Yellowstone population. But Yellowstone cannot endure adult female mortality much above natural
levels and expect to keep its grizzlies. The recorded grizzly deaths
were the only ones the agencies knew about. There are always
more.

No one knows how many grizzlies live in the NCDE. Estimates range from about three hundred to more than a thousand.
The population trend appears to be downward.

Other areas south of Canada have remnants that—without
help, such as augmenting the surviving population with bears
from the outside—are on their way toward extinction. In 1985
there was one last grizzly in the Sierra Madre of Mexico. An old
female grizzly was killed by an archer in 1979 on the upper Navajo
in southwestern Colorado. An extensive search in Colorado produced no additional grizzlies. A similar program of baiting and
trapping in Mexico had the same results. Of course, it is no
accident that the last grizzlies in an ecosystem cannot be trapped;
they did not survive as long as they did by being careless or
conventional.

There are three more ecosystems in the northern Rockies that
contain grizzlies, and a fourth in the Cascades where a rare griz

wanders down from Canada. The principal differences between
the Rocky Mountain ecosystems and the Pacific coastal mountain
ranges have to do with accessibility and the quality of the habitats
they contain.

North Cascades National Park is a good case in point. I
worked in the backcountry there for three summers in the seventies. North Cascades consisted of a couple of rugged, though not
particularly large, enclaves of towering peaks, glaciers, and permanent snowfields generally above the zone for commercially
harvestable timber. Before its designation as a national park, the
area was part of a much larger wilderness. But that wild core was
bisected by the new North Cascades highway, as part of the compromise we were told is always necessary when designating wild-
lands. The new road ran within ten miles of the subalpine basin in
which I camped for the summer and which, before 1968 when the
road was built and the last grizzly in Washington was shot and
killed there, used to be three times that distance from the nearest
trailhead. The relationship between the remoteness of the basin
and the presence of the last Washington grizzly was no accident:
grizzlies require larger wilderness areas than this bisected region to
survive. The basin was much tamer without the possibility of a
grizzly haunting the landscape.

Although there were plenty of rumors of grizzlies wandering
south from Canada into the North Cascades or the adjacent
Pasayten Wilderness, no reports have been "verified." Of course, a
"verified report" tends to be a dead bear, so it is just as well for
whatever grizzlies might be out there that confirmation has been
lacking.

The three Rocky Mountain areas contain better habitat and
would have a chance to sustain grizzlies if the timber and mining
industry would leave them alone and the U.S. Forest Service
would give them some protection. The Selkirk Mountains of
northern Idaho and adjacent Washington have the best chance
because they are on the border and there is interchange of grizzlies
with Canada. Still, there might be only two dozen grizzlies in the
area, which is currently being roaded to death by the Forest
Service. Farther east are the Cabinet Mountain and Yaak River
areas. Without augmentation, these grizzlies—there are perhaps

less than a dozen left—do not have a chance. The wilderness area on the Cabinet crest is as narrow as a mile wide and surrounded by clear-cuts right up to the tree line. If that is not enough, the mountains have silver deposits, and ASARCO (American Smelting and Refining Company) has proposed an enormous silver and copper operation at Chicago Peak, the core of the tiny wilderness area. The other ecosystem, the Selway-Bitterroot Wilderness on the Idaho-Montana border, is mostly a dream because it will not be populated until the Cabinet grizzlies recover and spill down into it.

9
BREAKUP

MAY (1980s)

The snow had melted off the flats and bottoms of the Yellow-stone Plateau. Most of the big meadow complexes were open, except for lenticular crescents of drifted snow lying on the lee sides of the sagebrush-covered hills. Mid-May was not too late to find some solitude here. The big crowds of bipeds come later.

I was back here on the edge of Wild Goose Valley to see if I could find some sign of the Bitter Creek Grizzly, to look for his crooked paw print on the last drifts of melting snow. My chances of locating him were poor, since this big grizzly disappears every year from the Goose Creek–Bitter Creek valley during late May—probably drawn or driven by the dynamics of mating, when adult male grizzlies range almost continually. If I did not find sign of him in a couple of days, I would give up looking and leave the Bitter Creek area for a place west of there where adult grizzlies often run together during the few weeks of their mating season. In a week, I would try to catch them on film.

Two hours after daylight, I surveyed the valley: three cow herds of bison with a total of eight three-week-old calves—orange toy critters on spindly legs nursing at their mothers' dark sides—grazed in the creek bottom; near the far tree line a half dozen cow elk stood watching the timber. The elk should begin to calve any day. New grasses and sedges sprouted along the creek. Western springbeauty, a lily with a tuberous stem, edible in its entirety, poked through the wet ground below receding snowbanks. The time of snow and dying had passed, the birthing season had arrived. Buffalo calved here in the first two weeks of May. Elk gave birth to their calves almost a month later, as did moose.

I swung my binoculars past the elk toward an adjacent finger meadow at which the elk seemed to be looking. A flock of ravens buzzed the edge of the meadow. Ravens? Ravens were messengers, Ravenese the universal language of the woods.

Among the sagebrush a large brown grizzly and her slightly darker yearling cub dug and tugged at the barren ground. The sow reared and swatted at the cloud of ravens, flailing away at the air with her paws. The ravens were teasing; they were there because of the grubs unearthed by the bears searching for pocket gophers or their seed caches, or, maybe, the dens of tiny voles, the *Microtus*. A coyote lurked in the shadows, awaiting any runaway rodent that escaped the grizzlies' attention.

I unpacked my camera and followed the bare ridges shielding cornices of deep snow, walking into the wind and skirting the timber up to the edge of the finger meadow. I stopped, set up my tripod and ran off a few feet of film. After twenty minutes, the sow suddenly stopped digging, reared, spun, and ran off into the trees with the yearling close behind. Shit. As far as I could tell I was well hidden, quiet, and downwind. But the sow picked up on something—the whirring of the camera, my scent on a stray gust of wind. Sorry, grizzer bears, I thought, had I known I'd blow it I would have stayed home.

Feeling downcast about spooking the sow and yearling, I dragged myself back along the ridge tops. I walked on the fringe of the melting cornices, leaving my boot prints on two inches of soft snow but not on the muddy undersoil. By tomorrow, I thought, the tracks will have melted and there will be no trace of my passage. I was unsettled about remaining too long in the Bitter Creek drainage that year. I still had not pinned down what it was about Tame Loon camp that had made me so nervous, and my running off the yearling grizzly and its mother intensified my uneasiness.

Maybe it's time for me to move on to new territory, I thought, leave the Bitter Creek Grizzly until fall and go to the place where the bears run together. I had nearly ten days before I needed to leave for the Blackfeet Reservation, and I would love to see some mating activity, but this valley was not the best place for it. A dozen miles northwest was another area that offered a better chance to see and film mating behavior. It was not too far from the spot where Gage and I saw all the elk. I had plenty of time to travel over there and set up on a hill.

Grizzlies mate from late May to early July, with most actual copulation taking place in the first two weeks of June. Since I was about a week early for the estrous period, I was looking for precopulatory behavior—adult grizzlies running and playing together.

Adult pairs of grizzlies had been seen there from mid-May all the way through to mid-July. The earliest I had seen adult pairs (in Yellowstone) was May 25; the latest (in Glacier National Park) was June 26. Others had sighted pairs from mid-May all the way through to mid-July. Grizzlies have been recorded mating between May 26 and July 9. The heat period of females is short, maybe around ten days, and there may be two estrous cycles separated by a week or so.

The one spot I knew where I might be able to film bears mating without disturbing them was a hilltop to the northwest, a little mountain overlooking yet another thermal area. I could have found better grizzly habitat, but none more complex and fascinating. Every late May and early June, adult grizzlies ran together through this gauntlet of steam, a place called Cinnabar Mountain.

Packing up my gear, I walked to the west along a high bluff running above Goose Creek. I reached the end of a meadow and spotted a long-legged bird near the creek bank. Through my field glasses, I saw a black stork. Of course black storks do not live here, but it didn't seem to be a heron, a crane, or an egret, so what else could it be?

I named the black stork the Bitter Creek Stork in honor of the nearby drainage and the great grizzly who frequented it. I left the huge meadow complex, striking out westerly along a string of narrow clearings and heavily used game trails. A foot or two of snow lingered under the lodgepoles, but bison and moose had opened the animal trails that cut through the deeper snows under the thickest timber. The walking was easy. I followed a trail through the last snow of spring into narrow meadows. The open ground at the edge of the clearing was beginning to green up; on the meadow side sprouted blades of grass and western spring-beauty. Back under the trees nothing grew; the grouse whortle-berry lay dormant. I picked a blade of grass and rolled it between my fingers. The angular stem rolled poorly; the grass was a sedge, and the sedges had already been grazed—by elk, if I read the sign correctly without tracks.

I moved on. Behind me a red squirrel chattered a tardy objection to my passing. Toward evening, I heard the distant honking of Canada geese. Ten minutes later I reached a bluff overlooking a meadow; beyond it, through a fringe of trees, lay the river. Deciding to go no farther, I sat back against a dying tree and watched a solitary white pelican fly upriver.

Finally the light faded. I moved back away from the river and set up another hidden camp deep in the timber. During the night, a thunderstorm rolled through. I was awakened by groaning lodgepoles rubbing in the sudden wind and by a single crack of lightning. A few minutes later, raindrops driven before the wind slapped into the tent fly. It rained hard. In fifteen minutes, the rain slackened and the storm passed over. I lay back and listened to the rain dripping off the pine boughs. Wide awake now, I relaxed and savored the night.

Back in Bitter Creek, a foreboding had crept into my sleep. No one—neither a twentieth-century biologist nor a tribal hunter—can say why bears do what they do. To allow that there might be more than we know, things unexplained or not understood, is not to spurn science. For example, Cinnabar Mountain has always seemed strange, haunted with its own mix of magic and spirits, not all of them good. It is one of the few spots on earth where my much-practiced, nearly infallible sense of direction breaks down. Within the space of a square mile of rolling, timbered hills broken by meadow bottoms and surrounding a highly visible plume of steam from the central thermal group, I have become temporarily lost any number of times.

Grizzlies have always used this island of cover and security, surrounded by open sagebrush hills of postglacial lacustrine origin. In the sixties, before the dumps were closed, it was possible to rouse half a dozen bears off day beds scooped out of the duff next to big lodgepole pine.

I have had a few minor problems with grizzlies at Cinnabar Mountain. Once I was approached by a big adult. Another time a sow with yearlings charged, but she stopped short and ran off with her cubs. More recently, a woman day hiker spotted a bison carcass and decided to approach the dead buffalo to see if anything had been feeding on it. Before she got there a mother grizzly came charging down, ears flattened back on the sides of her head, knocking the hiker to the ground. The woman screamed, "Oh no, oh no," and later remembered the grizzly moving around a lot on top of her, mauling her with teeth and claws. Realizing that her reaction, although natural, was a mistake, the woman stopped screaming. She played dead and the bear retreated to the top of a small hill. Again the bear charged downhill over the woman, stopping on the downhill side to turn the victim over with her claws. The hiker, knowledgeable about bear attacks, rolled over again so that she was facedown and balled up in a fetal position with her eyes closed. The grizzly rolled her over three times, and each time the woman ended up on her face, escaping further injury. Then the sow and her cub left.

There is no avoiding an occasional mauling of this sort. The victim did everything right once she realized her screams were exacerbating the attack. She might have been more cautious in approaching a summer carcass, although that could happen to anyone: surprising a bedded mother grizzly and her cubs is one of the most common causes of daytime bear attacks. The reason you don't hear more about it is that by the time the victim is aware of what is happening, it's too late: the grizzly is up and charging. Often the cubs are impossible to see, although this is more common in places like Glacier Park where the underbrush is thicker.

The wind died down and the beat of raindrops dripping off the trees onto the tent ceased. I nodded off. Sometime midmorning, I was awakened by the staccato cry of a shafted flicker. I got up, dressed quickly, and walked a hundred yards through the trees to the high bank overlooking the river. The grass was sopping from the previous night's thunderstorm, and low clouds hung just at the crest of the higher hills.

Again I heard the rapid, barking call of the flicker. I scanned the valley, and a minute later two half-grown grizzlies burst from the tree line into the meadow below. Wishing I had the camera with me, I believed for a second that I was watching a rare mating couple in May. After a few minutes I realized the bears were teenagers—three- or maybe four-year-olds.

The subadults chased each other across the flat, into the trees, and on into the next small clearing. The lead grizzly reached the center of the tiny meadow and suddenly spun on his rear paws, shaking his head vigorously from side to side. The second bear slowed to a walk and stepped up to its litter mate. Both grizzlies rose to a standing position with their paws on each other's shoulders. They wrestled and sparred, nipping each other on the neck and ears. The first bear pushed off, turned, and loped off toward the river. The other followed. I put all thought of filming out of my mind and raced through the trees. I didn't want to miss this.

Stepping beyond the line of lodgepole, I looked down on the river valley. A quarter-mile upstream, a flock of Canada geese honked angrily on a grassy island splitting the dark waters. In the deeper channel, opposite the geese, two brown heads bobbed and splashed like river otters. I raised my glasses and saw the two young grizzlies standing in the current. Just below the island a thin line of trees hugged the river terrace. I dropped into the valley, moving for the trees from which I could safely watch the bears play.

As I reached the edge of timber, the two wet animals pulled themselves up onto the grassy bank and ran the length of the small island. The first bear stopped at the tip. The second, close behind, crashed into the first, tumbling both into the swift, deep run. Twenty feet downstream, the bears caught hold of the river bottom and again stood up on their rear legs, sparring and wrestling.

Undetected at the edge of the lodgepoles, I watched the two 250-pound grizzlies romp and play for twenty minutes. Finally, one subadult climbed the far bank and ran downstream. The other chased, full tilt. At a bend of the river three hundred yards downstream, the two bears raced across the river, swam through channels, ran over shallow weed beds, and climbed a steep terrace without breaking stride. They disappeared over the lip of the slope into the timber.

A light drizzle began to fall. I remained hidden beneath the pines, watching the river, the rain, and the sky. The water had clouded noticeably since the day before. The river had not risen much but the roily water limited visibility. I could not see the bottom, two feet down. It was too risky to chance a crossing. But I did not really care: watching the grizzlies play had improved my mood considerably. The land had grown wild again, and my soggy spirits soared. Thanks, grizzer bears. The clouds closed in, the rain quickened. I retreated to my tent and crawled in.

Toward afternoon, I went even deeper into the forest and built a tiny fire, smoked my clothes, and nibbled some granola while wanting a fat tarragonned roasting chicken stuffed with a bulb of garlic. The lack of high-caloric food was deliberate and, unfortunately, necessary. I pinched the roll of belly fat around my waist and shook my head. I had returned to the trail of the Bitter Creek Griz ten pounds heavier, the result of the inevitable sloth and bloat that was part of the lecture circuit, which I occasionally join.

I puttered around until dark, trying to get my mind off the food I had not brought. I sat by the fire much later than usual, bringing my notebooks up to date. By the time I crawled into the tent, the stars were out.

The trip to Cinnabar Mountain required crossing the river at the crotch-deep ford four miles downstream. Once the ice broke up on the large lake through which the river ran, this trip would be impossible. Besides, the late spring breakup coincides with my leaving Yellowstone for northern Montana, and that would give me about a week. Cinnabar was only a day's travel, and I'd have a few days to just sit on a hilltop waiting for a pair of amorous grizzlies to pass through. If that didn't pan out, I'd head across the valley to the hot springs where Gage and I saw the elk.

By midmorning the next day I was moving, and by afternoon I had arrived at the ford: chilly, but no real problem. I had to cross the road, which I had been pretending did not exist. I waited below the edge of a high bank hidden behind a small grove of young pines, watching the sporadic flow of Winnebagos strung out along the highway. I did not want to be seen.

Whatever transcendence I had gained watching the grizzlies the day before slipped away as I crouched nervously below the road grade for fifteen minutes. I sank even lower into the trees as a ranger car passed. I didn't want to let them know I was about. If I got into serious trouble, I didn't want to be rescued. My considerable carcass could feed the bears.

Traffic thinned out. I darted across the pavement onto a buffalo trail cutting through the last bank of spring snow, leaving no tracks.

Uphill and hidden from the road, I took a minute to rest, breathless from the uphill sprint carrying a seventy-pound pack. What I consider proper behavior in the woods resembles outlaw living. The renegade escapes surveillance and evades capture once again. The desperado gains the safety of the mountain stronghold and regroups for one last raid.

I stood up and shook my head. I could hear the road traffic but I was safely out of sight. It would be clear sailing to the mountain.

Finding a hill from which I could survey the area, I stashed my gear and looked around. To the north, at the edge of the timber patch running a mile along Sour Creek, I spotted three light brown animals on the fresh green-up of the river terrace. They were a mile to the northwest, close to the hot creek where the elk were. I pulled out my binoculars and saw three distant grizzlies within 150 feet of each other. A few seconds later, two ran off toward the trees, the larger one chasing the first into the timber. The bigger bear turned back to the third grizzly. Then the two full-grown animals walked across the terrace and disappeared into the bottomland.

The first grizzly, the smallest of the three, may have been a two-and-a-half-year-old cub—the offspring of the third animal. It was so far away it was hard to tell. The two who walked off together seemed to be a mating pair, even though I did not see estrous behavior.

During the mating season adult males range all over the place looking for females in estrus. Once a sow comes into heat, there are likely to be several males around, and that's when dominance and the social hierarchy come into play. Boars do most of their fighting during these times, usually late May through the end of June. Actual combat is probably rarer than a subordinate bear's giving way to a larger male. Still, the ubiquitous scarred faces of big males belie this placidity. Since few human observers have been present, it's difficult to know. Males who know each other may signal submission by head and body positions; a head turned slightly to the side might indicate subordination, though bears victorious in brawls also sometimes turn away when they've finished. In any case, aggression is common among the big ones.

Females as young as three and one-half years of age may mate, but none south of Canada have bred successfully before their fifth summer. The average age is older, and some productive sows don't have cubs until they are eight or nine.

A mother grizzly may have a litter of cubs, usually two, every three or four years. Typically, they are born in late January or early February and are cared for by the mother grizzly for two and a half years, until about May, when she may wean them and mate again. Grizzlies have one of the lowest reproductive rates among land mammals, the primary reason they are so susceptible to local and regional extinctions.

Seeing grizzlies in an open meadow during midday was unusual for Yellowstone. Back when the major dump was open only a few miles from here, it had been common to see bears out in this large valley. Now they were not accustomed to the smell of people's garbage, and hikers and low-flying aircraft made undisturbed feeding by grizzlies a real luxury. The only time I saw bears using the centers of big meadows was the off-season, usually spring, before people showed up. My suspicion—totally unproven—was that the reason for the declining use of open areas by grizzlies from 1973 to 1975 was the increasingly frequent overflights by researchers.

The route to Cinnabar Mountain ran down a sagebrush-covered hillside southwest and on across a tiny draw into the trees beyond. The timber patch was not large, nor was the lodgepole forest especially dense. Nonetheless, it was one of those rare spots where I get turned around. I squinted off to my left, fixing the afternoon sun through the cracks in the cumulus cloud cover, then struck out through the tall pines.

Even on a cloudy day when you cannot follow the arc of the sun high across the southern sky, you could tell direction in that country by paying attention to the trees. The lodgepoles had a random average lean to the northeast, and, on slopes facing north with greater than a 20 percent grade, there was a slight increase in the frequency of fir and whitebark pine.

Fifteen minutes into the timber patch, the sun disappeared behind a dark cloud and I navigated by the darkness of the lichens on the bark of the lodgepole pines: they grow on the leeward side. Even this natural direction-finder vanished as I penetrated deeper into the timber, away from wind and sunlight. I was annoyed by a moment of disorientation, then remembered that the entire island of trees was less than a mile across and, since I was carrying everything I needed on my back, there was nothing from which to be lost. A minute later, a strong whiff of hydrogen sulfide wafted in on the breeze and I knew where I was. Farther on, the patches of spring snow had melted away and the lodgepoles became smaller and stunted. I looked across the white thermal flat, checking for bear tracks in the gray sinter along a hundred yards of tree line. Nothing. I decided to scramble up a hill for a better look.

I maintained my lookout on one of Cinnabar Mountain's highest hills into the late afternoon. From that vantage point I was able to watch a wide sweep of meadow, timber, and bottomland. Four bison herds were visible: two small herds of older bulls, a group of nine two- to four-year-old bull buffalo, and a cow herd. You can tell the age and sex of bison by their horns—cows' horns are more slender and curve toward the tip. Bulls' horns are thicker at the base and hook more symmetrically. Males younger than four often have spike horns. Through my field glasses, I could see four orange buffalo calves with the five cows.

I watched the fringe of the timber patches across the valley for sign of bears. Grizzlies use timber for security. As populations begin to drop toward extinction, their use of cover increases, and often the last survivors within an ecosystem are seldom seen before they disappear altogether.

Once a given population of grizzlies has been exterminated, they are gone from that ecosystem forever. There has been a lot of talk about reintroducing bears into areas they used to occupy. In

1978, a friend of mine did a feasibility study for North Cascades National Park on the reintroduction of grizzly bears there, and concluded it is technically possible. But as another report put it: "The requisite technology is available; the legal, social, political, economic, and philosophical requirements are not." This meant, in the case of the North Cascades area, that bureaucratic agencies were too chickenshit; they felt they had enough problems without the considerable legal liabilities grizzlies would entail.

The shadows crawled across the valley floor, and most of the buffalo got up and began grazing. I swung my glasses east and studied the snowfields on Avalanche Mountain. Farther to the south was the Two Ocean Plateau, a high, rolling flat running south out of Yellowstone Park, good fall habitat for grizzlies with whitebark pines growing along ridge tops—a place I visit every couple of years.

The amount of bear and elk sign falls off dramatically as you enter the national forest south of Yellowstone. Instead you see thousands of horseshoe prints, the leavings of the clients of commercial outfitters that the Forest Service allows to overrun much of the public land in northwest Wyoming. The trails are deeply rutted, and, during elk hunting season, there are little tent cities staked out every couple of miles along nearly every drainage. Occasionally these tent cities even include whiskey bars and whorehouses—all in the middle of what is supposed to be a wilderness. When a dude does blow away an elk, the gut pile is invariably thrown out, where it attracts bears who are themselves killed. This illegal activity is one of the three leading causes of grizzly deaths in the Yellowstone ecosystem.

The previous July I had passed one of the more notorious grizzly-killing outfitters riding off the Two Ocean Plateau into Pacific Creek with two pale-faced customers on horseback. This Wyoming outfitter had been suspected for years of killing grizzlies and had finally been nabbed dead to rights while killing a grizzly bear cub. Initially he tried to cover up the fact that he had fired at a group of bears in a meadow five hundred yards away. Later he admitted to shooting at the cub but claimed in defense that even if he had wanted to, it would have been impossible to shoot accurately at that distance, and his killing of the grizzly cub had been an accident.

I remembered hosing down on the Vietcong at Ba An. In all that misdirected, murderous rage, who were the real enemies? I remembered my vow: no more strangers, not even a dumbass grizzly-cub poacher whose horse I could gutshoot at half a mile. Five hundred yards—bullshit. As usual, the federal prosecutors pulled out and this outfitter was tried by his crony in the local court. The judge dismissed the charges and accepted a plea of "cruelty to animals." This judicial slap on the wrist was typical of grizzly-poaching cases everywhere in rural Wyoming and Montana, where illegal bear killing is almost a socially sanctioned activity.

I dropped down to explore the little mountain, half evenly timbered, half steaming rhyolite and broken andesite. Lying in a low area, surrounded by steam vents, was the skeleton of a bull bison dead for two or three months. Bears had probably fed upon it, although the sign was too old to be certain. I found a tiny hot drainage overflowing from a boiling spring. In the pool just below the spring were calcified, arrowhead-shaped pine needles. Farther downstream I found a coyote skull. Only a moment later, the yipping of coyotes broke the silence. Unsettled, I hurried back to my overlook.

Far away across the valley, coming out of another timber patch, a dark shape moved—it looked like a bear. I grabbed my glasses: it was a large, dark brown grizzly. A bit overeager, I dragged the heavy tripod and camera off the hill to another small summit under which the bear would pass. The grizzly reappeared in the sagebrush; I breathed heavily. The bear entered the thermal flat, walked directly below me, and rolled in a buffalo wallow, all four feet in the air. My camera jammed. Seconds became hours as I tried to calm myself after missing this rare footage. I felt for malfunctioning parts in the changing bag, and my fingers groped blindly over the camera. The grizzly moved out from below me and walked toward the higher hill, disappearing around the corner. I rewound the film by hand, replaced the Bolex on the tripod, and raced toward the other summit overlooking the old buffalo carcass.

I reached the top. The bear was still on the carcass, his entire head hidden in the rib cage of the dead animal. He played with it, curling the bones over with his feet like a seal with a beach ball. Finally he rolled in the carcass, coating his fur with rhyolitic ash and putrescence. I saw the naked bottoms of his humanlike rear paws. He shook off the dust and offal and walked across the white flat, into the sagebrush and the patchy snow beyond. I recorded all this on the remaining eighty feet of film. The bear never noticed me.

An hour before dusk, I left my cameras on the hilltop and dropped down for a walk in the gray light, which was too dim for film work. I moved warily through the area—it is always possible to stumble into a grizzly. I picked a black flake up off the light sinter of the thermal flat; a retouched blade of dark green translucent obsidian. The Indians were also fascinated with this place, if I had read correctly the pattern of obsidian chips they left behind. Sometimes I found projectile points or arrowheads in those hills, turtle-backed scrapers of obsidian over in Gneiss Creek or brown chalcedony skinning blades back in Bitter Creek.

Several days later, I was still waiting for a mating pair to come through. The big, dark grizzly had not returned. I was running short of time. It was still early for the bears, but close to the time I had to leave for northern Montana. I had promises to keep; I had told a biologist who studies grizzlies up there that I would go with him on a bushwhack across Glacier National Park on the trail of his radio-collared bear.

I decided to stash part of my gear and explore across the far side of the valley, one last spot where I had previously seen signs of mating. I took an early morning route along ridge tops within sight of the river. A pair of trumpeter swans glided in the current, backlit by the glare of the rising sun. I ran along the crusted snowdrifts for six miles, making the open ground near Sour Creek by late morning.

A dense stand of timber ran east along the south side of the creek. On the snow under the lodgepole I saw a muddy pattern of tracks coming off the creek bottom. I picked up the bear trail at the creek bank and followed it downstream. Tiny pools of water remained in the toe prints; the tracks were very fresh, an hour old at the most.

Cautiously, I began to follow the tracks of the grizzly into the timber, realizing the bear might be headed toward a day bed. A foot or two of snow lingered under most of the forest, and I broke through the crust every other step, making too much noise. The thought of the spooky ambush laid by the Bitter Creek Griz put an abrupt end to my curiosity. I gave up tracking the grizzly trail and struck out down the creek, guessing that the bear was moving parallel to the drainage, through the woods. I cut across a bend of the sluggish creek and stepped through a fringe of trees separating the two loops of water. At the edge of the timber I froze: on an open bench above the creek four hundred feet downstream, a four-hundred-pound brown grizzly nosed about the sagebrush, occasionally clawing at the earth. The bear might have been feeding on elk thistle, a pulpy forb preferred by grizzlies in summer. Some springs I saw scats full of horsetail and ants. Late spring food was more often grasses or, when available, mammals, especially elk. His back was toward me so I could not be sure.

I watched for perhaps five or six minutes; suddenly the grizzly looked around, then turned and bolted into the timber opposite the creek. Puzzled, I stepped into the clearing. Two seconds later, I heard the drone of an approaching airplane and dove back into the trees. The single engine craft passed. I could see the telemetry antennas attached to it. It was the biologist again, tracking radio-collared grizzlies or looking for unmarked bears from the air. The grizzly had heard the sound of the aircraft about four seconds before I had, confirming what I had always suspected about their hearing—that it is slightly superior to ours.

Climbing one of the main bluffs overlooking the valley, I found a sunny ridge from where I would spend a leisurely late afternoon watching animals. A bull herd of buffalo rolled up the creek and stopped just below me, sparring with one another in mock battle and rolling in the dust. One bull kicked a stick with his rear hoof. At the beginning of this century, we had just under two dozen free-ranging bison left of the sixty million or so that had roamed North America the century before. These twenty-three animals were part of a wild herd that no one had been able to catch in Yellowstone National Park. The bulls below me were their grandchildren, the only buffalo who have always been free-ranging and wild. Their kinship gives me pleasure.

Toward sunset I got up and climbed north over a sagebrush-covered saddle and looked down into the steaming creek bottom in which Gage and I had watched the ghostly herd of elk milling and bugling years ago. I dropped down and stuck my finger in the creek; the hot spring waters had been diluted by melting snow—the creek was warm but not hot enough for a soak. I hurried back down the creek toward the timber patch and my stashed gear. Just as I was about to wade across the creek I caught movement off to my left at the edge of the valley. I glassed the tree line and saw a small female grizzly and tiny cub nosing about the sagebrush. They seemed to be steadily if slowly working down the valley. I was curious about what they had been eating, although it was already too late to consider filming.

The sow and her cub disappeared along the tree line in the fading light. I marked the spot by a solitary pine tree. I moved rapidly upwind, then paused and checked the edge of the meadow for the bears. Nothing. I found their tracks and sign of grazing on grass and dandelions. Following the tracks in a wandering circle, I ended up back at the lone lodgepole. It appeared these bears had been eating dandelions.

I heard the rustling of sage back in the trees. Instinctively, I reached up and grabbed the first branch of the easily climbable pine. I was halfway into a one-arm pullup when I saw movement at the tree line twenty-five feet away. The female stepped out to the edge of the open slope, sniffing the air. She had definitely heard me, although the wind had been blowing in my direction. I did not dare breathe. This was as close as I had ever been to a grizzly with a cub.

The sow reared and lifted her nose into the night air. I saw the tiny cub move behind her. She slowly turned around and looked straight at me. I did not even blink; she was twenty feet away. She could see, but not smell or hear me. I knew it was too late to get up the tree. The grizzly stared right at me for what seemed a long time, then spun and dropped to all fours. I heard her whooshing through the sagebrush and the coughing gasps of the cub as he struggled to keep up. They were out of sight and running away.

I was strangely, perhaps stupidly, calm during the encounter, as if I had known all along that I was in no danger. The female grizzly certainly heard me and saw my outline. She must have trusted her nose more than her eyes. Violet clouds lay on the western horizon as I crossed the creek. I grabbed my extra gear and hurried into the timber, settling on the first open ground as a campsite.

The evening sky was clear. I threw my sleeping bag out under a tree and lay back watching the first stars come out. I had probably just been through a close call, though it did not feel like it. All the time I had been a stone's throw from the grizzly family, I had felt as if I were having an out-of-body experience. My mind drifted, and I remembered a time in this same valley, many springs ago. I remembered a charging grizzly. I had been hired by a magazine to take pictures for an article about grizzlies. I had some borrowed 35-mm cameras and long lenses, and Lisa and I were out on our first excursion of the year into grizzly country. It was late April. A friend, a winter keeper in Yellowstone, was with us. We had come around the edge of a timber patch, and, in the meadow beyond, a sow and her two yearlings were nosing out the winter nests of voles under the snow. The yearlings played while mom did the work of rooting out the grassy nests. They all gobbled up the tiny mammals. I photographed the grizzlies with a herd of bison behind, using a new camera I had not taken time to learn about. I finished shooting the roll, then realized that the hotdog professional photographer didn't know how to rewind the film.

My friend went to dig out the instruction manual from my pack and keep an eye on the bears. Lisa and I sat down on the bank of a tiny creek and fooled around with the camera. Suddenly I caught some movement out of the corner of my eye. My friend, the lookout, was silently backstepping, taking the longest strides I had ever seen. I looked down the creek. Fifty feet away the grizzly family slowly worked up the creek toward us. Oops.

I stood up and made a reflexive but futile move for a tree branch two feet away. Lisa followed suit. I heard the scraping of my rubber boots, which were useless for tree climbing. Lisa was doing only slightly better, although neither of us had a chance to climb high enough; the sow charged at the first sound of my scuffling boots. I thought the grizzly looked uncharacteristically small all stretched out, her ears back, crashing over the creek right toward us. The creek and downfalls slowed the bear slightly and gave me a chance to say something to her like "Aw shit, momma griz." I still was hanging from the tree branch like an overripe pear with my ass in perfect position to absorb the first bite. When she was twenty feet away from us, the sow veered without breaking pace and raced across the meadow with her yearlings in tow.

We were shaken but safe. I stole a sheepish glance at Lisa and thought she had never looked more beautiful. I wanted her to know the entire gamut of emotions a grizzly could generate, but I hadn't counted on this. I also knew I could not control them; grizzlies were beings you embraced in all their unpredictability.

I watched the stars through the branches of pine. Arcturus rose into the clearing and the celestial clock began its whirl around Polaris. Chilled, I sat up and started a fire. I stoked the tiny blaze, scribbling in my notebooks and staring into the fire until long after dark. My time here was growing short. I would trek to Cinnabar Mountain the next morning, then in a couple of days I'd have to get out.

I traveled the six miles back to Cinnabar slowly, following bison trails through the soft snow cornices lying just off the ridge tops. Detouring in a half-mile circle, I bypassed a pair of sandhill cranes plucking insects off the earthen casts of rodent dens melted out of the winter snow. On a distant snow cornice, I spotted zigzag patterns streaked in mud down the largest slope of snow remaining in the area. Something was wrong. My heart raced. All the old animal instincts and practiced caution rushed back as I crawled up to a rise and had a look. I eased up, crouching behind some sagebrush. I glassed the slopes: cross-country ski tracks, three sets, made the previous morning, etched on the last skiable snows of spring. I waited, hidden in the trees for two hours, listening, watching before I stepped into the thermal flat.

It took a minute to recover from the initial shock of seeing the first human tracks of the year. Moving into the open, I also saw fresh bear tracks—two sets of adult grizzly tracks traveling together, digging huge nonfunctional holes, running around and around a pine tree, and marks where they had been rolling together in the thermal mud. A mating pair. I studied the tracks for at least half an hour trying to read the scene: the two grizzlies pranced in a ten-foot circle, once rearing on their hind feet as if dancing, no doubt chewing on each other's necks and ears. The smaller female had run off with the boar close behind. She stopped and pretended to hide behind a tree. Both bears dug large holes nearby, including one excavation large enough to bury half a Volkswagen.

One of the three sets of human tracks was more curious than the other two; the Vibram prints followed the grizzly trail with skill. I followed these tracks—made by a man who was later to become my friend—up and beyond the lookout hill I had occupied two days earlier. Where the hell was I, I wondered, and why did I miss the two animals? Maybe they had come through during the night or after I had left.

Again I missed my big chance to film the grizzlies' mating behavior. Somehow, I was relieved. A tug of loneliness pulled at me, and I mapped a route in my mind out to the road, where I would hitch a ride to the nearest phone. A collect call to Oregon would bring Lisa out to pick me up in twenty-four hours.

I climbed the summit overlooking the river. Glassing the horizon, I could see huge blocks of ice floating on the river. The lake had broken up. This place, this season had been kind to me. It was time to leave.

10

TRACKING THE MEDICINE GRIZZLY

Early June in the northern Montana valleys was deeply verdant as I watched the country fly by. I looked out the window of the pickup truck for a magical line of demarcation between the High Plains and the sharp hills that become the Rocky Mountains. The ridges to the east are open and buckled, and the hills west are only slightly more folded and dissected, though timbered with thickets of aspen and conifers. The transition from the plains to the mountains is a crumbled zone of rolling country, rich in history and potential. The great northern herd of plains bison ranged here until 1883, when we wiped them out—here and everywhere else—as part of our final solution to the Indian problem.

Now a heavy silence has settled over these hills and cottonwood bottomlands once crawling with deer, elk, bear, wolves, and sheep. The slopes were black with the buffalo, the greatest herd of hoofed animals ever to roam the surface of the earth.

I was riding in an Idaho state vehicle with two friends, both biologists. One of them, Chad, studied the mountain pine beetle. The other, Bob, studied grizzly bears. In about two hours, Bob and I would step out of the truck in Alberta, Canada, shoulder our packs, and strike out south on a foot trail leading back across the border into Glacier National Park. There we would leave the hiking trails and bushwhack west across the Continental Divide. We would be on the trail of a young grizzly on whom Bob had fixed a radio collar. The trip should take about a week, because the drainages through which we would be bushwhacking have no trails and contain some of the thickest brush and densest downfalls in the park.

I had signed on this trip as a guide. It was about time, I thought, to see how biologists gather information on grizzly bears. Most current bear studies involve the use of radio tracking, and I had never seen this equipment in operation. Bob was also a first-rate botanist and I thought I could learn a lot from him. Besides, I had lost a friend and I needed a trip, an adventure of sorts. I was hoping we would run into a pair of grizzlies doing their courtship routine. In contrast with my spring trips to Yellowstone, where I was looking for the Bitter Creek Griz and other bears I knew from past years, there were no particular grizzlies I was looking for in Glacier. That northernmost slice of the park was a bit too far north for me to be familiar with individual grizzlies. But I hoped we might run into a mated pair.

I sucked down the dregs of the warm beer I was holding, crumpled the aluminum can, and threw it into the back of the pickup. We passed the bar in Babb, a place once written up as one of the ten toughest bars in the country. I used to stop in there every year, although I had missed the last few; I was getting old and tired. The bar's lowbrow reputation pleases my egalitarian sensibilities.

A cottonwood river bottom ran off to the northeast, with wet green meadows studded with blue camas, which was the most important food plant for the Indians in the northern Rockies. We turned off on a paved road running west, toward Chief Mountain.

We drove on in silence through the lush and lovely land, so barren of wildlife. I have had two friends who studied wildlife there on the east side of the Rockies; one was a mountain goat biologist, and Bob, sitting next to me, studied bighorn sheep. Both have ill-defined but lingering grudges against the people who live there, because "they shoot everything that moves."

This was Indian country, the Blackfeet Reservation. It may be one of the final ironies that the very people we look toward when we seek an American example of harmony with the natural world have themselves overhunted and killed off their animal relatives. It might have been worse. Down south, segments of the Hopi people were preparing to sell off Big Mountain to Peabody Coal.

Chief Mountain dominated the horizon. Set apart from the central chain, this peak is the sentinel for all the surrounding plains country, visible for a hundred miles. Chief Mountain was a holy spot to the Blackfeet and home of many sacred springs. Until recently, a painted buffalo skull faced east on its summit. The mountain sits on the boundary of the reservation and Glacier National Park. The Blackfeet, of course, believe that much of the eastern portion of the national park, their traditional hunting ground, is Indian land. This dispute was the basis of some animosity between the Blackfeet and the National Park Service. A few years earlier, two Glacier park rangers were badly beaten when they tried to serve an injunction against grazing cattle within the park on an Indian family who lived on the reservation. This enmity also accounts for a good deal of poaching, most of which involves sheep and elk, inside the park's eastern border. Reliable rumor had it that an Indian sheepherder at Chief Mountain illegally and secretly killed four grizzlies the year before.

I popped another beer, toasted the Medicine Grizzly, and thought about the elitist pipe dream the three of us in the truck sometimes shared, in which great expanses of land were reserved just for animals. We passed another cluster of tacky agency houses built for the Blackfeet, descendants of the survivors of the most cantankerous tribe of Plains Indians, who were finally subdued by smallpox. During the second half of the nineteenth century, their culture was fragmented by the decimation of the bison, from which they derived food, shelter, and tools. There was the usual reduction of territory through a litany of broken treaties and deceptions. Then, the survivors were thrust into a life of dependency, accompanied by poverty and alcoholism, through the reservation system.

These Northern Plains people were only a recent cultural development. Many of the tribes came in from the east, and all had had to wait until the 1700s for the introduction of the Spanish horse from the south, after the Great Pueblo Revolt. Scholars sometimes use this cultural transformation as one of the rare examples of a Neolithic or farming people reverting to a hunting and gathering culture.

In 1800 there were still some fifty million buffalo. By 1884, all but a couple of mountain herds were gone. The last herd of twelve hundred was found in western Dakota in 1883 by Sitting Bull and a thousand Sioux braves, who surrounded the herd and completed the final hunt before the white buffalo hunters could get them.

Blackfeet culture was based on the buffalo. The old men who hunted the buffalo last, who remembered and who passed on this dying knowledge to the young, were now themselves dead. What this break in continuity means to a culture largely dependent upon oral history can only be imagined.

We passed through the Chief Mountain customs station and on into Canada. Heavy cumulus clouds were throwing dark shadows over the spring green aspen groves as we wound our way around the mountains into Waterton. Early June weather patterns were like this, and the most we could expect for the next week was a couple of rain-free days—or snow free when we crossed the divide.

We swung past the Prince of Wales, a European-style hotel, drove through the townsite, and pressed on to the end of the road. There we threw on our packs, said good-bye to Chad, and staggered down the west side of the long glacial lake, glad to leave the little warren of tourist development behind.

The long, slow exit from Waterton took us past day hikers and a couple of fishermen. Finally the well-used trail narrowed and we had it to ourselves. It was past midday and the clouds were gathering. We walked past a small rivulet fringed on either side by a green carpet of horsetail. In the mud where the tiny stream washed across the trail, there was the eight-inch track of the rear paw of a bear. Suddenly this not-so-wild part of the park area came alive with possibilities; all the power of the animal lingered in its track.

We looked over our shoulders and checked the area for more sign. You cannot always distinguish a medium-size grizzly from a large black bear by its rear track if the toe marks are not clear. This track was not distinctive. We found a scat. This bear had been grazing on the dark tips of the male form of the sexually dimorphic plant, *Equestrium*.

Considerably more alert, we hiked down the trail paralleling the large lake. Like many roadless areas, this one was not as wild as it looks on the map. At the end of the lake was a Park Service compound housing a dozen or so seasonal employees and visited twice a day by a ferry carrying as many as three hundred tourists per trip during the summertime. Fortunately, they stay only an hour or so.

At the end of the lake the trail widened and again showed signs of heavy use. The Park Service paved it where it snakes through the compound. We hurried through the area, anxious to avoid having to explain ourselves to anyone who might be around. The trail turned to dirt again as it entered the woods. It began to rain and we came to a footbridge across the Bullshoe River. We paused on the bridge. We had to recross this river some ten miles upstream. The glacial stream was raging from spring runoff; there was no way the torrent could be forded. We would have to locate the logjam of avalanched trees we spotted from the air last week, when Bob was tracking his radio-collared bear from a single-engine plane. River crossings were our biggest problem and greatest danger this time of year, even more dangerous than tracking a male grizzly during the mating season.

Some males—usually big and presumably dominant, prime-year grizzlies—treat everything they encounter with aggression when the mating juices are running. "Everything" means mostly other grizzlies, but when bears are agitated they often redirect aggression without discrimination—like a dog during a fight, they could turn on you. Statistics on grizzly-inflicted human injuries do not reflect this, because few people ever penetrate the last strongholds of grizzlydom, where even fewer bears hang out during early June. Even among this group of adventurers, the risk of injury is slight, nothing really compared to commuting from Santa Monica, or riding subways, or drinking more than one Black Russian a decade in the Babb Bar.

Where grizzlies survive today, early June is a soggy, buggy month and comes just before the greatest influx of tourists. I have seen sign of nineteen mating bears running together and know of

many more. Only one pair was within three miles of a road. The
places where I generally run into mating grizzlies are the most
remote, far-out corners of the wilderness. When not concentrated
by food sources such as garbage dumps or carcasses, grizzlies
seem to prefer to mate in secluded areas.

We inched across the suspended bridge, already wondering
what crossing the logjam the next day would be like. The muddy
torrent boiled underneath. The ranger for this district had told
Bob that there was no way we would ever get across the Bullshoe
River. Maybe it was true.

From there on out the way got wilder. Once we succeeded in
finding a way across the river, we would embark on a course no
one had taken for years, for good reason. We had to bushwhack up
a valley filled with slide alder, climb up permanent snowfields to
the Continental Divide, and find a route down into a wild cirque
with near-vertical walls, then scramble out a drainage littered with
some of the worst downfalls in the park. It should take most of a
week. Crossing the divide would be possible because Bob's grizzly
had come over this way. We had seen his tracks on the snow from
the plane.

A soft rain fell on us as we plodded up the trail. Fresh moose
tracks half-filled with water splayed out in the mud. Where the
path crossed avalanche chutes, false hellebore plants unfolded and
studded the barren ground, showing that the snow had just
melted. Under winter alder, I saw two large snow mushrooms,
Gyromita gigas.

We stumbled onto a set of medium-size black bear tracks,
the short claw pricks showing close to the front pad mark. Half
an hour later I saw the track of a larger black bear heading the
other direction. This was more black bear habitat—densely timbered lowland forest—than grizzly country. At this time of year
grizzlies prefer new growth, slides, and disclimaxes, to mature
forests.

The trail disappeared under several feet of avalanched snow
for an eighth of a mile. Two-hundred-foot fir and spruce trees lay
uprooted, tossed like matchsticks by the force of the sliding snow.
The awesome power of the mountains spoke to me of my own
smallness and frailty. Men were inconsequential here. For the first

time that year, I sensed my own fear, a foreboding, probably about the river crossing.

I walked over the debris and looked up at the furrow in the mountain that had carried the avalanche. These were foothills compared to the peaks of the divide. We wound our way through and over the broken trees and honeycombed, coarse snow. On the far side of the avalanche we found the trail again and slogged up the slick, rocky grade.

I stopped and tested the wind by licking my index finger and poking it up into the still air: no breeze, nothing but a vertical drizzle. I looked up the trail at the muddy streaks, the six-inch swath of a sliding paw on the sloping trail that had caught my attention. It was an unusual, startling sign, too wide for a black bear. We inched forward cautiously until we found a clear track: a large grizzly bear had come this way yesterday. We followed the sign up the hill the bear had come down. It looked as though the grizzly had swung down the trail with the stiff-legged gait typical of big males during the mating season. The tracks were slightly pigeon-toed, and the front paw slid as it padded down the muddy trail.

The drizzle thickened into a cold rain. It was late, and we had been on the trail for ten hours, anxious to put as many miles as possible between us and the Canadian townsite. Only two more man-made structures remained before we entered the wild core of the mountains.

We crossed a footbridge over a creek lined with tall cotton-woods. Beyond was a small clearing with a log cabin set back against the trees. The cabin was tasteful enough; it just seemed out of place. It was an administrative patrol shelter used by rangers or other Park Service personnel when traveling or working in the backcountry. Parks like Glacier and Yellowstone have them strung along major trails. The Park Service says these buildings are here in case people like us get hurt.

Bob, who worked for the park as a research biologist, opened the door with his backcountry key, curious to read the logbook. The interior was dark from the bear-proof shutters covering the windows. A half-dozen mousetraps littered the floor, each containing a single small victim. Mice, apparently, were not granted the protection of more noble park animals. I checked out the larder and found it well stocked with Danish hams and other treats. Bob discovered that the ranger, whose tracks we had crossed, had made his initial visit. Although it was raining hard, Bob did not want to use the cabin since subdistrict rangers were often territorial and possessive about their backcountry fiefdoms.

Our official wildernesses, the National Parks, are being civilized. They stress scenery and standardized recreation. The Blackfeet used these mountains for vision quests; their medicine people sought their patron animal, Real Bear, as a spirit guide, because the grizzly was more than the animal wearing the fur coat, he was the Medicine Grizzly.

* * *

Halfway through my first hitch in Nam, I had to break in a new team CO on his first combat operation. The new captain had spent a year in Vietnam with some other unit and had never been shot at. The two of us accompanied twenty-five CIDGs out of Bato, mostly Hre Montagnards. He wanted to assault a hamlet, a village controlled by the Vietcong—a stupid mistake, like kicking an anthill. As expected, we got pinned down by sporadic crossfire before we even got out of the hamlet. Then we had about a kilometer of relatively open ground before we reached the safety of the trees.

Once we busted out of the village, we ran like hell. I was as weak as a kitten: I had had three recent bouts of acute malaria and should have evacuated myself weeks before then. I had lost over fifty pounds and just couldn't keep up. I found myself pinned down, listening to the distinctive bark of an AK-47, which was unusual because the village Vietcong did not have top-of-the-line weapons. The new captain and three Yards came back for me. I didn't think the rounds were coming that close until one of them pointed out the hole shot through one of the plastic canteens I carried on my hip.

It wasn't over yet. We reached the edge of a rice paddy at the foot of a steep jungle hillside. We all took turns darting around an exposed bend in the trail. Finally I took mine. As I turned the corner, I heard the simultaneous *pop* of a muzzle blast and *splat* of a bullet hitting the muddy trail next to my foot and looked up into the face of a Vietcong wincing with disappointment from his spiderhole. He had missed his big chance to bag an American at fifteen meters. The local VC didn't have enough ammo to practice. They were terrible shots. I dove into the bushes and crawled away.

The way out lay across two hundred meters of open rice paddy. It was like a shooting gallery with the shooters placed a sporting five hundred meters away. I was the last to cross. I was exhausted and simply didn't care. I couldn't run any farther. I staggered across one of the dikes, hearing bullets splash at my feet. I was moving too slowly, one of those bastards was going to drill me yet. I jumped down into the paddy, taking advantage of the low earthen wall for cover. Only my back and pack stuck up. I crawled on my hands and knees, my face just at the surface of the murky water. I could hear the *crack-boom* of the slugs breaking the sound barrier, followed by the noise of the muzzle blast telling you the VC were right on target.

One of those big snakelike paddy leeches somehow caught hold of my right cheek. I couldn't wipe it off because I was crawling for my life. More rounds cracked and splashed around me. The leech started to grow, sucking blood from the side of my face: I could see it get bigger out of the corner of my eye. I closed my eyes and scrambled through the filthy water. I crawled out the other side and ripped the leech off my face.

′ ′ ′

The patrol cabin bothered me. Everyone should be taking the same risks out here. When I was a backcountry ranger in the North Cascades, we used tents. What is missing from our woods and mountains is a spectrum of wilderness possibilities. We keep eliminating the wildest option: the original landscape we called home for all but a heartbeat of history. The trend is toward a homogeneously mediocre experience, a woods safe only for recreational diversion. Such a place need not include risk and unpredictable things like grizzly bears.

We crawled back into the brush and alder toward the river, as far from the cabin as we could. Everything dripped. The clouds had dropped and visibility was only a couple hundred feet. We were already soaked. I dug the cheap alpine tent out of my soggy backpack. We kicked back the bushes, making a muddy wallow where we would sleep.

While I pitched the tent, Bob pulled out his hand-held telemetric antenna, which he assembled in sections. He stuck the pieces together and plugged the apparatus into a portable receiver, adjusted the volume, and rotated the antenna perpendicular to the mouth of Morning Eagle Creek, the drainage in which we had last located the radio-collared grizzly. Bob rotated the rod 360 degrees: no beeps. I was not disappointed, since I was more interested in the bushwhack up trailless Morning Eagle Valley than I was in locating the bear. Besides, the grizzly could still be in there. All the silence meant was that the collared bear was more than a couple of miles away or around the corner of some rock outcrop.

Bob had originally trapped this bear near Sullivan Meadow the previous year with a loop of steel cable over a bait of rotting fish. He found it snared the next morning and tranquilized it with a shot of M99, an immobilizing agent. The male animal was young, not more than five years old. Bob had lost track of the bear until he received funding for overflights. In May he located it far up Ammonite Creek in the huge recesses of Silenos Cirque. Over a period of several weeks, he located him on various feeding and bedding sites. On June 1 the grizzly had taken off, climbing eastward out of the cirque. Bob had found it in Morning Eagle Creek. The second time he flew over Morning Eagle, I had been aboard. We found two sets of bear tracks crossing the Continental Divide on the snow. Bob's grizzly had a consort. From what we had seen of the pattern and size of tracks, Bob's bear traveled over the divide with a smaller female. For all we knew they were still running together up Morning Eagle Creek.

The clouds settled in low for the evening. Bob put his telemetry equipment away and I laid out my sleeping bag inside the sopping tent. Dinner was two handfuls of granola with a side of protein drink—bitter fare given the opulently stocked patrol cabin only a few hundred yards away.

The day the author returned from Vietnam.

The Blond Grizzly, Glacier National Park. Light striking the dark underhairs makes the bear appear darker than it is.

Sow with single yearling, Bitter Creek area, Yellowstone. Cubs generally come in pairs, but there is an unusually large number of single cubs here.

Three-year-old subadult, Glacier. The snap of the shutter spooked this bear.

Bear grazing on huckleberries, Glacier.

Happy Bear, at age four or five.

The bear that the author ambushed on the trail to his fire lookout in Glacier.

Fire Lookout, Glacier, where the author spent seven summers watching for fires and grizzlies.

Inside a natural cave in Baja, California.

Ten minutes after the picture was snapped, this sow charged Lisa and the author. Taken in Yellowstone, with bison in the background.

Dominant male that would not let the author near him. Frontal orientation of the head is a direct confrontation.

View from the Grizzly Hilton.

The Black Grizzly.

The days were long this time of year. I listened to the staccato beat of rain on the nylon tent and slowly chewed the stale granola, wishing I had not been so cheap and bought some fancy freeze-dried backpacking food. Better yet, I could have packed in a two-pound porterhouse, moistened with olive oil and a dash of soy and rubbed with garlic and pepper, which we would broil over coals from the patrol cabin we accidently burned to the ground. We would wash the rare beef down with a magnum of 1961 Gruaud-Larose.

Morning broke gray and dank, and the rain slackened to a drizzle. We packed up our wet gear and began bushwhacking downstream, toward the logjam we had spotted on the Bullshoe River. We trudged under tall cottonwood trees, through thickets of alder and patches of devil's club, until we reached the riverbank. The river raged, deep and fast, barely contained by its fifty-foot channel. There was no way we could swim it or manage a traverse with our heavy packs. We would have to find the logjam.

The river wandered westward in a broad meander through a swampy conifer forest. High above the trees, across the river, I saw the furrow of a snow gully running down between two meta-morphic spines. The avalanche scar intersected the river bend just a quarter mile ahead. With luck we would find our logjam there.

We slogged through the dripping brush and followed the roar of the spring deluge. The sound of the surging waters diminished as the river widened, slowed by the numerous trees and downfalls brought down year after year by snow from high up the mountain. We picked our way over the stacked trees looking for a way across the frigid river. Most of the broken and uprooted trees had been swept underwater or away from the bank. Finally we located a tall spruce tree spanning the larger of two channels to a small island where a raft of dead logs led safely across the smaller tributary. The trunk of the spruce narrowed to only a foot and hung inches above the water. At least the bark was still on the tree, making for surer footing on the wet surface.

I hate river crossings. My horoscope contains no water signs, and the one way I know I do not want to punch out is by drowning. In Vietnam we once got ambushed while wearing heavy packs and crossing a swollen river. I lost two men to the current during the panic. When we dragged them up two days later, I did not like the expression I saw on their faces. Nor did I like the look of another boy I discovered dead in a lake during more peaceful times.

Years ago, in the Wind Rivers, I would go to any lengths to avoid hazardous fording. Once I spent three days building a footbridge over a deep, narrow canyon. Later, when I worked as a backcountry ranger in the North Cascades, I felt my stomach tighten when the field radio had crackled the news that two bodies were hanging from short carabiner slings on the steel cable strung across the raging Chilliwack River. A father and son had tried to ford the river crossing, a difficult one even during normal water levels. The son had gone first, hooking a carabiner on the cable, and had been swept away and anchored helplessly in the raging water, inches out of reach of the metal hook that caused him to drown. Perhaps thinking to help, the father joined him.

The previous spring, closer to home, I defied astrological warnings and took Lisa down the main fork of Idaho's Salmon River in a raft piloted by my huge river-running friend, Ted. The river was cooking, as they say, moving right along at record flood stages. In the middle of the biggest rapid, Dutch Oven, the eighteen-foot raft folded in two, the oars shot out, and 270-pound Ted was lifted into the air. He grabbed onto me since I had, forewarned by my horoscope, a Gila monsterlike grip on the metal frame of the raft. The raft unfolded. I looked out. Lisa was out of the boat, bobbing along in the standing waves. Thinking the worst, I screamed to Ted, "Get Lisa."

"The hell with Lisa, get the oars," he yelled back.

I reached out for Lisa, knowing I was going to lose her. She grabbed my hand and I lifted her straight up and into the raft. She was smiling. Having grown up on the rivers of Oregon, she has a naturalness around water that eludes me.

I didn't tell Bob any of this, since I was supposed to be the older hand. Instead, I dragged the 120 feet of $^7/_{16}$-inch nylon climbing rope out of my pack and found a place where he could belay me back to shore if I fell off. I prepared to lead out across the slick, branching log. I tied a bowline around my waist and unhooked the belt on my backpack, which I would jettison if I hit the drink. Tentatively, I stepped out onto the spruce trunk. The log wobbled in the eddying current and my heart rose to my throat. I steadied myself on the handle of my ice axe. I inched around spruce boughs, which forced me to lean out over the water, and somehow resisted the temptation to drop to my hands and crawl along the log like a caterpillar. The tree trunk narrowed to a foot and sank to the level of the river, which surged over the log. Ten more feet of naked log to the island, where the rest of the crossing was easy. I began to tense up, knowing that if I took a swim, it would be here. I freed up the rope just in case and took a couple of short steps using the tip of my ice axe as a third foot. The narrow log wobbled and I lost my balance. I ran the last four feet then jumped for the island, which I missed by a foot, landing in waist-deep icy water. But I was across.

I took up the slack on the climbing rope and belayed Bob, who crossed smoothly until the last section, which he also ran across. The other channel of the Bullshoe River ran deep but was covered with a network of downed trees, which we crossed without incident.

We stood on the far bank of the river we had been told we would never get across and repacked our gear. Shouldering our loads, we contoured through the swampy bottomland leading to the mouth of Morning Eagle Creek. The alder had just begun to leaf out. We entered a section of mature timber. The mosaic of vegetative types and maturity there was typical of areas where catastrophic erosion and wildfire naturally create maximum diversity. It was also the best kind of mountain grizzly habitat.

I caught the pungent, heavy odor of a large animal ahead. A hundred yards farther, a yearling moose crashed away through the trees. Patches of snow remained under the timber. Morning Eagle Creek—a third the size of Bullshoe—was also swollen from spring runoff. Fording it was out of the question. This meant bushwhacking up the south side of the creek until we found another log to cross over. Meanwhile it would be slow going, as the south sides of the east-west drainages up here tended to be brushier and devoid of game trails.

Sometime around midday the rain stopped, but the clouds continued to hang around the mountaintops. We moved westward, close to the creek and along the base of steep slopes and low cliffs. We immediately ran into slide alder the size of a man's wrist and growing so thick we had to paw and pull our way through it at the rate of less than a mile every three hours. By late afternoon, it began to rain again and we were scarcely two miles through it. By evening exhaustion was crowding our judgment. We wanted badly to get across the creek and pick up the relatively well-used network of game trails. Beneath a bench lay a tiny island lined with willow. The bare trunk of a tree stretched across the wider channel of the creek. Maybe we could wade across holding on to the tree.

We dropped our packs and waded out to the little island, through waist-deep water. Wading across the deeper channel would be dangerous, maybe impossible. We had been stupid to think we had a chance. The rain was steady by then and turning colder. We stood knee-deep in the frigid water looking at the far bank we could not reach. Bob told me he thought he was getting hypothermic.

Cold and mentally sluggish, we waded back to our packs. I knew we had to get our blood pumping, so I climbed rapidly up the steep hill to the bench. Up on the tiny flat we gasped for breath, beyond the grasp of hypothermia. I got a small fire going and the breeze blew the smoke down the valley. We warmed ourselves, grateful to see the wind carry our scent away from where we thought Bob's bear might be.

I pitched the tent over low huckleberry bushes while Bob set up his antenna. Just before dark he pointed the receiving end up-valley, and we heard the faint *beep beep beep* of an inactive bear. The radio transmitted in two modes: the resting or inactive one, and the active signal when the bear was moving and the tiny beeps came faster.

I crawled into my soggy sleeping bag and tried to adjust to the uneven terrain. I thought of Bob's job out here and considered my ambivalent role in it. I was here to help him: he wanted to track his grizzly and I had more experience working close to wild bears. But we were not exactly of one mind; he was a wildlife biologist practicing his science, wanting to learn about grizzly bears by studying habitat relationships. He mapped bear movements and activities, and, to obtain data on this, he had snared and collared a grizzly bear. My own interest in animals was less scientific. I wanted to learn from the bears themselves and was wary of the limits of scientific inquiry. Traditional Blackfeet saw the natural world in terms of awe and mystery. Animals lived in metaphorical relationships to them; the creatures were other nations. Every plant and animal passed coded information to man. Part of the price western science has paid for analytical power is that it has transformed the natural world into something alien.

Like film-making, wildlife biology is also a business. Grizzly bears, who are disappearing, rake in more grants than cottontails, who are thriving. The rights of animals are subjugated—not unlike the way we handled the Indian. I did not begrudge Bob his solitary radio-collared bear. He and his park colleagues had shown admirable restraint in that respect. But both Bob and I saw a reciprocity in our respective work; we planned to give something back to the bears.

By morning the clouds were hanging only a couple of hundred feet above the trees. We pulled on our slimy boots and headed out into the first of several parallel strips of steep slide alder separated by thin wedges of fir and spruce. After two hours of struggling with the underbrush, we hit another long triangle of trees converging at the creek. A large spruce was crammed between two rocky walls, hanging twenty feet above Morning Eagle Creek.

The crossing was not nearly as tricky as Bullshoe. I tiptoed across using my ice axe as a staff, while Bob crawled over on his hands and knees. Safely across, we skirted a strip of timber uphill and almost immediately crossed a well-used animal trail, replete with sign of a single moose and several elk. Patches of snow lingered under the trees. The willow had budded, but cow parsnip, an important grizzly food, had only leafed at ground level. The plant phenology above us was still in its winter mode and holding.

Our game trail petered out. We traversed up through the timber and found another. Crossing a drift of spring snow, we stopped. Two sets of bear tracks were printed in mud on the melting snow. Both were grizzly, but they led in opposite directions. One set was fresh, perhaps from the previous night. The other, made by a smaller bear, was older. Neither track suggested a huge animal. The larger set could have been made by Bob's bear.

We walked on through a thin understory of alder and mountain ash under mature subalpine fir and Englemann spruce. In the forest duff, I found an old bear scat on a faint animal trail. The scat was a berry scat dropped late the previous summer, probably by a grizzly judging from the pie-size area of disintegrating mountain ash and huckleberries. The purple berry scat looked like caviar, like beluga, a caviar I loved far beyond my impoverished means. The red ash berries more closely resembled American salmon caviar, cheaper but also out of my price range. I staggered on through the forest, lost in fantasy, carrying a heavy pack with absolutely nothing good to eat in it. Back in Tucson I had spread the beluga on her belly, then lapped up the tiny roe with my tongue. The ova had burst audibly between my teeth. I had poured more champagne into her navel and licked it out. The champagne had been Spanish and inexpensive; we were saving so we could afford the beluga.

I snapped out of my daydream; Bob told me he wanted to stop. He set up his radio apparatus and again received a signal up-valley; it was stronger, but still in the inactive beeping pattern. We should catch up with the critter tonight if he keeps on sleeping, I thought. Bob was excited about getting his first real ground data and packed the radio gear on top so he could get to it every hour to monitor the bear.

About midafternoon it began to drizzle again. We did not especially care: the going was easy compared to the south side of the drainage. We crossed another avalanche scar tangled with alder. The game trail was faint but traceable. We paused on the open slope to take another reading; the young grizzly slept on not too far ahead. He could have been bedded in the very next strip of timber.

Entering the trees again, we found an older set of bear tracks, belonging to a larger grizzly. There also was the five-toed, clawed mark of a large weasel—a martin or perhaps a fisher. Bob took readings every five or ten minutes; he wanted to make sure we located this particular animal before we stumbled across him and ran him off his bed.

Grizzly bear day beds are reasonably predictable in the sort of subalpine mountain valley where we were. During June, grizzlies bed hidden in the thickest tangle of downfalls, next to trees and close to running water. They are very secure on day beds: solitary animals can be approached to within a hundred feet or so. Beds tend to be used as retreats, so if you are walking on well-used game or human trails, you probably will not run into a bedded grizzly. Beds are only reused for the few days the bear spends feeding in the area. But there are exceptions, and I know of bedding sites that are used for long seasons year after year.

Solitary grizzlies are not generally aggressive when disturbed on their day beds. The ones I have blundered upon ran away, often at the last minute. Other bears remained bedded, allowing me to pass, sometimes at less than a hundred feet. Some grizzlies, however, are like people who wake up cranky. The real danger lies in surprising a bedded grizzly at extremely close range, especially one bedded next to a carcass and or a mother bedded with cubs.

Bob did not trust my theories about bears on beds. It was a bit unscientific for him; and after all, it was the mating season. We moved on with care. Halfway into the half-mile-wide wedge of subalpine timber, the beeps got very loud. We turned down the volume so we would not alarm the grizzly. He was still bedded, but with only three hours of daylight left on a cool, damp day he could have gotten up to begin feeding or traveling at any time.

We stopped and discussed our strategy. Bob was understandably wary of walking up on an adult grizzly. My guess was that the bear was bedded so much because he was a young, subordinate animal living in the presence of larger males during the mating season. I thought he was hiding out and holing up.

Normally, Bob would have circled a location, taking a number of linear readings, which would then intersect in a point. But if we had done this, the grizzly would have smelled us and spooked. The alternative was to track the bear upwind, using the receiver until we got close enough to see him. Bob was hesitant. I felt confident about walking up on the young grizzly as long as he was on a day bed. This was an intuition born of some experience but hardly idiot-proof.

We dumped our packs near a small clearing far off the game trail and away from the path of traveling bears. Carrying the receiver and antenna, we edged down the game trail in the direction of the sleeping animal. Bob had his headphones on and we worked out a simple system of signals. I had no experience with radio telemetry but trusted Bob, who guessed the bear was less than a quarter mile off. We walked to within a hundred yards of the end of the timber strip and reached a small stream. Bob pointed down the slope from the game trail. He held his palms a foot apart to show me that we were not far away. I licked my finger and held it up, feeling the evaporative coolness on the windward side. I sniffed the air but got no sign of the grizzly. We padded on silently into the sparse ash and elderberry understory.

Windfalls of all kinds obstructed a direct path to the source of the signal. We circled and found ourselves surrounded by barricades of downfalls. Visibility was limited to the branches twenty feet away. I felt a hand on my shoulder. Bob was gesturing in a circle, which meant the signal was coming from every direction. He had explained that, when you get very close to the origin of the signal, the beeps seem to come from everywhere at once, because the radio waves bounce off trees, bushes, rocks. Frozen, we listened, peering under every deadfall and into every bush. I heard rustling twenty or thirty feet away but could see nothing through the maze of downfalls.

"He's going," Bob whispered, pointing beyond the entanglement. He swung his hand and pointed up-drainage. The young grizzly was running up the valley, away from us.

We were both disappointed and relieved. Bob had hoped to locate the bear on his day bed, then withdraw and let him sleep. Our chances of doing this probably had not been that good. We had startled the bear at about thirty feet and still had not gotten a glimpse of the animal. The gloomy day brightened as a beam of sunlight pierced the timber. We systematically searched for the bed. Finally we located a shallow, dish-shaped depression of matted brush at the foot of a big spruce tree. Frequently grizzlies scoop out the duff with their claws or even dig moderately deep depressions in the dirt or snow.

We followed the route of the fleeing bear to the edge of the trees. Bob took another reading and got a strong, active signal from perhaps a mile up the drainage. Looking over the top of the alder we saw the shining mountains of the Continental Divide still buried under a white blanket of snow lit by the oblique sunlight. We were more than halfway up this trailless drainage. By the next night, we would be poised for a crossing.

We had not seen a human sign since leaving the patrol cabin. People simply do not hike much off established trails to a place like this drainage. Which is as it should be: this fundamental lack of imagination and initiative is what protects the wilderness. Even in a place like Yellowstone, open country where you could walk anywhere, most folks stick to the Day-Glo orange markers of the constructed trails—if they leave their Winnebagos at all. The country where we were is so miserably thick with brush and littered with downfalls that you have to be strongly driven to do any bushwhacking off trails at all.

Mandatory permits for backcountry camping were initiated when I was a backcountry ranger in the North Cascades. I was ambivalent about the complete and unquestioned acceptance of the reservation system by the public. Nobody complained. The compliance made my job easier. Still, there was an element of sheeplike submission in this that I found appalling. I was torn between doing the real and necessary job of protecting the natural resources and following an innate tendency to resist regimentation and root for the outlaw. However, one of the reasons we still have a few pockets of wilderness left—and the grizzlies who live in them—is that backcountry users carry with them an idea of recreation that precludes the vital urgency that drives us through jungles of alder into the last wild basin.

I do not advocate anyone's leaving the well-used trail systems. The more we leave wilderness places alone, the better. But I hate trails and love to bushwhack, though I have an indolent nature that keeps me thinking about adventure more often than living it. When I do step off the human-traveled trails, I find myself leaving behind conventional expectations, launching myself into the thicket, pawing at the brush with anticipation, smelling discovery.

The sun sank behind the peaks of the divide and dark clouds closed in again. We looked for a place to set up the tent. We picked a spot under the trees, far from potential feeding areas or animal trails. Bob prepared to monitor his bear throughout the night at two-hour intervals, making use of the six-dollar pocket watch he bought in the touristy little townsite. Just at dark he took another reading: the young grizzly had bedded again farther up the valley.

I had gotten to know Bob at the Belton Bar in West Glacier, Montana. I knew he was some kind of a government researcher studying grizzly bear habitat, so I ignored him for a long time. But Bob won me over with his weakness for Wild Turkey, hound dogs, and redheads—reminding me of my own blemished character. As his boss said, Bob lacked "sensitivity in dealing with public relations situations." This meant that Bob had tried to bite a journalist from *People* magazine on the ass. His candor was seen by the Park Service as a lack of tact.

I know of no field of natural science half as political as grizzly bear biology. Whatever data you collect or studies you complete remain forever secondary to the political alliances you make and the bureaucratic power you wield. Bob naively believed that old-fashioned science would count, at least in the end, and that truth would triumph. The likelihood of his failure in the profession of biopolitics drew me to him.

I heard Bob turn on his receiver and fumble with the knobs, taking another fix on the bear. Half awake, I realized I had been dreaming. About war, I thought. The young grizzly's behavior reminded me of something. His reaction to the smell of danger—the presence of a larger boar or maybe the mating season in general—seemed to be to crawl back into the brush, hole up, and lie out this hazardous time. The same thing used to happen to me back in Southeast Asia: whenever the shit really hit the fan, when it looked as if we were about to be overrun and it became a matter of everyone for himself, my first impulse, or perhaps instinct, was to slide off alone into the jungle and keep going until I found vegetation thick enough to hide in, a sanctuary where I could ride out the hunt for Americans. So I thought I knew what it might feel like to be outgunned by bigger bears.

I did not share my thoughts with Bob, although I find this kind of thinking useful. Humans are so strongly discouraged from comparing their lives with those of other animals. Yet everything I had experienced taught me that metaphor is the fundamental path of imagining, a first line of inquiry into the lives of other creatures that sheds light on our own. As a species we started out that way, learning our ties to countless other species and discovering the fundamental parallelism that first pried open the secrets of our own intelligence.

By dawn the clouds had settled in and we looked forward to a wet day. I pulled on my Mickey Mouse boots, half wishing I had worn my hiking boots instead. The boots were hard on the feet, and I had the blisters to prove it. But they were good for fording streams and snow of the kind we would encounter when we crossed the divide. My feet had been a bit timid ever since I suffered a mild case of frostbite in Algonquin Park, Canada, during a cold December. I wolfed down more stale granola, our only food except a bag of protein powder. Bob carried no food. He was following my diet as an experiment. When I am out in grizzly country I do not care about the lack of variety in food because I like to devote my time to the country around me.

I looked out at the bleak day, the low gray clouds, the dark cliffs beyond. I sat and stared, then quickly stood and shouldered my pack. I left a note for Bob telling him where I would meet him at dusk. I struck off on a game trail, scarcely aware of my surroundings, walking for hours without looking up until the gloomy light grew dim again. Although tired and hungry, I could not shake my black mood. I made camp and turned in without eating, hoping that Bob would find the tent.

During the night the young boar moved on. Bob could pick up only the faintest of signals. He thought the bear had bedded again in the upper reaches of the valley in one of the last stands of timber. That meant it would be a short day, since we did not have enough time to cross the divide. We would have to do that the next day. The day before, we made a total of four whole miles. That day, it made sense to knock out the distance to the end of the valley in a couple of hours.

A light rain fell. We left the cover of the trees and crossed a brushy avalanche scar. Deep snow remained in the bottom, covering the creek with a series of snow bridges. Subalpine meadows dotted the slides and south-facing slopes. A few of them showed the beginning of spring green-up. Ahead of us, upslope, a dark brown bear grazed on a green flat. A grizzly that was big by Glacier standards—we guessed 400 or 450 pounds—nibbled at green shoots and the leafy nub of cow parsnip. The bear fed boldly and confidently in the open seventy-five yards from us. The big brown animal with a slightly silver-tipped neck was probably a male. We watched for about fifteen minutes. The bear moved off into the brush. We followed the game trail across the slide, passing below the grizzly and on up the valley beyond him.

We made good time. The several small animal trails had coalesced into one large path. Around midday we entered the last sizable timber patch remaining in the upper valley and picked up the strong signal of Bob's bedded bear. We decided to set up our tent, get out of the rain, and monitor his activities throughout the rest of the day. Tomorrow we would cross the divide.

In the snow under the timber we came across the tracks of three different grizzlies. We moved as far away from the trail and tracks as we could and set up camp. Bob dug out his radio gear and I kindled a tiny fire over which we hoped to dry our sleeping bags and clothing before climbing over the snowy divide. Bob monitored the bear, who slept perhaps half a mile up the creek. Along about four o'clock, a small storm cell settled in and blew the smoke up the drainage. Five minutes later Bob received an active signal. The young grizzly was moving. The signal came from directly up-valley. The beeps grew fainter: the bear was running away. He was probably leaving the drainage and going over the divide.

I was a little surprised at the speed with which the little grizzly left. Although he was not the first bear I had seen run from smoke, I was disappointed. I had not wanted to run him off. We cured the disease but killed the patient. Nonetheless, Bob was pleased at the number of fixes he had gotten on the bear. He had not really expected his radio-collared grizzly to be in that drainage and had only intended to investigate those sites where he had located the animal from the air.

This bear is one of the first to be tracked by radio in Glacier National Park. Radio telemetry has become the standard technique used by biologists to determine movements and habitat use. Not much was known about Glacier's grizzlies. A considerable amount of data, however, has been gathered on Yellowstone's bears.

The bedrock study of Yellowstone's grizzlies was done by the Craighead brothers beginning in 1959. Pioneering and using radio telemetry, they conducted their work largely out of the open-pit dumps where the Park Service disposed of their garbage. This practice had decades of tradition behind it, and most of Yellowstone's bears frequented the dumps. The Craigheads rightly saw the congregation of bears as a goldmine of data.

Since that time, telemetry has been used to study grizzlies in Canada, Alaska, Northern Montana, and around Yellowstone. This data is integrated with information collected from aerial surveys, hunter kills, scat analysis, direct observation, and habitat studies.

Telemetry is most useful in collecting data on movements and habitat use, less so in determining population trends and reproductive rates, where large samples or "statistically significant" information is necessary.

Most of the methods of analyzing telemetry data were originally developed for small territorial animals. The home or seasonal range of grizzlies, who are not territorial, is less distinct because it includes all those corridors of movement through "sterile" country—though no less important than any to a grizzly. For example, one Yellowstone male grizzly's home range varied between 1,917 and 286 square miles, depending on the method of calculation used. The smaller area, the "minimum area method," is more useful for grizzlies who may travel as far as fifty miles as the raven flies between seasonal forage ranges.

Within these "home ranges," usually calculated on a one-year basis, lie all kinds of seasonal forage ranges for berries or pine nuts and sometimes "biological or ecocenters," defined in the telemetry business as a clumping of fixes or radio-locations in relatively small areas such as a garbage dump or salmon stream. Also, home ranges change from year to year and over the life of an individual bear, sometimes dramatically. All the areas overlap with ranges of other bears. The areas tend to enlarge in lean years and shrink in lush times.

Grizzlies have extensive spatial needs and may range almost continually. Average home ranges generally reflect the relative quality of different ecosystems, such as food and den site availability. Individual variation is tremendous. Males use more area than females—maybe two or three times as much.

In the wetter regions of the Rockies, such as in Glacier National Park, where weather is influenced by maritime climate, male grizzlies get by on average ranges of about 150 square miles; in a drier climate, like Yellowstone, they might range over twice that area. A home range with lots of berries and salmon runs could be very small—around five square miles on Kodiak Island and maybe forty on Admiralty in Alaska. But these are averages for a species known for its individualism. The actual home ranges in Yellowstone vary from three square miles to one thousand.

Densities are expressed in square miles per grizzly. On Kodiak, there could be a brown bear every half a square mile, while up on the Arctic tundra the density is closer to a grizzly every fifty. Down in Glacier Park, the density might be as high as one grizzly every eight square miles; in Yellowstone, an average of thirty to forty square miles per bear.

Of course, all these numbers are extrapolations of sample studies of areas chosen by researchers in part because they were good places to study grizzlies and are therefore not exactly a random sample of the bear population. Also, the research upon which the extrapolations are based varies in methodology and quality. Some are not much more than guesses. But, in a general way, these densities do indicate the productivity of the different areas.

In comparison to most studies, Bob's one-man, hand-held telemetry operation was decidedly small potatoes. His low budget required him to drag his ass out in the thickest brush and push the object of his inquiry off day beds twenty-five feet away.

Bob checked the place where he had last gotten a fix on his young boar—a shallow bed under a tangle of dead spruce—then backtracked on the game trail to where we had been drying our clothes. Bob was still puzzled about why the bear had left the valley. Maybe it had been the wood smoke. Earlier, the grizzly had moved only a short distance, a half mile or so, after we had jumped him on his day bed. He seemed especially skittish. The day before, he had spent over twenty-two hours on his day bed.

I wandered off beyond the trees, down to the creek where I listened to the hollow wind sweeping the empty spaces and watched the water disappear under snow bridges. On these trips I tend to leave my human troubles behind. Out here, it's the lives of other creatures I want to adopt.

But this time I could not get out of myself. I tried to let the wild mountain beauty wash over me, but I failed. The dark frigid water disappeared under the snow. The huge basin was so empty. That alpine cirque felt as alien as did the tunnels of the Song Cai Valley. Our crossing of the Bullshoe River now seemed impossible.

* * *

I am fly-fishing my favorite bend on the Madison, casting a weighted nymph up and across the current, mending the line and letting it dredge the bottom of the swift run opposite where I wade. I have been at it an hour and a half and have caught and released three two-pound rainbows. Lisa has been watching me from the edge of the campground two hundred yards away for the past forty-five minutes. She gets up and walks down the grassy bank. I reel in my line and wade toward shore. I stand in the shallow water next to the grass. She tells me the news: Gage has cured his pain with a shotgun.

* * *

In the fading light of the snow-filled valley I got a grip on myself. After all this time I still handled death so poorly. So what if he had not died on schedule? That, I told myself, was his privilege. But I remembered our talks; so little time, so much evil in the world. He might have gotten Pol Pot in his gunsights: he could have taken a bad man with him.

11

THE SACRED BEAR
OF THE BLACKFEET

Scholars believe that bears provided the original model of spiritual renewal. The bear showed early man how to get through the little death of winter by burial, emerging from the cold in spring, sometimes with new life in the form of bear cubs. The bear showed the way of survival and renewal as part of the cycle of life.

The reason the bear plays a role beyond other sacred animals in this hemisphere has its origins in the biochemistry of the bear's belly. The example of his ascetic behavior in the den—where he neither eats nor excretes—and his rebirth, timed to the solar calendar, is the result of the biology of the grizzly's carnivore gut.

American thinker and scholar Paul Shepard, writing with his colleague Barry Sanders, has said the Blackfeet myth of the bear has roots in some of the oldest of Asian religious traditions, customs which, like the American Indians', had a common origin in the prehistoric world and which live on in the language and ceremonies of the native peoples of the circumpolar north. The most pervasive of these traditions was the ceremony of the bear and the Myth of the Bear Mother, which Shepard and Sanders think might be the most persistent and widely told tale ever devised for education and entertainment. In the Bear Mother story, a woman marries a bear and their children become the ancestors of all people. As kin, both bears and people are part animal and part human. The Bear Husband, a divinity, dies for the good of the people, and his flesh provides sacramental food. The Bear Sons, also divine, are intermediaries of the hunt and teach men that success in hunting depends not so much on power but humility.

Elements of the Bear Mother story and other bear traditions are ubiquitous in prehistory and the ethnographic record. Across the top of the world, the native peoples of Finland, Siberia, Hokkaido, British Columbia, Alaska, and Labrador retained elaborate rituals centering on a sacrificial feast of a young bear who willingly passes into the afterlife. These circumpolar ceremonies, often called the Cult of the Master Bear, are remarkable in their similarities and in their suggestion that the good things in life are not seized but given. The symbolic bear, both black and brown, becomes the model of renewal and immortality, in undergoing burial and resurrection.

This is part of the spiritual celebration of the bear that survives today among traditional Blackfeet. In tracking the mythological bear you invariably come across the Real Bear of flesh and fur. One leads to the other. Real grizzlies have healthy hearts, do not die of cancer, and have fewer parasites than humans during an average lifetime. If men do not kill them, grizzlies lead an active, vigorous, sexual life until their twenties. Above all, they heal well. The Blackfeet and earlier cultures paid attention to all of this.

To the ancient Blackfeet the grizzly, whom they called Real Bear, was the most esteemed of all animals. Many surviving tales evolved from elements of the much older traditions of the Spirit Bear, the most common of which are variations in the story of the Medicine Grizzly.

The great bear was a healer and the source of power of the medicine pipe. The Blackfeet, following the way of the grizzly, held the pipe in both hands. Real Bear was killed only as a sacred enemy, and during such hunts the name of the bear was never spoken. Instead—and this indirect reference to bears occurred throughout the tribal cultures of circumpolar Europe, Asia, and North America—he was called Old Grandfather, Old Man, Old Honey Paws, or Crooked Tail.

Most of the American ethnographic record dates no earlier than 1880, and the bulk of it is after 1900. Very little is recorded on what Indians thought of grizzlies. Most of what is known comes out of folklore, mythology, and song as preserved in the reports and bulletins of the Bureau of American Ethnology. By the time anyone got around to studying native peoples, the buffalo were gone, the grizzlies were going, and so were the traditions.

The differences between the ways the High Plains Blackfeet and the Pacific Coast Indians regarded the grizzly are small compared to their similarities—so far as these are reflected by the historical record. Grizzlies were considered our closest animal relative. On the rare occasion when they were hunted, a formal conciliatory song or speech preceded the kill, which was often followed by a ceremonial feast.

Among the Flathead and Kootenai, fear of grizzlies resulted in a more malevolent and destructive portrayal than the Blackfeet's Real Bear; this perhaps was the result of a more myopic forest perspective where bears were encountered on close, brushy trails up salmon rivers. The Salish believed that the terrifying power of the grizzly could be resisted only by magic. Among the Kootenai, a dream of bears was a sign to lead a ceremony to ask for immunity from bear attacks and for protection against enemies by the bear warrior. Fear of the grizzly appeared strongest among the Indians of California, the southern branch of the Pacific Northwest culture.

Unlike the West Coast Indians, the Blackfeet and their neighbors on the east side of the divide revered the grizzly and never hunted him during hibernation. They saw him more as a healer than a threat—as the Medicine Grizzly. Since the passing of the traditional Indian, the attitude of the dominant culture toward grizzlies has been one of unmitigated hostility. Whatever the Blackfeet, along with nearly all other ancient peoples of America, knew of or learned from the grizzly has been lost. By the time we got around to finding out about these people, they, like the grizzly, were mostly gone.

12
ACROSS
THE DIVIDE

At dawn, I walked back up the snowy basin and watched the morning light creep into the valley. The snow-filled amphitheater seemed less ominous. We had to find a route over the divide, and we hoped Bob's bear would show us the way. I saw the paw prints on the snow and picked up the line of bear tracks above the timber, traversing the white ledges and climbing up to the blanket of snow covering the upper drainage of Morning Eagle. He was traveling alone; there was no sign of the smaller bear with whom he crossed the divide. His trail crossed the creek and climbed steeply south and east out of the U-shaped valley. We would be following his spoor.

We broke camp in silence. Bob packed away his equipment after trying to monitor the bear. I shook the dew off the tent, rolled it into a sloppy cylinder, and stuffed it into my backpack. Passing the last big trees in the valley, I picked a route over a series of snowy ledges, roughly following the tracks of the grizzly, contouring up and out of the upper basin. We walked as much as possible on the snow, which was still deep enough to cover the alder. We crossed the bear tracks, which led west, and continued climbing south along the ledges.

All of a sudden we found ourselves staring up at a vertical section of rock and brush—not exactly a technical climb but an awkward and arduous one considering our sixty-pound packs. Stupidly I had wandered too far south, beyond the cascade of gradual ledges leading down from the divide. I should have stayed on the track of the grizzly, who knew where he was going.

I relaxed a bit. My mood lightened as I concentrated on the mountain. Lisa, who was already an accomplished technical climber when I met her, would have welcomed a challenge like this. For years now I had gone up the easy sides of mountain peaks. Too stubborn to turn around, we decided to keep climbing up the steplike cliffs. The rock was mixed with a jumble of glacial moraine, partially weathered into thin soil, making the trip up to the ridge miserable and filthy. We paused on a slick, muddy ledge and looked up at five-needle evergreens, whitebark, or limber pine, indicating that we were approaching the ridge top. It could not be more than a couple of hundred feet above us.

We climbed over the lip of the last rotten cliff into the shade of the deep green trees. Breathing and sweating heavily, I sat on the three feet of snow lingering under the timber and cooled off. This was as wild as the country gets in the lower forty-eight. All that is necessary to control human impact on a place like this is to leave the mountain valleys without constructed foot trails. It's cheap and democratic. I wonder why the park and forest services have not figured out that if you leave every other backcountry drainage without trails, you create entire regions to which animals like grizzlies can escape during the peak months of human travel.

There are precious few drainages, mesas, or playas within our so-called wilderness areas in the lower forty-eight that are not crisscrossed by an extensive network of foot trails. The valleys and passes through which we had just traveled were hardly remote; they simply did not have developed trail systems. They received just the right amount of human visitation without the imposition of management: the animals had a sanctuary, a place to which even the shiest ones, like grizzlies, could retreat and be left undisturbed. Man has been a member of grizzly bear biotic communities for at least the last twelve thousand years—so it's quite natural to have a few *Homo sapiens* pass through.

The pines thinned out as we scrambled over the moguls of crusted snow onto the open ridge. We found a short, steep pitch of packed snow where Bob practiced an ice axe arrest—a technique for stopping yourself if you fall and start sliding down a steep slope of snow. It's a good tool when crossing the Great Divide in early June, and a new one to Bob. I had some earlier practice, having once done three unsuccessful ice axe arrests on a fall down a frozen eight-hundred-foot snow gully: the fourth one bit in and held a hundred feet from the bottom, where the chute dropped into a boulder field. That was one of two climbing records I held in the North Cascades. The other was when I fell into a crevasse on a glacier while traveling alone. Luckily I landed on a snow bridge twelve feet down and was able to claw myself out without embarrassment, since no one was watching. I blamed my horoscope, which said I was accident-prone. I was sure such mountaineering ignominy happened all the time, though no one else advertised. I neglected to fill Lisa in on this, as I was putting the move on her and had my image to protect.

The ridge climbed out to a huge sloping slab of snow and ice, dotted by a few clumps of dwarf alpine trees. We hurried into the nearest timber, a patch of stunted fir trees, as a storm squall swept across the whiteness, blowing stinging hail into our faces. It appeared these little storms would continue throughout the day, so we waited this one out. Above us were a string of small snow-covered glaciers, below which I planned on passing. Above the snowfields stretched the divide itself, undulating and gently sloping to the east, but dropping off abruptly to the west into the hidden recesses of Silenos Cirque three thousand feet below. Finding a route in there would normally have been our biggest problem on this trip. Instead, I was trusting the trail of the young bear to lead us safely to the bottom.

We waited out another snow squall, which restricted our visibility. The grizzly trail led south over the snow, around the foot of towering snow fields, and climbed toward a low pass between two peaks. We passed two tiny azure tarns beginning to melt in the weak spring sunlight filtering through the breaks in the clouds. This pass was the route Bob's bear and his consort had taken the week before. Snow covered the old spoor; only the previous day's tracks remained. He was going down into Silenos by himself.

About midday, the snow began to melt and we wallowed,

breaking through the crust to our knees. We had only about a mile to go to the pass. We kicked steps up a moderate incline, walked out onto a small flat, and looked out into space. We were there: the Continental Divide, the highpoint of our trip.

A forest of windswept stunted pine trees clung to a partially melted-out ridge on the southwestern exposures. Before us the country dropped off into a large glacial valley thousands of feet below, which ran off twenty miles into the gray distance of the North Fork of the Flathead River. I could have stayed there forever, but bad weather was on the way in from the west. We sat on a mat of heather with our feet dangling down toward Silenos.

The shallow valley bottom of the North Fork and its mosaic of low meadows stretched toward Canada. Bob had studied the vegetation of these meadowlands, some of which are fallow fields from early homesteads, and said there was more grizzly food in those old farmlands than any other place he had studied in Glacier National Park. Other meadows lay over old alluvial channels of the river and were rich in cow parsnip in the spring and sweetvetch in the fall. This complex of open areas along the North Fork is the most important spring habitat for grizzlies down here, especially in April and May, when higher areas are under snow. By June, grizzlies begin to disperse, drawn by spring green-up and the dynamics of the mating season.

I owned an acre of land somewhere down there. I bought it from another whacko-Nam vet whose trust I won by bailing him out of the slammer after he got busted on an old deer-poaching rap. I had no plans for improvement or development; I bought the place only so no one else would. The whole idea of owning the land was still alien to me. I bought it for Lisa and my dog during a period when I was not particularly happy, to hedge my bets against mortality and cut the inevitable losses. I knew that the land would last.

We lingered between storms, enjoying this enchanted swale where the snowfields began. I wandered off looking for the trail of the bear. On a cornice of snow overhanging a dizzying abyss, I found a set of tracks five inches long with the clawed thumbprint registering in the soft snow: a wolverine shared the snowy pass with Bob's bear. That part of Montana around Glacier National

Park is the last place left in the contiguous states where all the
Rocky Mountain megafauna that was here when the white man
showed up on the East Coast can still be found: the wolf, the
wolverine, the woodland caribou, and the grizzly.

We started down off the pass into the huge cirque, the head of
which was hidden behind sheer cliffs. The bottom reportedly
contained the most impenetrable jumble of downfalls in the region, having been overprotected from wildfires, which would
otherwise burn through it every thirty years or so and keep the
timber open. The steep slopes of Silenos provided some of the best
late spring and early summer habitat for grizzlies. Dropping rapidly, we slipped and slid a thousand feet down the gulch, then
contoured north at the foot of the cliffs above the awful mix of
brush and downed timber.

Slowly we made our way below the steep cliffs and edged
down toward the trees, where Bob wanted to check out a bedding
spot on which he had located his bear from the air the previous
week. He stopped and dug out his radio gear while I glassed the
wild basin. A black bear was grazing beneath the far cliffs despite
my expecting to see nothing but grizzlies up there. Bob rotated his
antenna and heard a faint signal from somewhere far off in a distant
corner of the cirque. The transmission bounced off the cliffs and
bedrock, so that he could not pinpoint the young grizzly.

Following the animal path we made the best time we had
made in five days. The sun dropped behind low clouds in the
western sky. It must have been past midafternoon. Bob took out
his topographic maps and located a radio fix where his bear had
bedded the week before. The spot lay directly below us, in an
angle of timber a thousand feet below. As much as we hated to
leave this facilitating game trail for the agonies of bushwhacking,
our job was to do ground investigations of all the sites Bob had
marked.

We entered the trees and almost immediately ran into a vertical jungle of downfalls stacked twenty feet in the air. We spent half
an hour looking for the specific bed site. It could have been
anywhere in that maze. We dropped down to the bottom of the
small creek hoping for easier going. Instead, we found the laby-
rinth of windfalls piled high with uprooted trees and the debris of

countless avalanches coming off the opposite slope. It began to
rain. We tottered along the spines of slippery deadfalls, leaning on
our ice axes for stability as we leapt down to the next tier of dead
wood. By evening we had not come much more than a mile. We
were tired, frustrated, and irritable. I told Bob that he was heading
in the wrong direction.

"Fuck you, all you want to do is go up to that lake and go
fishing."

"Go die alone, asshole," I said. "I'm not going into that valley
bottom."

We decided to take the shortest route to the creek, since we
needed to find water and make camp. We launched ourselves into
another vertical stack of downed timber, slipping on the treacherous sections of wet, naked logs. We fell a dozen times apiece but
were too loose and inebriated by fatigue to injure ourselves. The
rain continued. Just at dark we hit the creek and forded the knee-
deep water. I found a soggy campsite within a few feet of the
glacial stream, which I hoped would not rise during the night. I
pitched the tent in a puddle of water and we crawled into our wet
sleeping bags. We shared a canteen-cupful of murky protein powder, which ended our bickering.

I felt for a hip-shaped depression in the sump over which we
had put up the tent. I was too weary to sleep deeply. My stomach
growled and I conjured up a vision of leg of lamb stuffed with
many cloves of garlic, basted with oil and rosemary, and roasted
over mesquite coals. Of course I try to boycott lamb because the
sheep industry has the habit of poisoning or shooting every bear,
coyote, or eagle in rifle range. Running sheep is incompatible with
grizzly habitat. A grizzly will wade through a herd of woollies tossing the mangled carcasses left and right. The whining and bleating
and endless run of excreta seems to trigger something in the bear's
predatory wiring to make him attack solely out of irritation.

The next morning found us sore and bruised but in better
spirits. The rain had stopped, and, despite the fact that we had
covered only a mile and a half in six hours the previous day, we
were on our way out. The bushwhack down the side of the big lake
in the valley would, we thought, take only two or three days.

Meanwhile, as a result of my unceasing lobbying, we started upstream to visit Silenos Lake.

We scaled the last latticework of branches and trunks and stepped into a meadow of false hellebore and cow parsnip. Three minutes later we gazed across the cerulean waters of Silenos Lake and the half dozen waterfalls pouring off the ice and rock into this great hole. The lake was free of ice, though large snowfields lingered at the northern end. Bob caught movement high up the eastern wall, just below the snow line. A brown grizzly sow, with one of the smallest cubs I had ever seen, moved directly across a snow patch into avalanche brush and disappeared. She was too far away to notice us. The cub was what I call a spring cub, a guess on my part that the tiny bear might have been born a few weeks after the normal birthing time of late January and February.

We returned to the lake shore and cut long willow poles. I tied on ten feet of fly line attached to another eight feet of nylon leader and let a small, orange-bellied streamer drift out at the mouth of one of the feeder creeks. I always carry line, leader, and a few flies. Once, in Alaska, I lived for seven days on the grayling I caught on a dwarfed willow pole. This time the willow fly pole did not pan out.

We gave it up and walked along the shore. The openness of the alpine cirque, the turquoise water, and the sky beyond were salve to our soggy souls. The clouds, brush, and dark forests had worn us down. I savored these moments in the heart of our journey, this wild basin from which a river of ice flowed.

Stepping up on a slab of baked claystone, I surveyed the far corner of the lake. On the fan of snow alongside the lake below the glacier were patterns of tracks and networks of patterns. Even at that distance there was no mistaking the sign of adult bears. We moved in for a closer look. Long, large, sliding tracks—like those on Bullshoe trail—streaked down a slope. Sets of tracks ran together in at least two distinctive gaits. The front track of a smaller grizzly disappeared, and at one point the tracks of a large running grizzly were etched on the snow—claws digging and rear pads straining forward. There was much more than I could read. What I did not understand I imagined.

The sow was young, four and a half or five and a half years old. Although she had mated before, the breeding had not been successful. She had returned to this cirque, where she had spent much time as a cub and yearling, from the wet meadows twenty miles west, where, throughout the spring, she had fed on grass and forbs along the riparian zone of the major river. She had been aware of the boar browsing upwind for some time, but she grazed on unconcerned.

The male grizzly was fully mature and fairly large—about 450 pounds. By the time the big bear noticed the female, they fed only a hundred yards apart. Without hesitation he approached directly with his stiff-legged swagger, his neck arched and his head held low. She stood motionless until he came close; she lowered her head and shoulders, pointing her nose in the air. They stood side by side like this for a long time. The boar sniffed along the side of her head and rubbed his flanks against her. She moved off a few feet and pretended to graze. He nuzzled her and tried to herd her away from her feeding, but she persisted. They spent several hours nibbling the fresh green leaves of *Heracleum*; the female did most of the feeding while he attended her. They bedded close together in the slide alder during the middle of the day.

The shadows fell over the great amphitheater of Silenos and the pair rose and moved. They loped and romped over the open areas, sometimes side by side, sometimes with the female in the lead. Within minutes they reached the snowfield at the head of the lake below the glacier. She broke into a short run. He followed, his swaggering gait greatly exaggerated now. The boar appeared to lick the female's ears. She turned back with her jaws open like a cowering, playful shepherd dog. He mounted her, grasping her flanks with his front legs. They remained motionless for a while. He leaned forward and nibbled at her neck. He was salivating and his rear legs were wet with urine. She turned back toward him and they exchanged bites. She knelt at one point, then got up and shuffled forward on the snow. The copulation went on for twenty minutes. Afterward they stood quietly.

Suddenly the boar bowed his neck and lowered his head. He snorted, arched his neck, and took long, stiff-legged strides on the snow, swinging his large head violently from side to side.

* * *

I reread the scene with my binoculars one more time from about 120 yards away. That was the closest we should be. This white flat was the arena below the great amphitheater of Silenos, the wild stage on which the grizzlies danced for no one; this was a mating area.

Distinctive breeding grounds for grizzlies have not been identified, but that doesn't mean they do not exist. They were perhaps like elephant burial grounds, sacred ground, at least for me: I wanted my reverence to buy me an ounce of grace. I buried the orange streamer at the edge of the lake as a token offering.

We packed up and crawled back down the creek into the tangle of brush and dead trees. By midday we passed the previous night's camp and picked up our stashed equipment. Straining under full packs, we struggled up and over the piles of ancient timber. We told ourselves what we had been saying each successive day: This was the worst bushwhacking we had ever seen.

By late afternoon we reached the head of a long, narrow lake filling a glacial trough. We picked up a game trail along the north shore of the lake and made good time until dusk. A cascading creek ran off the mountain, depositing a small alluvial delta at the edge of the lake. We stepped out on the spit and watched the sun set over the distant shore.

The dawn was a flat gray over the calm waters. We pushed out early, knowing that we were only a long day's travel to the nearest trail and that it was going to rain. With some luck and steady humping, we would be out by dark. We climbed above steep rocky cliffs that plunged into the lake, struggling upward on the dry southeast-facing slope until we reached a mixed forest of pine and fir. Animal trails traced the contour of the ridge. Our game trail faded out and we scrambled higher on the hill looking for another. Climbing too high on the ridge we found ourselves lost in a sea of little gullies undulating endlessly across the breast of the mountainside. We rolled up and down the convoluted landscape for an hour, then found a rock promontory from which we could survey the area.

We sat on the rock studying the country. The route we should have taken lay below us a few hundred feet. The rest of the way out would be easy. We looked back at the divide, at the wild snowy pass we came through two days earlier. The odds were that neither of us would ever come this way again.

13

GRIZZLY BEAR
RESEARCH

Research on grizzly bear biology is embryonic. Until the development of tranquilizing guns around 1959, bears were difficult to get close to. By the time biologists got around to studying them, few grizzlies remained and they were hard to find. Most of the information about grizzlies has been gathered through the use of telemetry, as with Bob's bear. This technology, although invaluable in providing information on ranges and movements, has received criticism because handling and collaring are stressful to this threatened animal and may alter its behavior.

Telemetry has been the very bread and butter of grizzly bear biology, and its use often determines whether or not a researcher receives funds and garners credibility. Younger field-workers sometimes complain that they have been denied their chance by older "experts" who have already had theirs.

The process of radio-collaring a grizzly entails some risks. First, the animal must be trapped in a culvert trap or foot snare. Then a muscle relaxing or anesthetic drug must be administered. Free-ranging grizzlies, mostly in the far North, are shot with tranquilizing guns directly from helicopters. Next, measurements are taken and a tooth, a premolar, is pulled for determination of the bear's age. The animal is then outfitted with a radio transmitter.

All bear biologists I know have at least one horror story to tell about trying to instrument their animals. Grizzlies have been injured or killed in snares and traps. During arctic helicopter operations, more than a few cubs have been permanently separated from their mothers. And the tranquilizers can be fatal: most accidental deaths occur as a result of drug overdosages, bad reactions, or the mistaken injection of an opiatelike drug into a major blood vessel.

Grizzlies that are snared, trapped, or otherwise immobilized for radio-collaring are also not necessarily a random sample. Trapping favors bears who range widely, more males than females, and bears accustomed to humans. Bears have distinct personalities, and, just as the intolerance of some grizzlies for others keeps them away from dumps, salmon streams, and berry patches, there are those bears who avoid man, his smells, his traps. In areas of some national parks where people often hike unarmed, many bears learn that the hikers mean them no harm and that grizzly nutrition is served by getting used to people. But some bears in these areas never habituate—not even a little bit.

Then there are drug side effects. In 1983 one of the more frequently handled and tranquilized bears in Yellowstone killed and partially consumed a camper at Hebgen Lake. This bear had been shot many times with the animal tranquilizer phencyclidine hydrochloride—better known on the streets as angel dust. Angel dust makes humans violent and psychotic, but nobody knows exactly what it does to bears. This particular grizzly, known as "Fifteen," was trapped and identified at the kill site the next day. The publicity generated by this death raised questions about the inner lives of grizzlies. Some experts called for restraint in drugging bears. Some bear biologists gathered evidence that they felt vindicated them in using Sernylan, or angel dust. Others thought that Sernylan made Fifteen aggressive or irritable. This grizzly was a predatory male and a bear accustomed to eating human garbage. The killing occurred on the heels of a spring drought when natural food was scarce. It was the mating season for grizzlies and this predatory male was entering the dominant stage of his life—he was about a dozen years old—an explosive combination that made an event like this almost inevitable.

Nearly all radio tracking of grizzly bears is conducted from aircraft because of the vast extents of rugged terrain the bears occupy. On top of lingering effects from drugs, the outfitted animals are subjected to whatever stress comes from being buzzed by an airplane three times a week. Some biologists claim the bears get used to it.

A few authorities insist that the basic biological data collected in Yellowstone and elsewhere can be applied to other populations and that extensive additional handling of grizzlies is unnecessary.

Nonetheless, the tendency persists to put off crucial and difficult decisions until more data comes in. These decisions—especially the political ones dealing with attrition of grizzly habitat, official designation of "critical habitat," and listing the bear as "endangered" throughout much of his former range—need to be made immediately to protect the last populations south of Canada. As things stand now, the final information on grizzlies will roll in long after the last great bear has disappeared from the lower forty-eight.

In the end, there are limits to what may be quantified. The bear is tied by delicate threads to other animals, from the raven with whom he hunts food, to the coyote and wolverine with whom he shares meals, and to the elk and mountain goat who become objects of that hunt. Individual grizzlies are twisted by irritation and jerked around by weather patterns. Whole populations or segments of populations may evolve socially over time; bears adapt, habituate, and change their behavior and habits when exposed to other bears and human beings for periods of time—as the parent species, *Ursus arctos,* adapted to the proximity of people in places like Japan, Italy, and Spain.

In North America, the initial behavioral response to open country and the presence of other predators was probably increased aggressiveness in grizzly bears. How much, if at all, have they changed some 15,000 to 50,000 years later? And what role has man, especially in the last 120 years following the invention of the repeating rifle, played in this change?

At the time of European contact, the grizzly—who is extremely adaptable at exploiting new habitats—was probably in the process of expanding his range southward into tropical regions of Mexico and Central America, perhaps poised for a crossing into the Andes. Given time, the brown bear also may have moved east across the Mississippi. Could the grizzly, so adaptive, even flexible, in other ways, learn to get along with us if we elected to give him a chance? So far the bear hasn't had this option, so we don't know. Nor do we know how quickly these kinds of changes take place—or how much of this would ever be conveyed by a radio collar.

14

A SUMMER WALK

AUGUST (1980s)

On the fifth of August, Lisa and I took a ride in the back of Ed Abbey's pickup and cruised upstream along the major creek that drains the heart of Glacier National Park. We swept past lowland groves of big western hemlock and red cedar, cottonwood bottoms waist-high in cow parsnip, and on up beyond the foot of avalanche fields gaudy with wildflowers, to the mountainside where tiny patches of snow lingered above shrunken waterfalls.

We turned off on a narrow secondary road and bounced through a quarter of a mile of fireweed and alder, to a dead end a hundred yards farther at a backcountry horse barn. There we shouldered our packs, said good-bye to Ed and Clarke Abbey, stepped onto the trail, and started out on a week-long trip along and over the Continental Divide—the heart of Glacier Park's best summer grizzly habitat. We were on vacation; Lisa was on leave from her job as a pastry cook at the Belton, a local eating and drinking establishment, and I was taking time off from my job as a fire lookout. We had looked forward to this trip for years.

The trail cut through a muddy wallow that showed the recent passage of several moose and two black bears. It crossed one creek and followed along another. It was an hour of easy hiking. Abruptly we left the dewy lowland and followed the trail up a timbered, rocky slope terraced by blocky cliffs of gray dolomite.

The late morning was still cool. Later, these dark outcrops would radiate heat absorbed from the brief flame of a Rocky Mountain summer. The trail climbed, cutting a darker sill of mottled diorite, and topped out among stands of spruce and sub-alpine fir.

We had already reached the high country. A distant raven croaked, barely audible over the roar of a small waterfall. Through my binoculars I scanned the sheer cliffs of the Piegan Range three miles to the northeast. One solitary immature golden eagle was visible through the branches of subalpine fir. For the next week we would be traversing the subalpine and alpine zones of this Great Divide, exploring country we had never seen before.

The terrain leveled out along the top of a huge, mesalike ridge running up and abutting the naked spine of the divide. The forest was studded with snags left over from the most recent fire, some twenty years ago. The blue-red communities of lupine, Indian paintbrush, and larkspur filled narrow, finger-shaped meadows that seemed clawed out on great parallel courses across the ridgetop.

Ten minutes after topping out we ran into grizzly sign. There were furrows and pockets dug into the shallow mountain soil along the edge of the first meadow. The digs were several weeks old. Grizzlies were likely to be on the move this time of year. The first berries were beginning to ripen at lower elevations, and some of the bears had dropped down to the valley bottoms or had begun to travel to areas where forest fires burn through and berries grow in reliable abundance. One of these places was near my fire look-out, a spot I called the Grizzly Hilton.

I poked at the bear digs, trying to figure out what the grizzlies were after—maybe rodents, or the roots and bulbs of plants. I found a bear scat nearby. A familiar alertness crept up my spine, squelching my initial curiosity. I looked around with the sensate concentration that automatically turns on when I come across bear signs, even old ones. It is immediate, mandatory humility, some-thing you do not get any more hiking down the Sierra Crest or anywhere now in Colorado, Utah, or Arizona. When you shoul-der your backpack there and step down the trail, you are top dog. But in grizzly country, human status is second-rate, and these places are the last ones on the continent where a person can enter an ecosystem and not be the dominant critter.

I scanned the tree line, then looked back at Lisa and smiled. She knows what a pile of griz shit means to me. She looked radiant in her hiking shorts, standing in a field of flowers. I picked up my old backpack and we stepped back on the trail leading into a forest of scattered fir with berry brush growing underneath.

We climbed onto the highest part of the flat-topped ridge and started descending through a series of elongated meadows. We found more fresh grizzly sign. One of the meadows looked as if it had been plowed. The digs were three or four days old, made just after the last hard rain. I tried to find out what the bears were feeding on. A root or two had been bitten, but no pattern emerged. The food habits of grizzlies can get complicated this time of year.

After the faster life-style of the mating season winds down, grizzlies' movements are determined mostly by the availability of food, especially edible plants. From about mid-July on, bears begin to put on weight. This seasonal metabolic stage is called hyperphagia, meaning that they eat excessively to lay in the twenty thousand calories a day necessary to get them ready for hibernation. On the west slopes of the northern Rockies, the succulence of forbs, graminoids, roots, or tubers provides most of their sustenance. They are found in moist parks, avalanche chutes, damper meadows, and in bottomlands—the riparian zones. Since the big river valleys tend to be settled, Glacier's bears go elsewhere to avoid people, often high into the subalpine zones. Glacier is not a large area to animals like grizzlies; even in the heart of the park's wildest parts, you're always within twenty-five miles of a paved road or a park boundary.

Bear diet can be peculiar. A few eat small mammals during summer, and I know of one who killed and ate deer and elk. Despite this, most Glacier grizzlies are strongly vegetarian during the summer except for the occasional feast on ants and other insects.

Lisa and I sat in the clearing looking north to where the country falls off into a long drainage leading to Canada. The shadows ran before us; the sun dropped below the western peaks. I glassed the wall of the Piegan Range for goats, then shifted the heavy binoculars to the big subalpine flat below. A brown bear moved across the grasses followed by two smaller bundles of fur. The grizzly and her two cubs ambled to the edge of the flat, where the mother began digging along a grassy ledge. The seven-month-old cubs chased each other among the boulders and around fir trees. One cub fled, the other followed, and both disappeared into a tangle of stunted alpine trees. They reappeared, their roles reversed. The cubs collided and rolled off a ledge, nipping each other and sparring with their mouths open. They leaned back, interrupting their play, and sniffed the air. They resumed the wrestling until one of them broke free and turned away. The other cub sat on its haunches waiting. After five seconds of patience, he attacked his sibling's flank with fresh determination.

I sat among bluebells and showy daisies; a gentle wind rustled the dry grasses. Lisa joined me and I passed her the field glasses. Watching her face I could tell the little bears were still playing.

We spent the late afternoon on the ridge top watching the grizzly family. Dark clouds edged into the western skies. We would have to drop into the basin and set up camp before it got dark. The weather should hold for an hour or two, I thought.

The big brown sow and her cubs continued to dig in the shadows on the edge of the great slab of subalpine flat. I watched through the binoculars as two subadult bears, panda-colored two- or three-year-olds, walked out of a clump of fir trees to within thirty feet of the sow and her cubs. The sow displayed no sign of alarm. The subadults approached the family, then stopped and grazed only twenty feet away. I could scarcely believe the sow tolerated the pair in such close proximity to her cubs. The bears fed together for ten minutes. The cubs began to tussle again. The two-year-olds pushed each other up onto their hind legs and traded bites on the neck and swats to the side of the head. The sow looked up once and leaped in place, but did not join in the play.

This collection of bears was what is called an atypical grouping. Grizzlies are not territorial animals; rather, joint occupation and free wandering are the rule. There is a pecking order; smaller bears usually avoid larger ones. Each individual, family, or grouping normally stays to itself. Unless abundant food is available, you seldom see grizzlies within two or three hundred yards of each other, and when they do graze, browse, or dig where they are drawn together by food concentrations, there is often visible uneasiness and increased alertness or wariness.

When groupings extending beyond the immediate family members, siblings, or mates do occur, they almost always involve a mother with young. The most common configuration is a mother with young cubs or yearlings with other subadult grizzlies nearby. These teenage grizzly bears are usually a past litter of the sow. The other common group is of two or more families bonding together. In Glacier Park I once observed three mothers with four cubs and yearlings and a solitary subadult. These families were about thirty feet apart and there was some apprehension on the part of one of the females. There are exceptions to any generalization about groupings; grizzlies all seem to know one another, where they stand in the hierarchy, and which bears to avoid, tolerate, or dominate. And all this is influenced at every moment by what they stand to gain; the lure of abundant nutrition diminishes mutual intolerance.

The two pairs of young bears did not seem to want to play with each other. They kept to themselves, to their own litter mate, each having worked out the rules and limits of play long ago, and were not anxious to try their game with relative strangers. The little cubs wrestled vigorously and persistently. The larger two-year-olds battled more roughly but with more caution.

The sow and her two cubs turned and looked at the two subadults; the larger succeeded in flipping and pinning the other, who lay belly-up and submissive. The bears' ears were straight up and their mouths were open, indicating the play-wrestling had not turned into a real fight.

The two-year-olds moved off thirty feet and began to graze in the meadow. The sow clawed at rootlets at the fringe of the meadow while her cubs cavorted around, occasionally nosing about in the freshly turned earth looking for something to eat.

I passed the binoculars to Lisa, dug out my notebook, and scribbled a few notes. We lay back against our backpacks. The sun dropped behind dark thunderheads. We pulled on sweaters and prepared to drop down off the ridge into the timber where, anticipating thunderstorms and showers, we would look for a good place to pitch our tent. Just as we left, I glassed the hillside again; the subadults were now out of sight but the sow and her two cubs dug on. Fifty feet away were three large grizzly bears.

These bears completed the atypical grouping I had heard rumor of but had not believed. This was a herd. Only once, apart from dumps and salmon streams, had I seen this many bears together, and that was when berries provided an abundant source of food. Even then they were not as close together. Up where we were, there was scarcely rich foraging and nothing special about the place. These grizzlies were together because they wanted to be.

I took one last look at the grizzlies. The three big bears stood together. One of them nuzzled another's side. The trio were behaving like subadults; they were probably big four-year-olds. I lowered the binoculars and stuffed them into my backpack, which I shouldered. It was getting dark.

We dropped into the wooded swale, where we reached a long flat at the head of a small drainage. I checked the area for bear trails, then decided on an island of trees away from possible grizzly paths—including the main hiking trail, which was often used by bears.

Of course, the spot we chose was not an official camping area; the designated campsite was higher up in good bear habitat. I consider it one of the two most dangerous camps in Glacier Park. Two people had been mauled by grizzlies near this one; at the other, a young woman was killed.

I was amazed this group of bears was hanging around near one of the most popular backcountry areas in Glacier. A river of high-trekking hikers flowed by every decent day of summer. The trail was less than a mile from the area used by the bears. Yet there had never been a problem, at least not with these grizzlies.

Until recently, the only times the bear-risky campsite had been closed was when a griz had walked through it—to the bear it was indistinguishable from any other good subalpine habitat. The incident occurred when a couple from Los Angeles walked up to a grizzly feeding on summer berries and tried to drive him off.

Whatever they did was perceived by the bear as aggressive, since the young grizzly charged and mauled them both. Later they hired a world-class tort lawyer to sue the government for $2 million for bad bear management, inadequate warnings, and perhaps making the grizzly crazy by shooting it up with angel dust. This, of course, is utter bullshit: getting mauled is in the configuration of possibilities anytime one is in grizzly country. The only ones not filing lawsuits were the grizzlies, who would be the only ones to suffer so long as people could sue land managers as a result of avalanches, lightning strikes, and grizzly attacks.

Grizzlies virtually never assault people without provocation. The exceptions to this rule—and they are exceedingly rare—are apparent predatory attacks. Otherwise, blundering upon a bedded or feeding grizzly at very close range may elicit a reflexive charge resulting in a mauling. The rest of the time there is a chance to walk off without injuries depending on your actions. It has been my experience that a charging grizzly is still in the process of deciding if it wants to conclude that charge. So what you do is important.

During confrontations with bears, you must show the grizzly your intentions are peaceful without showing docility or weakness. You must remain still and inoffensive and yet defensive. Don't make sudden movements or loud noises. This includes hollering and waving.

The biggest single cause of griz maulings is the result of people running and trying to climb trees. It is too late to climb a tree once the bear is aware of you. Government handouts are wrong on this point. Forget about trees. A griz in Denali was clocked at 41 miles per hour. Some think climbing trees is a submissive sign. Maybe, but any grizzly who would allow you to climb a tree can be deferred to on the ground with appropriate body postures and moves—by standing your ground, perhaps with your arms outstretched to appear bigger, with your head turned off to the side, and all the time talking to, not shouting at, the bear. For every grizzly who would stand there watching you scramble up a pine tree, there are a dozen others who are irresistibly triggered by your frantic scrambling to take a bite out of your rear. Once you're face to face with a grizzly bear, only

calm and dignified behavior combined with a dose of luck can
save you.

Lisa and I finished putting up the dome tent and pushed it under a
thicket of mature Engelmann spruce. We nibbled on our dried
fruit and other dehydrated food with some ceremony. Although a
vacation, this journey was more than a chance to see some grizzlies
and explore new terrain. Lisa has been both my partner in this
grizzly project for over half a decade and my closest friend in other
ways. The light faded and we talked softly in the heavier air of
evening, but not of bear maulings. Lisa marveled over the univer-
sality of play among young animals, young mammals anyway.
You could learn a lot about bears by watching almost any litter of
young carnivores, domestic or wild.

   Nobody talks much about play among grizzlies. Although
older naturalists observed and reported on grizzlies at play, con-
temporary bear biology is more caught up in quantifiable aspects
of their behavior. Some solitary adult grizzlies spend time at play,
although play is more often a shared activity. Among litter mates
and some mothers, wrestling, along with the attendant sparring
and chasing, is the most common form. Within litters the larger
bears are more playful. As bears grow up, the sparring can get
rough, more cautious, and eventually tends to resemble the real
thing. Among adults, play is usually confined to mating pairs,
though all play increases when there is an abundance of food.

   From what I've read, play has most often been observed in
wolves, some whales and dolphins, otters, lions, elephants, bears,
and primates, including man. All are smart critters with either a
well-defined social life or an inclination to wander widely and
exploit a variety of habitats for food. Seeing play as simple re-
hearsal for future activity, such as predation or strife, does not
explain everything. Too much of the grizzly bears' playing is
nonfunctional and undirected. Play encourages flexibility, experi-
mentation, and creativity, and serves animals who need to make
adjustments to the world around them as they go about their
business.

   I dragged myself into the tent, still sweaty from the rapid

descent into the timbered saddle. Lisa zipped our sleeping bags together and I stripped off my wet clothes. I scooted into the down bag and snuggled in.

I woke in the middle of a hazy dream about deadly combat and bullets fumbled at critical moments. The patter of rain on the tent fly threw a chill down my body and I leaned against Lisa's warmth. The rain might bugger our plan to leave the trail the next day and bushwhack up to another broad, mesalike mountain. If we had to lay back a day and wait out the weather, I would try to locate the bear family again.

Lightning boomed and the yellow underside of the tent flashed like a lantern. The storm passed. I heard another behind it, rolling into the mountains. Lisa slumbered on my shoulder. I heard the soft rain slack off, then drip from the branches of the spruce. At first light, I unzipped the tent and peered out into a cloud. A poor day for a bushwhack. We prepared a breakfast of jerky and protein drink, dressed slowly, and stepped out into the tentative weather. The grass glistened and the trees dripped. We started off for the big flat where we had spotted the eight grizzlies the previous day. The wide, hard-packed trail made for quick, dry travel—altogether too easy to get to.

We passed the official designated campground—a depressing place, complete with bear pole, outhouse, metal signs, and almost an acre of denuded subalpine meadow. I found an old bear dig less than a hundred feet away. Camping sites in grizzly country should be hacked out of thick timber, preferably at lower elevations, away from all sign of bear activity. Still, I try to respect the difficult job of agencies like the Park Service, who think they have to manage every inch of wild country in order to protect it. Maybe they do. I try to keep a balanced view, valuing freedom most. Not freedom to molest and trample but freedom to take total responsibility for your own ass. Even if a bear chews it off: no lawsuits, please.

We dropped into a brushy gully and climbed through the dripping foliage until we reached the edge of the flat. Fresh bear digs were everywhere, especially along the grassy ledges bordering the big meadow. I found a grass-scat but could not identify any of the green stuff. I am a careless botanist and my plant taxonomy is crude: grasses are green, sedges have edges, and rushes are round.

This bear turd was still warm. I tensed and looked around back over my shoulder. The grizzlies had to be here somewhere, maybe bedded by now, in any of the little clumps of subalpine fir around us. Unlike Bob's docile bear, or other solitary adults on their day beds, sows with young are extremely dangerous, and it is possible to walk up on a sleeping sow before she hears or smells you. At close distances, her protective instincts take over and she nails you.

I wanted to find the sow or the three big subadults, but we were too close. I was intruding on the grizzlies' limited forage area, which this season tended to be these high meadows and ledges. And Lisa was with me.

We backed off, sticking to the center of the broad alpine flat where we knew no bears were bedded. The fog had lifted and it would probably turn out to be a typical August day in the mountains. We pushed through a thin break of fir trees and entered a tiny circular meadow covered with fleshy pale mushroom buttons. I picked up one mindlessly thinking it was a puffball and took a bite. The cross section cut by my incisors revealed gills, a ring, and a cup, meaning that I had bitten into the cap of a young amanita. Whoops. White amanitas are the only deadly mushrooms in America. Then I remembered white amanitas do not grow up here; one of the first things you learn in practical mycology is never to mistake an amanita button for a puffball. We cut back to camp through a series of meadows separated by linear thickets of subalpine fir. More bright mushrooms decorated the clearings, a bumper year for the fly agaric.

The clouds were building again in the western sky as we reached the hollow where our tent was pitched. Somewhere in the distance thunder reverberated. We crawled into the dome-style structure and waited for the rain.

Morning. I peeped out. A thin blanket of ground fog lay draped over the basin, but patches of clear blue sky stared through holes in the fog bank. We stuffed our bags, broke down the tent, and stashed the gear in our backpacks. We dropped down a game trail to the bottom of the hollow, then climbed up through the wet brush over a ladder of eroded cliffs until we topped out, panting in the cool morning air.

From there on we left the trails and backpackers behind. We stuck to the western nose of the broad ridge, aiming for the highest point on the flat-topped mesa. We reached the first of several long finger meadows strung together in parallel rows separated by breaks of fir, all with a peculiar northwesterly bent.

The meadows were great grizzly habitat and the timber breaks perfect cover. This was as good a place as any to creep up on a wild bear. I groped around in the huge single sack of my backpack and pulled out a 35-mm camera and lenses. I took a 200-mm lens with an extender and mounted it on the camera.

I was obliged to take some pictures out here. The national magazine that had hired me wanted good grizzly shots as well as scenics. As with my motion picture filming, I have mixed feelings about taking money for anything I do with bears. But I was broke again and thinking about starting a family, and there would be rent to pay. I get these jobs not because I am a hotshot photographer but because I know how to find griz and work around them without getting into trouble.

Climbing a gentle grade to the wide spine of the ridge, we moved carefully with the wind across our faces to the edge of each successive line of trees, peering up and down the long, narrow clearings. Grizzly sign was all over the place and some of it was fresh. We crossed the third finger meadow and entered the next strip of trees. I stepped to the edge and looked to my left, into the gentle morning breeze. About two hundred feet away I saw the back of a small grizzly bear.

I motioned to Lisa, who was a few feet behind me with the binoculars. She joined me and we watched the 150- to 200-pound animal, whose lower half was hidden below the slope of the meadow. The grizzly was soon joined by another subadult. They nosed about the flowers, sometimes grazing, not moving more than a few feet each time.

I decided to try to move closer and get some pictures. Lisa remained at the tree line. We had a system of hand signals worked out long ago that we use to tell where the bears are and what they are doing. I backtracked twenty feet to the strip of meadow and circled, stalking toward the two grizzlies now hidden by the line of trees.

A hundred feet down the meadow I turned back into the band of subalpine fir separating the two long clearings. Silently I moved to the edge of the trees, camera cocked and ready. The narrow meadow opened up; the bears were nowhere in sight.

I looked back up at Lisa. She held two fingers up over her head and two more out at her eyebrows; the two subadults saw me.

My heart leaped and I resisted an urge either to jump back into the timber or run. I remained motionless except for my eyeballs, which scanned the open ground and tree line. Almost straight across the sixty-foot-wide meadow, looking out of the thicket of the fir, were the two grizzlies. Side by side, they stared at me for forty or fifty seconds, once glancing in Lisa's direction.

The camera was in my hand at my waist. Ever so slowly, I inched the viewfinder up toward my eye. It took maybe fifteen seconds. I gradually lifted my left hand to steady the lens. The hand was at the level of my mouth when one bear woofed. Simultaneously, both young grizzlies wheeled and ran ten feet down the meadow edge and turned back into the trees.

It happened so fast I never squeezed off a frame. The sounds of bear running and breathing faded; the breeze rustled the boughs near my head. I looked back up the meadow at Lisa. She shrugged her shoulders; skunked again.

15
PHOTOGRAPHING GRIZZLY BEARS

Unlike their cousins two airline miles away, these grizzlies were totally unused to humans. They seemed as wild as any. Or maybe these two bears act one way when they do not expect people to be around, and another when they do. Grizzlies are capable of making such distinctions.

The previous October I had been up in this same mountain range trying to get a great bear shot—a cover picture—for a *National Geographic* article my friend the goat biologist had written. Whenever I get these film or photography jobs, I try to turn in a professional performance. There are still times when I find it difficult to take the work seriously. Just as movies of animals are no substitute for the real thing, bagging a grizzly with a camera is not hunting. The dangerous temptation of wildlife films is that they can lull us into thinking we can get by without the original models—that we might not need wild animals in the flesh.

I doubt that stalking and shooting wildlife with cameras is a substitute for big game hunting: there is a visceral connection missing. But, in the twentieth century, sport hunting itself presents a moral dilemma. What kind of authentic experience of nature is possible when you are hunting with a weapon capable of bringing down a 747?

Despite my own ambivalence about my motives, I still

wanted the cover picture. I had been after this shot since August. September had been wet and cold and October had been freezing. I climbed up to a big subalpine flat, hauling the heavy camera gear up a steep series of cliffs and ledges.

By the time I climbed over the lip of the last cliff onto the flat, I was soaked in sweat. I immediately stripped off my wet clothes and air-dried for a few minutes in the subfreezing wind. A couple of inches of snow had blanketed the north-facing slopes. I dressed in every piece of clothing I had in my pack and found a little knoll from which I could see much of the flat. Within minutes, in spite of two sweaters, a down coat, a wool hat and gloves, I was cold. I screwed the camera and long telephoto lens onto the tripod, found an angle of rock out of the wind, and lay back against the stone.

The cumulus parted and the sun poked through, warming the temperature to almost freezing. The warmth on my face made me drowsy. I dozed, waking every few minutes to check the distant slopes for grizzlies.

I drifted off far longer than I should have. I lay on tufts of beargrass spread out along the bottom of a low rock shelf. Through the blades of beargrass, I imagined I saw the chocolate back and head of a grizzly bear backlit by the sun between two little fir trees only fifty feet away. I had to blink to keep my eyes open; I was still sleepy. In a of couple seconds I propped my head up. The bear was gone. I was not sure if I had dreamed it.

I groped for my binoculars and moved away from the camera toward the small trees. Out of the snow-covered brush stepped the most beautiful grizzly I had seen all year, seventy feet away, the silver-tipping of his fresh brown autumn coat a halo of light.

The grizzly had not seen me yet; I had not moved. The camera, mounted and ready, was less than five feet behind me. The bear stopped next to a mountain ash bush and looked right at me. I thought about how lovely a scene it was: the red ash berries, fresh snow, chocolate bear, and brilliant hoarfrost of the cliffs beyond. Scarcely believing my luck, I moved carefully back toward the camera. By the time I turned around, the apparition had disappeared. Had I not found his tracks in the snow, I never would have been sure I saw it.

At least I have a picture of that magnificent grizzly imprinted in my memory. At other times, I have spent too much time with my eye glued to the viewfinder and have ended up missing both the image of the mind and that on film. Twice I have stood spellbound and forgotten to snap the picture. Once I froze, camera in hand, twenty feet from a sow grizzly and her cub, who of course saw me but, because they could not smell me and I was not moving a muscle, couldn't quite make out what I was. I knew that if I raised the camera or snapped the shutter, I probably would have precipitated a charge and most certainly—at that close range—gotten myself mauled.

I should explain something. Although I have my problems, I am not in love with death. Walking up on or getting close to a grizzly is stupid, and I seldom do it intentionally. At the same time, this is the one kind of blunder I tend to repeat. I have accidentally walked up on bears a bunch of times, more than I like to admit. On all but a very few of these, I truly believed the grizzly had not seen me. This has turned out to be wrong. Film shot by Lisa, who was thirty feet behind me one of those times, clearly showed the bear looking at me, moving his mouth or jaw and otherwise signaling me to move off. During other close encounters I was ignored by grizzlies who probably knew I was there. With bears who are used to some human contact, it is hard to tell if they are unaware of your presence or just ignoring you.

Stumbling on bears like this usually happens when I am preoccupied with photographing or filming. I push too hard when stalking griz with a camera, trying to get closer, figuring that every frame is the last shot. This kind of proximity is not good either for bears or photographers. Yet every magazine picture editor in the world will tell you your shots are not tight enough. Sorry, Mr. Freelance, but you must get closer. We will not be able to use your pictures. You will have to find another way to pay the rent this month.

Sneaking up on so-called habituated bears is easier than grizzlies who seldom see humans, though I have done it with both. Almost every time that I wound up within fifty feet of a grizzly, I thought it was an accident. It's hard for me to see the pattern of this spatial blunder, but I do not doubt that there is one. When I want to get within a hundred feet of a grizzly without the bear's knowing I

am around, I always move into the wind and as quietly as possible.
I wait until the grizzly has its head down or turned away before I
move, or else I use cover. When I get too close, it is usually on a
mountain hillside with gullies and a few trees. In such terrain, you
do not always know where you will end up when you make a
move. If the bear is also moving and you cannot see it, you increase
the odds of landing far closer to a grizzly than you ever cared to.

There is no way to get a great picture of a truly wild griz—
with the exception of the blurred freeze-frame of the charging bear
who is about to maul your ass—without a huge infusion of good
luck. You cannot get close enough to wild grizzlies to use
medium-telephoto lenses; the grizzlies either run away or charge.
If you are within the range for a good medium-telephoto—
anything up to about a 300-mm lens—the odds that a grizzly, even
a solitary adult or subadult, will charge are quite high. If the bear is
a mother with young, she is probably going to charge you. If you
run, you will be mauled; if you struggle or fight back, you may be
killed. Most cameras are noisy, and bears can hear their clicking
from several hundred feet across a still mountain basin. So you end
up with long, unwieldy telephoto lenses, which absorb light and
shorten depth of focus. They require heavy, steady tripods. The
package is worthless in low light or where things move quickly.

There is nothing creative about such photography because
you do not control anything. You simply set up the cumbersome
monstrosity, get the bear focused in the frame, and shoot away like
a chimpanzee. Even with a cable release on a sunny day, you will
be lucky to get a sharp image. The best way to photograph grizzlies is to rent one in Heber City and bang away with a wide-angle
lens. Otherwise, like most professionals, you will have to ride the
buses in Denali National Park or submit to the state-run lottery to
draw a spot at McNeil Falls in Alaska.

16

WALKING
OUT

Miles from the nearest human trail, Lisa and I moved across the giant slab of tundra and fir—the gentle subalpine habitat. We reached the highest point of the flat-topped mountain; the waters ran off north to the Atlantic, south to the Pacific. We needed only to drift along these high meadows, the Continental Divide, to the next range of peaks and then contour along its flanks northward.

The day warmed to seventy as the sun burned off the last of the morning fog. One meadow gave way to another; they grew to about a mile long and a hundred yards across. We stepped across flats littered with mushrooms, which bears sometimes eat—although not these. Each open area showed sign of grizzly activity. I found many digs and two sets of tracks: the nine-inch rear pad of an adult and the smaller print of a subadult grizzly. We floated along as if in a dream, alive to a perfect summer day. I squinted into the midday sun watching Lisa's long hair halo her face. Each new meadow promised new discovery and a fresh chance at glimpsing a wild bear.

We began to descend, following the trail of a young bear who had turned over every other large rock looking for grubs or something. We crossed a saddle and a marshy, shallow pond and started up a timbered gully following the sign of more grizzlies—digs and rolled boulders. Climbing through a thicket of dwarf fir and stunted spruce, we arrived on a grassy slope overlooking a hidden alpine lake lying in a small basin. We dropped down to a tiny cove between two points of land and threw down our packs. We pitched the tent to dry off the morning dew and lighten our loads.

A few cumulus clouds built on the western horizon. We basked in the rare warmth, stripping off our clothes and dipping in the chilly waters. We lingered in the sun. Gentle waves lapped at the shore. We hung on to each other for a long time under the mountain sky, and then broke away to bathe again in the frigid waters.

Lisa and I rolled up the tent and stuffed it back into my pack. This lovely shore had been kind to us, and we left it reluctantly and with a silent reverence. We stood looking out over the lake until a cloud passed over the sun, chilling us. We had to be moving on; we had open alpine slopes to traverse before afternoon storms rolled in again.

Skirting the far corner of the lake, we climbed through the trees and stepped into the rolling meadows of a small pass leading north. Near the summit, we caught movement across the meadow. An odd-shaped, straw-colored, emaciated bear loped across the slope above us, far enough away so that she probably could not see us, although she acted as if she had got a scent. A moment later two dark brown black bear cubs ran up behind her. If it had not been for the cubs I would never have been sure that this strange-looking animal was a black bear. You could scarcely tell that it was a bear. What was it doing up here in grizzly country?

I have run into hundreds of black bears while traveling the woods and mountains but am not an expert about them. Although black bears are not nearly as ferocious or powerful as grizzlies, they are more than a match for humans when they choose to be: many more people are injured by black bears than grizzlies. Of course, there are ten times as many black bears as grizzlies in North America, and 90 percent of the injuries they inflict are minor. The reason that black bears do better than grizzlies around people is that they adapt better. Black bears are creatures of the forest and still live in forty states. Their reproductive rate is higher. They can live almost anywhere that is not paved or plowed, and they have expanded into grizzly habitats in places like the high Sierra.

As with any wild animal, I try not to bother black bears, unless I have to, but I do not back away from them either. I have met several dozen under circumstances where I have had to run them off, mostly on trails. Even mothers with cubs complied. A few times, in developed campgrounds, I have physically assaulted black bears—each time with my weapon of choice, a long-handled broom—in defense of dogs and children, and they have run off submissively. This smaller species of bear loves garbage and gets used to begging for food where permitted to do so.

But black bears can also be dangerous, even deadly. Black bears have killed a score of people in this century. What is troubling is that most of the time the humans involved were treated like prey. Worse still, the fatal attacks by black bears, unlike those of grizzlies, tend to be in broad daylight and almost half the time involve children or, at least, not fully grown humans. One should watch the kids and act aggressively, not like prey.

We moved on across these wild meadows near the upper zone of trees. Patches of Krummholz dotted the steppes. Thunder rumbled somewhere off to the west. A perfect fairy ring of *Agaricus,* possibly the common meadow mushroom though unusually robust, ornamented a small, bear-dug slab of tundra clinging to the coarse talus at the foot of the Stanley Range. The lightning boomed closer and we looked for cover. The first beads of sleet stung our faces. We hit the clump of trees just as a hard rain began to fall.

I stepped into a depression; under my feet was a three-foot-wide, shallow hole clawed out of the duff—a grizzly bed. I thought the diggings looked rather fresh. This bed had probably been used as recently as the day before, and we were lucky it was not being used then.

"Jesus Christ, baby, see this? We almost stepped into a world of shit," I called over to Lisa.

She arched her eyebrows and pointed down. Under the trees

beneath which she was waiting out the storm were two more beds, miniatures of the first—a sow with two cubs or yearlings. We would have been in a real fix if we had stumbled in here when they were occupied.

Within ten minutes the storm passed and we stepped back into the wet grass, then contoured north around the shoulder of a metamorphic spire. We climbed over a rocky ridge and looked down into a tiny alpine cirque filled with ice and water surrounded by a boulder field. Up on the cliff I caught movement and spotted a beast the color of snow running on a narrow ledge. The mountain goat stopped. High above, I saw the broad wings that had startled the bovid; a golden eagle soared over the range.

The big bird dropped something as it rose into the sun. I brought my field glasses up and saw tiny legs churning, falling hundreds of feet. It looked like a Columbian ground squirrel or a small marmot. Just as the rodent was about to smash on the rocks, the eagle swooped down and caught it. The golden bird flew toward the sun and again dropped the squirming, terrified animal. The eagle climbed and dove twice more, and the rodent no longer struggled.

We descended into the small cirque, dropping rapidly over the steep, rugged terrain, climbing over boulders the size of boxcars. We reached the rocky shore of the little lake and stared off into the hazy distance of a glacial valley a giant step below. The frigid waters were only recently free of ice. Only the mountain goats on the cliff above moved; everything else spoke quietly of rock and ten months of winter.

Skirting the boulder-strewn edge of the tiny lake, we contoured on around the shoulder of the mountain, hugging the steep slope, toward Sinopah Pass. A few dwarf trees clung tenaciously to the unsorted glacial debris. We were wet and wanted to get out of the chilling wind. There was little vegetation of any kind, let alone trees, growing out of this garden of boulders.

A spine of dolomite ran off the range of peaks and continued down the mountain as a bedrock ridge. Below the escarpment, a huge trapezoidal rock had split off. Next to the face of the rock, a green patch of low sedge pioneered the primitive soil lying in the sump. We had gone far enough. We set up our tent, locating it out of the wind on the carpet of Carex. We were above the foraging ranges of bears; morainal litter supports little plant growth. We sat in the jagged silhouette of the divide hovering fifteen hundred feet above us. Looking east toward the Great Plains, we saw towering thunderheads that already reflected the pastels of the approaching sunset.

The Continental Divide was the traditional boundary between the Flathead and Blackfeet Indians, who ruled the territory before the white man showed up. There is not a lot of evidence that either tribe, or their ancestors, used the mountains much, nor is there any indication that they avoided them except for the obvious reasons of bad weather and rugged terrain. Unless in quest of a vision, the Indians did not need to come here: there was so much game everywhere, a richness and diversity that can only be imagined today.

The Lewis and Clark expedition considered the High Plains of the upper Missouri much wilder, richer country than the Continental Divide. There, in Blackfeet territory, they saw the endless herds of bison, the eagle nests, huge springs filled with watercress, and fat wolves and fearless bears feeding on the carcasses of drowned buffalo. Those High Plains and cottonwood bottoms to our west were just as wild then as the mountains are now. In fact, the whole concept of "wild" was decidedly European, one not shared by the original inhabitants of this continent. What we called "wilderness" was to the Indian a homeland, "abiding loveliness" in Salish or Piegan. The land was not something to be feared or conquered, and "wildlife" were neither wild nor alien; they were relatives. Luther Standing Bear, the Oglala Sioux, said: "Only to the white man was nature a wilderness and only to him was the land infested with wild animals and savage people. To us it was tame. Earth was bountiful and we were surrounded with the blessings of the Great Mystery."

The next morning Lisa and I crawled out of the tent and looked down on an ice-age landscape of morainal boulders and frozen tarns. The dawn was chilly. We were halfway through our summer walk: as the goshawk flies, it was only about twenty miles out to the North Fork of the Flathead River. By the time we found a route along the divide and bushwhacked out to a trail, that distance would double. We could make it to the road in three days if we pushed a bit.

Sunlight pierced dark clouds on the horizon. We stuffed our bags and packed our rucksacks and climbed down over the coarse scree to a series of ledges that rose gently northward toward Sinopah Pass. Hardy specimens of phlox and saxifrage pried apart stress fractures in the red argillite. We walked the easy ledges, scrambling over the talus from one to the next. Finally we stepped out onto a bedrock ledge and suddenly the great cirque of Sinopah lay below us. The sound of avalanching rock broke the silence as fragments of the glacially plucked wall fell, boulders pried loose by freezing nights and thawing days. To our left the amphitheater crawled steeply to the grassy pass that was our destination.

A few scudding clouds lay near the lip of the waterfall draining the cerulean depths of Sinopah, two thousand feet below the vertical wall opposite us. The faint southerly breeze dried our clothes, damp from dewy vegetation, and cooled us.

Far below I heard the barely audible sounds of splashing water. Lisa pointed down to the outlet of the lake. It looked as if someone was swimming just offshore. Swimming? The ice never completely melts off the shaded corners of the cirque, and it is seldom visited by people.

Through my binoculars I could see a head splashing and bobbing ten feet from the logjam across the outlet of the turquoise lake. It was a dark brown grizzly, an adult, and I could see his ivory claws and canines as he stood shoulder-deep in the lake, mouth open, slashing at the surface of the lake with his jaws.

The bear was a long way off, at least a thousand feet below. I passed the glasses to Lisa. The faint resonance of paws hitting the water, like stones dropped from a great height, drifted up on the gentle breeze. Far below, the dark shape moved to the shoreline then back into the lake. The end of what looked like a pole stuck out of the water.

"He's playing with that log," Lisa said. "He's holding it with both paws and kicking it with one foot."

She passed back the binoculars. I watched the grizzly play with the fencepost-size pole, holding it out of the water with both paws. Somehow he maneuvered the log behind his neck, holding each end with his long claws. The nearly four-hundred-pound bear moved the log back and forth. He was scratching his neck, or rather, he was using the six-foot-long log to scratch his neck. Grizzlies are not supposed to be able to do that: we had a tool-using bear on our hands.

We watched for ten minutes, until the sun cleared the low cloud banks. The dark grizzly pulled himself up on a log and climbed out on the logjam. He stepped off and walked along the grassy shoreline.

"That sure looks like Happy Bear," I told Lisa. "Look at that bull-legged walk."

I handed the glasses over to Lisa. She knew the grizzly I was talking about. She first saw Happy Bear in 1976 and once after that. I had seen him every summer but one at the Grizzly Hilton.

One of the things I was hoping to find out was whether any of the grizzlies here made the annual trip to the huckleberry shrub-fields near the Grizzly Hilton. It is often difficult to tell one bear from the next, but I believed I had identified two bear families, in distant drainages of this same mountain range, who traveled fifteen and twenty-five air miles, respectively, to berry range near the Grizzly Hilton in late summer. Of course the bear I wonder about most is the Black Grizzly; I have no idea where he spends his year except for those few weeks he visits and terrorizes the Grizzly Hilton. Bob, my biologist friend, monitored a radio-collared female grizzly who moved fourteen miles to the same range.

My own experience with grizzlies in the Glacier Park area leads me to believe there are a number of seasonal concentrations of bears, of differing numbers and for different foods. If so, there must be migratory corridors across large areas not otherwise utilized by grizzlies. But here, in the high interior of Glacier Park, bears have seldom been radio-collared. Ordinarily it is difficult, often impossible, to be certain you are seeing the same grizzly on different occasions. Although I thought the dark grizzly with the white claws and odd gait was Happy Bear, I could never be sure. He was a long way off. I watched the amazing tool-using grizzly disappear into the timber at the foot of the sky blue lake.

The pass toward which we were heading was at the same elevation, so I tried to contour across the near-vertical slope. I used my ice axe to dig into the treacherous mix of mud and scree made slick by recent thunderstorms. After fifteen minutes of scrambling, I found myself on a dead-end ledge staring off into space. This was not the way to the pass, which now lay far below me. The spectacular view, however, compensated for my stupidity.

I motioned Lisa forward and she crept up to the abyss. We looked over the edge, back south into a hidden basin where four cold lakes sat perched on a broad shoulder of the mountain. Before us lay the wide flat of the pass—a high saddle of sparse timber fringing two shallow lakes. I wondered if anyone had ever visited those four lonely tarns.

I recorded the unnamed basin on my checklist of places I think about visiting—but never will—and turned back. The real value of such spots lies in a leap of imagination, the jolt of memory still possible until senility. We backtracked on the slick slope, slipping twice but catching ourselves with our axes.

This time we dropped down into the giant amphitheater and contoured below the cliffs. We inched up a steep slope of temporarily arrested talus, on up a grassy pitch, to a tiny knoll covered with stunted fir trees.

Sinopah Pass.

At the saddle I found a grizzly scat. It was fresh, maybe two days old, and was half grass, half barely ripened huckleberries. Berries were ripe only far below us, mostly below five thousand feet. This bear had been moving right along. I wondered whether he was traveling east toward the Rocky Mountain Front or west toward the Grizzly Hilton. I poked around the timbered knob finding more grizzly sign.

Bears tend to be on the move during late summer. Grizzlies travel from subalpine zones and the tops of avalanche slopes to lower elevations where several species of berries are ripening, the most important of which are the Vacciniums, the larger blueberries or huckleberries. Where we were and west of the Continental Divide, the sugars of these berries are the grizzlies' most important source of energy. In other places, like Yellowstone, berries are not as abundant, and bears derive most of their nutrition from grass and sedge.

We swung off the rocky knoll, down the steep grassy slope peppered with violet-blue harebells, and rolled down onto the broad flat of the pass area. Again we crossed ground clawed up by grizzlies. Off to the west thunderheads began to rise into the afternoon sky. Just below us lay stands of subalpine fir and the two lakes. We had gone as far as we wanted to that day. It had been a special day for us, and we needed to look for a spectacular camp, one in keeping with the last several days.

My own ideas about where you throw your sleeping bag or pitch your tent are a blend of paranoia, bear lore, and backcountry etiquette. I would never set up for the night in a location someone might stumble on or spot from the air. I do not want other people to know I am around: it gives one the feeling the country is larger. All my gear is camouflaged and I seldom squat in the open. I would never camp on a site likely to be visited by bears. But that night I suppressed my instinct to crawl into dense, impenetrable thickets and gave in to Lisa's wish to wake up near the shore of the steel blue lake. We had decided to marry later that winter, and the trip was our raised glass to each other. With my field glasses I surveyed the rocky shoreline of the lake, its pearly surface reflecting the fading light. Framed between two clumps of stunted trees was a tiny clearing. I examined the area for bear sign. The small meadows were full of old digs, the most recent being about a month old. Camping there should present no problem. The grizzlies were long gone, most of them anyway, and the site was far off probable routes of travel.

We hiked along the rocky shore of the lake to the small clearing and put up our tent. We had gone less than a dozen miles that day, but it felt like more. We nestled in the down bags. It seemed like luxury to share such a place. We had just passed through the heart of Montana's high country, arriving on this wild mountain pass far from any trail. The evening wind rose and we zipped up the windward side of the tent, looking out the opposite flap to the cold surface of the alpine lake. Living was a privilege, the day a gift, nature so magnificently harsh—the eagle dropping the ground squirrel.

We used my penlight to read our large-scale topographic maps, looking for a route out of there. The way out led north, up to a basin far above the timber, contoured high above the rim of a cirque, then dropped into another high north-trending basin, which in turn led up onto the Continental Divide again. From there, the route passed below a series of small glaciers and snow-fields, eventually joining an old miner's trail leading west to the North Fork of the Flathead River.

The bottomland of that river is the boundary between the park and Flathead National Forest. A road runs up it, and the lowlands are checkerboarded with private land and the usual rural inhabitants. We sometimes live down there ourselves. The riparian zone of that river is also prime grizzly habitat, especially in the spring and the fall. Throughout the history of the settlement of the West, those rich river bottoms were the first places humans competed and conflicted with bears.

There is a place along the river, north of where we planned to come out, where I watch grizzlies in October. The bears come down to eat sweetvetch, the taproot of *Hedysarum*, usually after a hard frost. Pea root is an important food north of here, although the farthest south I have seen evidence of its extensive use by bears is thirty miles below Canada, where it grows on the alluvial gravel of old river channels. The place I go attracts half a dozen bears to an area of a square mile or so. It's another seasonal concentration, a small one, where the starchy taproot of *Hedysarum* tempts the griz to shed some of their mutual intolerance. The number of grizzlies who come to dig pea root varies from year to year mostly depending on how many bears are illegally killed by humans.

Two autumns ago, sign of timber wolves was all over these meadows and bottomlands. The wolves had returned to Montana and formed a pack. They preyed upon mule deer there; up north, in Canada, they had been taking mostly moose and elk. I imagined the killing potential of lone wolves rising exponentially as they joined the pack; the efficiency of pack predation seemed much greater than the sum of all its members. I saw remains of seven deer carcasses in the immediate vicinity of the sweetvetch patches used by bears. Grizzlies had visited every single wolf-killed deer at some point. Deer hair was in nearly every bear scat. Something symbiotic was going on there with wolves and griz. Reintroducing wolves to a place like Yellowstone might make for a lot of extra grizzly food.

In the tent, Lisa and I planned the next day's journey. We went over the sheet as we might a treasure map, searching each contour wrinkle for hidden gulches. The route was high and rocky and all too barren of vegetation for good grizzly country. Only rarely during that time of year, when the army cutworm moths proliferate, do bears show up there. The few scats I had found up above seven thousand feet were composed almost entirely of casts of cutworm moths. These insects constitute another seasonal food source for grizzlies, although the preferred food in this region during the month of August is the ripening huckleberry crop.

The light died and a steady wind blew in from across the lake. We listened for the rumble of distant storms, but the evening skies were quiet. The next morning, a thick bank of clouds hung just above us. The route we were going to take had disappeared into the gray clouds shrouding the peaks. There was nothing to do but wait for the fog to break up. Route finding up there would be too chancy with five-foot visibility in a landscape where each ledge was indistinguishable from the lip of an abyss.

We sat around our camp waiting for the cloud above us to dissipate. By early afternoon the cloud was still there and I was about a day behind on my nonschedule. I had already laid over one day and did not especially want to write off a second one. The country to the west fell off two thousand feet into a cirque, then down a chain of lakes leading out. We decided to drop off, bushwhack down and look for a spot to camp near one of the upper lakes. We packed up and headed out through fields of faded wildflowers—dying lupine and paintbrush, asters, mariposa lilies, and showy daisies. We stepped out on a grassy ledge and looked down into another lake perched on the rim of the great basin to the west. A cascading waterfall fell down the hundred feet in three white steps.

Reluctantly we left this hard-earned world of high meadows

and lakes, where all the walking was easy and the vistas were grand. It might take three days of bushwhacking to get down to the nearest road. I climbed down the green strip of sedge growing along the waterfall and checked out what looked like fresh digging. Tufts of sod and moss lay along the watercourse all the way to the bottom. The bear sign was very fresh—about a day, at the most. The digs could have been made that morning. I dropped down with extra care, knowing a grizzly might be nearby. We reached the lower lake and stood on its lip looking out into the great trench that had been scoured out by the valley glacier thousands of years before. Below, a typical summer day was passing; up above, the cold, gray cloud bank hung over the peaks.

We walked the shore to the outlet of the lake, then started down again along the slick, grassy ribbon of water, following the spoor of a young grizzly who had left his subadult-size track in a pile of loose dirt. I examined the print more closely, finding a line of pad marks on the fringe of grass. Within the inside of the track, the dew had been wiped off the grass blades. This grizzly sign was minutes old.

I held a palm up to Lisa, signaling her to stop. The roar of water rendered quiet conversation impossible. I made a raking or digging motion with my fingers, meaning griz, and mouthed the word "wait." I eased down along the cascading ribbon of water and looked down at the next terrace of grass. Fifty feet below us a 250-pound silver grizzly was grazing. The bear could not hear me because of the noise of the waterfalls and could not smell me because the wind was blowing my scent back up the mountain. We watched the grizzly without moving for a couple of minutes. He looked to be about three years old. The bear was slowly grazing his way up the waterfall, coming straight toward us.

There really was no good way out of the situation. It was too late to get out of the way. I stood on the shelf of rock only a pebble's throw from the young grizzly, who by then looked enormous.

"Hey Grizzer Bear, we're right up here above you and we'd like to come down," I said, giving one of my usual lame speeches. The bear did not look up. He could not hear me over the roar of the water. We were already in trouble, and the closer the grizzly came before he discovered us, the greater the odds of getting mauled.

I kicked loose a cantaloupe-size boulder, sending it rolling down toward the bear. At the same time I waved my arms. This time the grizzly saw me. For a brief instant he froze. I followed his example by standing motionless with my arms out to the side and my head bowed slightly off center. Lisa was a few steps behind, partially out of his view.

The bear turned and ran downhill about ten feet, then spun and reared at the same time. I held my breath while he tried to make me out. Again I talked to him, this time louder, but he did not seem to hear above the wind and water.

After three or four seconds, the young griz dropped to all fours, lowered his head a few inches, and charged straight for me. In two bounds he covered a third of the distance between us, coming to an abrupt stop by slamming both forepaws on the slope. I kept talking to him, almost shouting, making sure he could hear me over the din of the cascades.

Again he made a short charge, leaping up and sliding to a stop. By now the grizzly was only sixty feet below us. I turned my head back and faced directly toward the bear, who flared his nostrils and chomped his jaws. He still did not appear to know what we were. The grizzly made another hopping charge but did not come any closer.

I reached for my sheath knife—a useless move, since ninety-nine times out of a hundred I would lose the stabbing and chewing match with the bear. I continued to babble and stare directly at the three-year-old, holding onto the handle of the silly knife. After maybe five seconds, he looked off to the side. The grizzly turned his head in the opposite direction, pivoted, and ran off down the steep gully.

Subadult grizzlies, teenagers or juveniles less than five years old, are probably less predictable than older bears because their behavioral patterns are still in a formative stage. These younger grizzlies are looking for their own territory after weaning and trying to figure out where they fit into the pecking order, so there's a lot of trial and error going on. Subadult females often set up home ranges near or on the fringe of their mother's, while young males wander more widely, sometimes beyond the range of occupied grizzly habitat.

I doubt that this three-year-old knew much about humans. He was trying to move us out of his way. Most of a bear's aggressive repertoire, especially among young animals, consists of threat postures and bluffs. The short, hopping charge is common when young grizzlies do not know where they stand with people and use behavior aimed at dominating the encounter. He had been testing us.

For this reason, I almost never allow subadult grizzlies to get away with backing or running me off in an area like Glacier National Park where they are likely to run into humans again. If you subordinate yourself to the young bear, you only embolden him for future interactions with other people. The next person the grizzly runs into may pay for your meekness. This is especially true if you try to run from the bear—a response that may trigger a chase and a catalogue of painful possibilities.

Although it is best not to permit subadult grizzlies to intimidate you, I do not mean to imply these young animals are not dangerous. Many knowledgeable people consider them the most dangerous bears because of their unpredictability. Younger grizzlies have injured many people and have been implicated in half of all the fatal maulings in Glacier. Even a small subadult grizzly is powerful enough to tear a human to pieces.

Despite this knowledge I imagined myself ready to take on this 250-pound carnivore with my six-inch sheath knife, defending my beautiful mate and dying a glorious death in the first 99 battles. In the last fight, the one I win, I see myself chewed and mangled—although victorious—staggering into the Babb Bar wearing my hard-earned necklace of fresh bloodstained grizzly claws. The place is full of beer-drinking Blackfeet who look at me wide-eyed with naked fear, and with new respect.

A gust of wind brought the smell of the forest up and me back to the world. I looked back at Lisa, who joined me on the ledge overlooking the chute of water. Our hearts pounded from the adrenaline generated by the close encounter with the bear. In all our trips into grizzly country together, Lisa and I had been that close to a bear on only two other occasions. We held on to each other and settled down, planning the bushwhack down the waterfall.

The first hundred feet were easy. As we dropped down,

leaving the subalpine zone behind, the vegetation pinched back in. Thick mats of alder and willow clung to the wet wall. We reached a vertical section and were forced to climb down the face of the waterfall, through thickets of alder, holding on to stunted fir trees. The water drenched us and our packs. By the time we reached the bottom, we were soaked, filthy, and exhausted. Late afternoon thundershowers were building and we needed to find a place to hole up and pitch the tent. We crawled around the head of a tiny lake through a patch of wild raspberry, *Rubus idaeus,* picking a few of the tasty red berries. We continued our bushwhack down the valley looking for an open spot to set up camp.

Lightning flashed and I counted seconds as the boom of the thunder arrived. We had about ten minutes to find a place to get out of the storm. We burst through the brush to the edge of the lake. Across the inlet I saw a low grassy bench along the alluvial shoreline. We clawed through the thick brush. I pushed ahead like a bull moose, leaving hunks of flesh and blood on every third bush. We waded across the creek at the outlet and along the marshy shore to the bench. Thunder reverberated. A bolt of fire hurtled down to a tall snag a quarter of a mile to the northwest. Quickly I threw up the tent. We sat on our sleeping bags as the storm swung over us and passed on.

The last light faded. The forest felt oppressive after the open alpine meadows, but fortunately, fatigue took over. It was hard to believe that we had only covered five miles that day; it felt like twenty. We comforted each other and listened to the water wash up on the cobbles only a few feet away.

The next morning the sun dried a thick dew off the tent. Up high, around 7,400 feet, the same steel gray clouds covered the mountains. We had made the right decision after all: we would never have found our way along all the cliffs and basins in the fog. We would save them for another year.

I consulted the map, then struck out through the brush in the direction of an old fire trail, which would save us two days of bushwhacking. We picked up a game trail: fresh moose tracks leading through the fern and timber. Another hundred yards and I saw an old axe scar on a tree root; the fire trail. From there on walking out would be easy.

The trail led to another, larger lake. We followed the path along the shore. Foot-long western slope cutthroat trout fed in the shallows. Near the foot of the lake I rounded a corner and almost walked into the hindquarter of a two-hundred-pound black bear. I asked him to leave and he bolted into the brush. He had been feeding on huckleberries, which were beginning to ripen down there.

The trail led back into the trees for another mile, then out to the shore of a huge finger-shaped glacial lake. We stood and glassed the distant side of the lake. Lisa grabbed my arm as a giant bird lifted out of a tall tree on the shoreline. We held hands and watched the bald eagle soar across the lake toward a high spruce with a saucer-shaped pile of sticks in the top. A second bird, his mate, left the nest and joined him. Together they circled up toward the morning sun.

17

THE
LOOKOUT

(1980s)

The bushes parted and a chocolate brown grizzly stepped into the mountain clearing. Cautiously he ambled over the downed timber, swinging his huge dish-shaped face from side to side. He stopped. He stiffened and thrust his nose up into the cool evening air, reaching for a scent of the intruder. He reared, jaws agape, and slowly spun on his hind legs as if in a gentle dance. Suddenly he bolted down the mountain, through the basin, huffing and rolling over the deadfalls as easily as water cascading over rapids. His vast flanks rippled, disappearing as he reached the timber.

I watched from the ridge top on the spine of a tiny mountain range. This was only the beginning. It was the last of August, and within the week this Montana high country would be crawling with more grizzly bears than I could count.

Off to the southwest tall, anvil-shaped thunderheads rumbled. An electrical storm was heading my way. This naked ridge top was a poor place to be during a thunderstorm. I saw a distant flash of lightning and counted from the flash to the arrival of the sound: nearly twenty seconds, which meant that the storm was still about five miles away. Since I was more than an hour from the closest safe route off the top of the range, I knew I was going to get it.

I crammed my binoculars and notebooks into my small canvas pack and struck back up the ridge, striding along the game trail on the top of it. Behind me lightning struck. The interval between the flash and boom was now less than five seconds, and I needed to get off the treeless spine. Before me the ridge rolled up into a minor summit, then dropped off to the east. I picked a route below the top, contouring through the sidehill shrubfields—hardly an inviting bushwhack in the nearly impenetrable elk-high vegetation.

I dropped off the narrow ridge, sliding down the steep slope until I reached the highest stand of subalpine fir trees. A horizontal rain stung my face and neck. I dug a cheap green slicker out of the pack and squatted among the fir. The rain turned to hail. I shivered, then forgot about the cold as a lightning bolt exploded close by. A man standing on the ridge would be a lightning rod. I shrank even lower into the brush.

The bolts slammed into the mountain for ten minutes, then slacked off. The storm was moving on, though another was on the way. Soaking wet and cold, but still leery of walking the ridge top, I decided to continue contouring through the dense undergrowth along the side of the mountain, then down a spur ridge to the foot trail that led out. The brush was sopping, and every few minutes I slid a ways down the slick hillside. Nonetheless I made decent time, anxious to reach the relative security of the trail by dark.

Something made me freeze—maybe a scent, a subliminal sound. I listened. An animal was moving in the brush just ahead, about forty feet away. I may have made a bad mistake. Over the sound of the rustling underbrush I could clearly hear the breathing of a large animal. I had blundered onto a bedded bear, probably a grizzly. I did not understand why the animal did not charge or flee. I stood motionless for three minutes, watching the wind blow across the thick tangle of mountain ash and huckleberry, looking for some sign of the animal I could hear so clearly. Distant thunder rolled far to the west. My stomach knotted, but the initial sickly, panicky feeling at nearly stepping on a grizzly bear gave way to a growing confidence as I slowly comprehended that the bear neither feared me nor meant me harm. The invisible animal in the brush sounded lethargic, as grizzlies sometimes are when they retreat to day beds just before severe storms.

I slowly backed up the slope stopping every few seconds to listen for the bear, who seemed to be moving in the opposite direction. Although I usually talked to grizzlies when I accidentally stumbled on them, I was silent with this bear. We had just shared a lightning storm. Quiet was better.

In five minutes I reached the crest of the range again and moved rapidly northward, hoping to pass safely above the bear and drop down to the trail ahead of him. The hell with the approaching storm, I thought; I was less concerned with lightning at that point than I was about running into another grizzly.

The mountain crest rose to a small summit. I veered off and started down the open ridge, back to the trail, when the bear from the brush—a medium-size light grizzly—burst into the open. The bear looked up at me, then turned and loped down the ridge, disappearing into the bushes again. It was a beautiful blond bear with ink-dipped forepaws and ears, a Siamese or panda color pattern not uncommon in this part of Montana, especially among younger animals.

I hurried down the side ridge, reaching the foot trail just as it began to rain again. The bear had vanished into the darkness, and I raced up the trail as fast as I dared, trusting my feet to find the dim but familiar path. Rounding the last corner on the trail, I saw a stark two-story pagoda, perched on a mountain top. At last.

I reached the foot of the lookout just at dark; the ridge carried more light than the gloomy north slopes of mountains. My fire lookout was a wooden structure built in the early thirties just after the forest fire of 1929. My twelve-foot-square living quarters were framed on all sides by glass windows and surrounded by a catwalk outside just high enough to be out of the reach of the tallest grizzly. It had been my summer home, my only home, since 1976.

I stumbled up the steps in the dark, glad to be home and happy to be living in the midst of a glut of grizzlies again. I stripped off my wet clothes and lit a Coleman lantern. A miniature wood stove sat in one corner with a prelaid fire ready to torch. I struck another match and lit it to take off the chill. Lightning flashed in the southern sky. This was a special night: the grizzlies had begun to gather in the high shrubfields of this small mountain range, and my real work was about to begin. Within a week, I would close up the lookout, sign off the government register, and drag my old movie camera up into the mountains, where I would spend the following few weeks living with and filming bears at the Grizzly Hilton. Sometime in mid-September, the Black Grizzly would arrive and all hell would break loose. He was sufficiently big, cantankerous, and dominant to drive most other bears and myself out of the range. He charged animals almost reflexively. He was also my favorite bear, the paragon of grizzlies: a wild force, as indomitable and recalcitrant as the wind.

Meanwhile there was cause to celebrate. I dug under the army cot for a C-ration box. Inside were four good bottles of wine. I picked out the one I had in mind for welcoming the bears back—a 1970 Les Forts de Latour. I popped the cork and set the bottle near the stove to warm slightly, letting it breathe while I fixed a bisque of the wild chanterelle mushrooms I had picked under lodgepole pines on my last trip down the mountain. My tiny propane refrigerator was well stocked with necessary condiments—garlic, shallots, butter, limes, and canned milk. I could not believe the government paid me more than four dollars an hour eight hours a day to live up here. Like getting thrown into the briar patch. To the south a storm cell rained lightning on Teapot Mountain. I mechanically marked the strikes on my fire-finder map in the middle of the lookout. It was a bit late in a relatively wet year to worry about forest fires. The storm was headed my way, though, and would provide some dazzling pyrotechnics.

I poured a glass of wine and stepped over to an inexpensive portable tape recorder hooked up by phone wire to a series of "D" batteries taped to two parallel pieces of broken broomstick—my dork battery pack. Nosing the wine, I picked out and inserted a cassette, and the tiny glass house was filled with a Bach cello solo. Outside the lightning flashed and a drizzle of rain ran down the panes. The warmth of the wine and the fire rose to my head. By the third glass I was slightly giddy, a cheap drunk on an empty stomach. The stark music was punctuated by approaching booms of thunder. I felt like Captain Nemo in my mountaintop glass house. I whipped the flour into the butter, then stuck the roux in a

350-degree oven with a bay leaf to let it thicken. The wind gusted, the lanterns swung, and the entire wooden structure creaked and swayed in the wind. The aroma of freshly sauteed chanterelles filled the lookout. I poured another glass of wine. It was tough up here in the mountains.

The next morning I was beginning to pack up the lookout when I caught movement far down the slope east of the tower. Stepping out on the catwalk, I glassed the burned-over open hillside. A brown sow grizzly with two lighter cubs of the year moved rapidly and nervously across the exposed ground. The cubs had trouble keeping up. Sows with young were usually the wariest and shyest of other grizzlies, especially during a social gathering. The greatest danger to a young grizzly, excepting man, was another, larger bear, adult boars in particular.

The interactions in this seasonal congregation of grizzlies in prime huckleberry range were not as intense and frequent as those along salmon streams in Alaska. But this gathering was characterized by a dominance hierarchy in which only the largest males would cross an exposed patch of terrain with absolute security. You can tell where an animal fits into this social hierarchy by watching the way it moves, feeds, and plays. Body language allows bears to communicate their intentions and positions on the social hierarchy. I do not pretend to understand all of it. But the bears do; they all appear to know one another. Such behavior probably evolved through these gatherings for food.

The only species of animal that tries to get by in the wilderness without interspecific tact or communication is the human critter. All other animals take stock of what others do and make adjustments in their lives for the behavior and presence of the rest of the animal kingdom. Bears have a body language in which the mere style of gait communicates mood, aggressiveness, and even changes in season. A young brown bear on a salmon stream can tell at a glance if he should flee the big boar who is still 150 yards away. Elk know when grizzlies are predatory and when they can stand fifty feet away watching as a bear walks through the middle of their herd to the next berry patch.

Grizzlies communicate with their size, posture, mouths, ears, and eyes. A grizzly standing on its rear feet swinging its head is only trying to see and smell better. Bears *whoosh* when alarmed but are no threat to humans. A bear who *woofs* but does not run away is. If the grizzly opens and closes its jaw, and slobbers, it's time to leave. A grizzly with its head lowered near or across a forepaw and looking off to the side is indicating a willingness to move on peacefully if you do. If the bear's head is turned off to the side, you can still get out without getting chewed. Once the head is lowered straight on and the ears are flat back, you're probably going to get charged. If the eyes fix at the last moment and turn cold, you're in a world of shit. The icy stare is caused by the eyelids retracting to the corner of the eyes, revealing the yellow sclera. It happens only at the last second and is the final signal you'll see before flying fur.

The grizzly family hit the bottom of the open basin and followed a thin string of trees up the south side, where they rolled over the ridge to reach the safety of the timber that the 1967 forest fire had missed. The cubs wanted to stop and play. They started wrestling but were quickly left behind by their mother, who wanted no part of open ground during the middle of a hot day. Usually bears bed during the heat of these August days, but females with young can often be seen feeding or moving around.

These bears came from somewhere north of this small mountain range, perhaps from the Livingston Range of Glacier National Park or, less likely, from the Whitefish Range of Flathead National Forest. Precisely where they had spent their springs and summers I would never know. They came for the berries that grow here in reliable abundance. Huckleberries are the most important fruit, although bears also eat serviceberry, mountain ash, buffalo berry, hawthorn, and salmonberry. The key to great berry habitat is wildfire.

I moved a folding chair outside and sat shirtless in the warmth of the late summer sun. From this vantage point I had, in past seasons, seen as many as a dozen grizzlies a week moving into the range during late summer. The brown sow with her young cubs moved with purpose to a spot already picked out in the south of the range. Over the years, many generations of grizzlies had been introduced to this particular huckleberry habitat. Mothers brought their young as cubs and yearlings, who returned as sub-adults and then adult grizzlies, some with families of their own. In prime years, as many as a hundred grizzlies visited these mountains. One year I saw seventy-one different bears, a number subject to some degree of error since solitary grizzlies are difficult to tell apart but still one hell of a lot of bears.

From inside the lookout the radio growled. I turned up the volume and adjusted the squelch.

"730 Scalplock, 720 Control."

It was the first time in a month anybody except the Fire Cache had radioed me.

"This is 730 Scalplock, 720."

"730, your pack-out date is confirmed for September first. The mules will be up Friday. Also, be advised that Lisa will be hiking up tomorrow."

"Ten-four, 720. Thanks for the message. 730."

Despite all the years I had worked seasonally for the Park Service, I still found talking on the radio unnatural. I went back outside, leaned into the wind, and tried to regain my sense of solitude. Far below, a large dark hawk rode the currents blowing up the steep flanks of the mountain off the meandering channel of the Flathead River. I swung the glasses onto his slightly mottled deep brown back. An immature golden eagle. Good. I loved to look down on the backs of eagles. I flew with him for a while, effortlessly soaring over the fluted ridges and gullies. The Indians had called this summit Eagle Peak.

The day was hot for late summer. I was officially on duty looking for fires until four-thirty, but work was slow since the forests were soggy with heavy August rain. I decided to use up some of the precious water I had hoarded by filling garbage cans with snow and letting the sun melt it. Besides, grizzlies had the preeminent noses in the animal kingdom and Lisa was coming to visit. I needed a bath.

I stood naked on the catwalk and splashed water on my body from a tin wash basin sitting on the railing. The warm water ran off my toes and was blown away by the wind. The warmth of the

sun and chill of the wind made me feel exceptionally clean. I felt
ready for anything. Tonight I would walk down the ridge again
and look for bears in Sullivan Creek. Grizzly bears were arriving
there daily now, and I would be looking for old acquaintances,
especially the Black Grizzly, though I did not expect him to show
up for another ten days or more. In the meantime I would close up
the lookout, drop down off the mountain for a couple of days of
serious sloth and bloat, check in with the boys at the Belton, and
get ready to go up to the Grizzly Hilton and film bears with the
Bolex.

A pair of kestrels hovered over the saddle just before Sullivan
Creek, hanging nearly motionless in the late afternoon wind. I
climbed the last rise and the whole of Sullivan Creek drainage
opened up before me. The creek led out to a broad expanse of
lodgepole, larch, and western white pine, which in turn swept
back up onto the shoulders of the snowcapped Livingston Range
twenty miles away. Beyond the Livingstons there are high basins
and subalpine flats: the heart of Glacier National Park and prime
summer grizzly habitat. Then there is another range with hanging
glaciers and valleys that eventually drain onto the High Plains,
which used to be buffalo country, wolf country, and the best griz
country of all until we shot them all out in the 1880s.

Patches of the hundreds of square miles of uncut timber
looked rusted in the oblique late summer sunlight. The blotches of
off-colored orange lodgepole were caused by pine beetle, which
had spread up the North Fork in epidemic proportions in recent
years, probably precipitated by overprotection of forests from
wildfire.

A dark, medium-size bear crossed an outcrop of rock on the
opposite hillside. I brought up the binoculars and saw a good-sized
black bear, *Ursus americanus,* sniffing the air and looking around.
The bear was nervous about something. I was far away and across
wind so I guessed that it was another bear. I glassed the slopes
where the black bear seemed to be looking. Nothing. Another ten
minutes passed. The black bear, who had not moved, suddenly
loped off toward the heavily timbered creek bottom. I caught a
flash of silver among the berry brush. A small, light-colored grizzly walked out on a white windfall, leaning out to either side,

stripping the berries from their bushes with its teeth. After a minute the bear was joined by an identical twin. The two looked yearling size. Sure enough, a great, blond head of a sow grizzly popped up above the brush thirty yards away.

The shadows lengthened. I had a good night. I started back along the trail to the lookout and rounded the corner where the lookout loomed against the purple sky. I paused at the bend, admiring the view, and heard rustling in the brush below the trail. Another bear. The place was already swarming with them. I quickly skirted on by, wondering what Lisa would run into. Probably not much during the middle of a warm day. She had spent more time with grizzlies than all but a handful of Montanans. Still, I found myself worrying. In about ten days, she would be beginning her eighth month of pregnancy and should start slowing down.

I lit two candles, whose flames wavered in the slight breath of wind that always found its way through the chinks in the lookout wall. It was amazing that the structure had withstood the full brunt of forty Montana winters with the loss of only one roof. To the south, I could see beyond Wild Horse Island to the far shore of Flathead Lake, a blue-gray plain in the fading light. To the north, the mountains of Canada were already hidden in the dark sky. A faint column of light shot vertically from the horizon: the aurora borealis. The northern lights would flash across the sky, throwing their luminous beams and curtains from the horizon to the heavens.

I had summered on that mountaintop for seven years. These past seven years, the grizzly years, had been a time of relative grace. I would not be coming back the following year. It was time to move on, time to leave these bears alone. I would go back up to the Grizzly Hilton one more time and wait for the Black Grizzly, then go where I could film a grizzly close up. Once that business was concluded it would be time to slack off, go to the Yellowstone country, fish and track a last bear to its den, then go south, Chihuahua maybe, look for the last Mexican grizzly and winter on the Sea of Cortés and the Piedras Negras desert. The following year I thought I might try the north country again: the Yukon or Alaska.

All morning the radio had been squawking with cryptic messages. Someone had received puncture wounds on his chest and extremities. The Arrowroot drainage had been closed and armed rangers dispatched into the area. It was, no doubt, a bear incident, although the Park Service, like most insular agencies, was naturally paranoid about adverse publicity and tended to disguise their radio traffic in bureaucratese. The words *bear* or *mauling* were never mentioned. I would not find out what really happened until I came back to Syphilization and solicited the information at the Belton.

I was sitting at my table, bringing my notebooks up to date, when I saw something white moving on the far hillside. Grabbing the binocks, I ran outside. On the distant trail, Lisa's big belly led her up the narrow trail through the brush; even at this distance the maternal waddle was distinctive. I raced off the mountain to meet her at the saddle and carry her pack up the last leg of the trail.

"Hi, baby," I said, grabbing her by both shoulders. We kissed. She was breathless, still gasping for air because of the three-thousand-foot climb and the child she was carrying. Beads of perspiration dotted her forehead. "Let me take your pack."

I lifted her Forest Service pack, surprisingly heavy with special treats and goodies for our last two days at the lookout. She managed a smile as we sat back on the edge of the trail while she caught her breath. "How was the hike up?" I finally asked.

"Okay," she said, taking my hand, "but I'm slowing down. This time up may be my last for a while. Don't worry, everything below is just fine. All the news is good."

I am one of those who, upon receiving a letter from an old friend, will skim it for bad news before reading it. My first concern was to know no calamity had taken place in the valley while I had been on my mountain.

"I saw bears," Lisa said. She meant grizzlies, of course. "They were in the last gully before the trees stop. I think the baby knew. It started kicking just as I spotted a straw-colored mom and two little cubs. She was very skittish and protective. She didn't see me, but she seemed to know something was wrong. The cubs kept rearing and trying to climb up on her back. They were awfully tiny. Like spring cubs. Just little balls of fur."

A gust of wind raised goose bumps on Lisa's slim, muscular legs. "Do you want to move on?" I asked. "You look cold."

"All right. Let's take it slow. It's good to be back up here."

We walked slowly up the ridge to the lookout, the gentle breeze blowing out Lisa's long hair on this warm, end-of-summer day. It was one of those rare mild days, everything important to me was near, I had no regrets and only a few lingering scores to settle.

We climbed up the steps of the tower and I closed the small gate that said PRIVATE QUARTERS. PLEASE KNOCK. Actually, visiting hikers were a rarity that late in the season, when the area had a good reputation for bad bears.

I fixed hot tea and opened a tin of smoked oysters. Lisa lay back on the cot while I started the first procedures of what would end up as Montana Pizza later that night. We selected another bottle of my Bordeaux stash, a 1967 Chateau Margeaux, and let it warm to room temperature in the afternoon sun. I dug out my stethoscope from my green-beret medic days and a cloth measuring tape. I listened to the faint pulse of life: about 120 tiny beats per minute. I measured the distance from the top of her pelvic bone to the top of the uterus, 33 cm. She was right on schedule, two centimeters' growth since we had measured it two weeks ago. This was new business to me, having arrived rather late at parenthood.

I popped the cork on the wine. A chocolatey bouquet, big enough to fill the room, opened up. We toasted each other. Lisa had been many things to me, most important an ally, a friend and supporter in the endless skirmishes I fought around bears and wild country. I slurped a splash of wine out of Lisa's belly button, almost nonexistent now, for old times' sake. She napped in the sunlight pouring through the continuous ring of windows. I dug out the rest of the chanterelles and began cooking. The aroma of garlic, oregano, and basil blended with the Bordeaux. A pinch of sage, a little thyme. I loved cooking for people I liked in my lookout. The tower lent itself to certain indulgences as easily as it did austerity. Small celebrations of the flesh, like sharing food and drink—humble rituals performed before all the majesty and wildness of grizzly country—became religious moments. Or so it seemed as I poured the fourth glass of wine. Lisa's intake was limited to a glass per day. Splitting a bottle of wine with a pregnant woman was a deal.

By next morning we were in a cloud. Visibility was less than a hundred feet. I turned on the radio hoping to learn more about the bear mauling. The Arrowroot drainage was still closed and patrols were out, but beyond a few stark facts little information was transmitted. I worried about the Park Service overreacting. Usually, when someone was injured by a bear the area was closed and an attempt was made to trap or dispatch—bureaucratese for kill— the offending animal. It is nearly impossible, though, to be certain which bear is responsible. Bears, especially grizzlies, are on the move at that time of year. The upper Arrowroot drainage was, as far as I had been able to determine, emptied of bears by late summer. They had all come over to the lookout, and they had to pass the area where the National Park Service would be trapping or snaring, using smelly bait nearly irresistible to bears. Chances were they would snare the wrong grizzly.

We spent the day packing away the mundane articles that made this cold structure into a home every year. It was a melancholy time, since we assumed we would not return. The restricted vistas, the gray rim of lookout railing, the damp fog and surging light clouds reflected our mood. Darkness fell early under the clouds. We turned in, silent and downcast, and lit candles to illuminate the gloom.

The next morning the clouds had broken up. Far below, I saw the string of white packs on the backs of six mules led by a single horseman with a Moose River hat: it was Stu Sorenson, the packer. I stepped out on the porch to greet him.

"See any critters on the way up?"

"Saw a big brown grizzly in the first gully. He just stood there looking at me. The mules saw him first."

We unloaded the pack boxes. I helped as Stu tied in our gear with neat diamond hitches and reloaded the boxes.

"What're you going to do next, go down south?" asked Stu.

"Going to look for my favorite griz for a couple weeks, then go fly-fish the Madison and drop down to the Sonoran desert by Thanksgiving. Want to go to Mexico. Maybe go look for the last

Mexican griz left back in the Sierra Madre. Keep hearing reports of tracks down there."

The pack string departed. We placed the shutter over the last exposed window for the winter and reluctantly followed the mules. At the switchback we paused, looking back at the tiny house on the mountaintop. It had been a good summer, but it was time to move on. The Grizzly Hilton awaited.

18

THE
BELTON

Pale September sunlight drifted through the leaded windows into the smoky taproom of the Belton Bar. I stared out at the mountains I would have to climb the next day to film bears and wait for the Black Grizzly. The bartender drew on his cigarette and dealt me another hand of cribbage. I was losing badly. Except for his eyes and high, intelligent forehead, the bartender might have been a character out of *Deliverance,* a towering man with huge hands and a black, scraggly beard.

"You're gonna get skunked, Peacock."

"Gimme another beer," I countered.

I continued gazing out the window, hoping to appear preoccupied, so I could lose with some grace. Goliath stopped just short of gloating. He made international news a few years ago when he stopped a charging grizzly by popping an umbrella in her face. He and two women were taking a day hike on one of Glacier Park's more popular trails. They topped out in a little subalpine clearing. About a hundred feet away, a sow grizzly and her two cubs grazed. The bears did not see Goliath at first. His two friends found trees and tried to climb them. One of the women could not get up her tree, and the noise they made alarmed the grizzly family. The sow stared at Goliath, who stood protectively on the trail in front of the two young women. After a couple of seconds, the grizzly charged straight at Goliath, who roared back. When the sow was twenty feet away, Goliath popped open the little purple-and-pink-flowered umbrella Lisa had given him as a joke and which he carried when it looked like rain. Goliath ducked his head and part of his large body behind the parasol. The grizzly stopped dead in her tracks, ten feet away. The bear walked a few steps toward Goliath and sniffed the umbrella, then turned and raced back to her cubs. All three grizzlies disappeared into a brushy ravine.

The door opened and two men walked into the room, deserted except for me and Goliath. They were friends, naturally, as this particular drinking establishment was largely avoided by company loggers, grizzly bear poachers, and higher ranking officials of the Department of Interior. The clientele was more likely to consist of a ragged and unkempt assortment of Vietnam veterans, each bearing private grudges, using their limited disability pensions to live close to the last wilderness areas.

This pair, Lucas and Whitebird, certainly fit that description. They greeted the sleeping collie we had smuggled into the taproom, then walked over to the bar.

"Hey, Peacock, hear about that oil exploration helicopter working up Trial Creek? Somebody blew the shit out of it. Burned it to a crisp at the airport last Thursday night."

All of us laughed knowingly.

"Don't suppose you know anything about it, do you, Peacock?" grinned Lucas.

"Not me, man. I was on my lookout."

More laughter. Shit-eating grins on black bewhiskered faces. The mood picked up considerably. I bought the house a round. It was impossible to know who knew what. Good. A small piece of the world had been corrected. Those scumsucking oil pimps had been buzzing prime grizzly habitat up north for weeks. They even buzzed my lookout twice.

"By the way, Steve," interrupted Goliath, a bit sarcastically, "would you like me to check your weapons?"

"Aye," smiled Whitebird, taking the model 1911 Colt .45 and army-issue machete off his web belting and passing them up over the bar. Whitebird was, as always, in uniform, dressed in camouflaged fatigues, jungle boots, and an old bush hat with a recon patch on it. Steve was slight, with long stringy black hair and a Fu Manchu beard.

"This was definitely a rear echelon establishment," said Whitebird, good humored and smiling as always.

I asked what the newspaper had said about the helicopter bombing.

"They traced the chopper to a rental outfit in Salt Lake City. The exploration company was out of Shithead City too, but the principals were unknown, whatever that means," answered Steve.

"Principals unknown, those greasy, greedy sumbitches think they can get away with anything."

"Are the Feds out yet?" I asked Whitebird.

"The FBI is mounting a search-and-destroy operation up the North Fork. I heard they questioned Trapper Don but he was clean," said the slender soldier.

Trapper Don was another partially disabled Montana Vietnam vet and bonafide VC POW with a reputation for blowing up bridges on Idaho logging roads he didn't authorize and, unfortunately, a record of being pulled over with blasting caps in the back of his pickup. His name comes up first on the FBI computer.

"The one thing you can count on with the FBI is incompetence. Hell, they even gave me a security clearance," I said.

Steve unscrewed the cap on his Forest Service canteen and passed it to me. I sniffed the mouth then slugged down a stiff belt of Canadian whiskey. The Belton was not a whiskey bar, so we brought our own. I felt the warmth of the sun, the glow of Black Velvet in my belly, and the pleasure of pissing away a late summer afternoon with my friends. Our unspoken solidarity grew out of an unfinished war that we still seemed to be fighting.

I had never considered readjusting to society a particularly noble calling, but my buddies in Montana feel even less a tie. The Northern Rockies feel like the sole option south of Canada for a warrior who still values his deadly skills yet considers himself exiled from the society he was trained to serve. It is an antidote to the powerlessness that elsewhere might make him sit alone in front of a television, drinking into the night, aiming a pistol in bottomless frustration at random figures and dreaming of the absolute power of the Mafia chieftain who, with the snap of his fingers, wipes out a roomful of enemies. These men speak of retribution for injustice in terms of taking out several enemies at once, then punching out themselves in a hail of bullets. Take an asshole with you, they say. None have ever done so, but they are not quite bluffing either.

Vietnam gave us a useful pessimism, a pragmatic irreverence I can wear comfortably down any bear trail. No one can ever show me a photo of a mutilated body or dead child again and tell me it is the way of the world. I can't live in that world, but I do want to live. If this is a wound, it doesn't want mending.

"Did you hear anything about the mauling up Arrowroot?" I asked Lucas.

"Only that the sucker made the mistake of trying to climb a tree after jumping a griz thirty feet away at the head of the trail to Christianson Meadow," he said.

"How badly was he messed up?"

"The poor bastard got his lung punctured but was cool enough to drive himself to the ranger station. Said he did some goddamn yoga to slow his breathing down. An Oregon hippie, sounds like. He's okay."

"What did the park do?"

"Put out a trap. They didn't get anything though. I think they still have it out there. Want me to take care of it?" Bud asked.

"Naw, I was just worried they'd get the wrong bear again. I think Lisa saw the griz that mauled that guy on the way up to the lookout. It was a sow with two cubs."

"The hippie didn't see any cubs. They probably were hidden in the ferns," said Lucas.

"Probably. You wanna visit me at the Hilton?"

"If I can get off work. You just watch your ass with that big black grizzly tomorrow. That bastard is mean. He'll chew you a new asshole."

19

THE BLACK
GRIZZLY

SEPTEMBER (1980s)

The leaves of the bushes along the narrow game trail had been knocked off, telling me that there had been considerable traffic, most of it bears. I was moving slowly, weighed down with the big Trailwise full of 16-mm camera equipment and enough camping gear for a week. The only thing I was short on was food: like the bears, I would live for the next six or seven days on huckleberries. Between the upper branches of the towering larch and spruce, survivors of the last two cycles of forest fire, wedges of a distant hillside flashed by, mottled in brilliant red and yellow. Fall had already touched the high country.

I waded across a tiny creek and filled my three gallon canteens, since the upper reaches of this small mountain range were poorly watered and the few cool spring holes were favorite bedding spots for grizzly bears. The brush along the creek, mostly alder and dried stalks of cow parsnip, was trampled and broken by the recent passage of many animals. I started upstream, leaning into the brush more cautiously, making just enough noise to forewarn any bear napping in the creek bottom. I skirted the muddy edge of a marshy area, reading the tracks of a moose, a large black bear, and at least five different grizzlies who passed through in the previous ten days. It looked like a sow with two cubs, a subadult, and a huge adult grizzly. I would be glad when I climbed up out of this brush onto the ridge top.

The timber opened onto the tail of an old avalanche scar. The bushes of the nearest ravine moved and a fat brown bear, glistening with silver-tipped guard hairs, moved into the sunlight. I wasn't sure if I recognized him. This area attracts a lot of large grizzlies and it's hard to tell them apart.

The grizzly was too far away to see me. I turned and struck off down an even more obscure game trail, leaving an obvious boot track in the fork not taken out of ancient habit, pulling myself up by bushes and alder trees for twenty minutes, then topping out on a narrow, open, rocky ridge top.

I stopped before a huge huckleberry scat, wondering if I knew the proportionately large bear who had dropped it. There were only three or four animals that size, and one of them was the Black Grizzly.

A sound startled me. I froze and leaned my better ear into the wind. A brash bawling drifted along the timbered valley, coming from the upper reaches of the basin. Again the cry shattered the mountain stillness. The sound seemed to be moving toward me, down the small drainage. I glassed the openings and avalanche chutes for movement. Nothing. I dropped my pack and crawled to the edge of the ridge, scanning the creek bed at the bottom of the small valley. I heard the rhythmic crunch of brush under the weight of a large animal running.

A medium-size brown grizzly rushed into an opening in the timber three hundred yards below me, spun, and reared. A second later two brown cubs ran underneath her. It was the family I had seen from the lookout the previous week. She and the cubs turned and bolted into the trees. Just as they passed below me, one of the cubs, unable to keep up with his mother, let loose a panicked and mournful cry. What they were running from I could only guess, though it was probably another bear. Whenever bears congregate, first-year cub mortality can range up to about a third. The litter size of bears at the Grizzly Hilton is low: over a six-year period, more than fifty grizzly families averaged 1.3 to 1.4 cubs and yearlings per productive female. Generally, it should be about two.

The bulk of the cubs are likely killed by other grizzlies, and the Black Grizzly probably figures significantly in this.

I realized I was sitting in a small saddle grizzlies used to cross from one drainage to another. Last year I had gotten into trouble there: I had set up my tripod and camera to film close-ups of mountain ash berries, and just as I was about to run the Bolex, I heard movement in the brush below me. Seventy feet away across the open slope was a brown grizzly and her small cub. They had not seen or smelled me, but they continued nibbling huckleberries and were headed straight for me. At that range, any sudden movement would make the sow charge, so I had no choice but to stand my ground and let the family know I was there. I turned on the Bolex. If I was going to get my ass chewed, I wanted it on film. The sow had fed on when the noisy camera started. The cub looked imploringly into his mother's face. Within a heartbeat she turned in the direction of the metallic clicking, gnashing her teeth and popping her jaws. Without moving or taking my eye away from the viewfinder, I began talking to the grizzly in what I hoped was a soothing tone.

The sow reared and looked right at me. She dropped back to all fours and took little steps in my direction. I kept on babbling. Still moving her mouth, the bear looked back toward the trees. She didn't know what to do any more than I did. I rewound the Bolex for another twenty-eight-second run, and the two bears wandered across the open slope to my right. Once more the sow rose on her hind legs. Through the viewfinder I watched the brown backsides of grizzlies bounce through the bear grass.

One close call in that saddle was enough. Now I moved in case the sow and her two cubs decided to use this gully again. I grabbed my pack and the tripod and pushed on up the ridge, climbing to a level just below the highest summits. Finally I reached a saddle overlooking a tiny tarn with a larger, deeper valley that fell off to the north. I set up on a flat ridge, restricting myself to an area about thirty feet square to minimize disturbance to the grizzlies. I had been coming here since 1975. I always returned to the same place so that the few grizzlies who had detected my presence could predict where I would be and what I would be doing.

I took the pair of big navy glasses from my pack and began searching the slopes. Although it was the hottest part of a warm September day, the grizzlies were active. A big brown sow and two fat blond yearlings browsed in the shadows just upslope from the tarn. Up the hill 150 yards, a pair of four-year-old silvertips fed together. They might have been a previous litter of the brown sow, but I am never sure about relationships where there are so many bears. Below me, in the timber covering the bottom of the drainage, I caught dark movement in the shadows. I glassed the thicket of spruce and fir. A huge dark brown head popped into the sunlight. I breathed a sigh of relief: it was not the Black Grizzly, but a familiar big brown boar. He was bedded, waiting for the shadows to fall before he ventured forth to feed.

The brown bear ignored the family of yearlings who, nonetheless, avoided violating the boar's "individual space," the distance within which a bear would charge or otherwise defend his territory. Grizzlies are not territorial, the way wolves are, but they do have a preference for certain seasonal ranges and share these forage areas with other bears. Grizzlies are secure and tolerant on day beds. I have seen the big brown boar allow smaller bears to pass within fifty feet while he was bedded.

Meanwhile the trio browsed rapidly downslope toward the shallow pond. I dug into the pack for the old Bolex, set it on the tripod head, and screwed on a 300-mm lens. The bears rolled over the last brush and into the open, walking over a jumble of deadfalls toward the water. As the grizzly family neared the tarn, the yearlings' usually taut discipline broke. They threw themselves into the pond, beating the water with their paws and leaving brown mud trails as they stirred up the bottom. The sow cautiously scented the air, then walked out on a bleached log and dove into the water. The two yearlings flailed away at each other with their paws from either side of another snag. They bit each other's ears and nipped like wrestling puppies. The mother joined them and all three bears rolled in the froth and spray.

The sow tried to disengage herself and was attacked from the rear by one of her yearlings. She shook the smaller bear off and crawled out onto a log. Despite her playfulness, she remained alert. It was only a matter of minutes before foreign odors would drift through the valley: smells of ornery male grizzlies and, then, the stench of man.

Suddenly she scented the air and bolted with the yearlings close behind. Racing across the open ground, she circled once in an attempt to locate the scent, then lumbered over the tangle of deadfalls with the muscles of her flank rippling. Through the viewfinder of the Bolex, I watched her flight, feeling regret, awe, and admiration. The air currents were fickle here, blowing over the ridges, curling into the basins, and diffusing in every direction. Some trace of human odor had reached the sow. I screwed up. I should have noticed the cold air flowing off the ridges.

Feeling remiss, I decided to visit the Grizzly Hilton before I stirred things up any more. The Grizzly Hilton is simply the clump of trees I make my camp in—a thicket of fir lying on a little knoll apart from the ridge-top game trail the bears sometimes use. There was no berry habitat in the immediate vicinity, and I had never seen sign of any grizzly bedding where I camped. It's about as bear-free as any place can be that's crawling with griz.

With the afternoon sun behind me, I climbed the highest local summit, sat, and glassed the shrub fields. Nine bears were visible on the distant slopes: two family groups with a single offspring each and five other adults. The shadows lengthened. Two more grizzlies came off their day beds to begin feeding as the air cooled. One subadult fed too close to a larger bear that made a short charge to drive off the youngster. Usually these grizzlies behave more like bison: a dominant animal browses his way in and the subordinate bear merely moves on a bit.

But all this was happening at a considerable distance away: it lacked the intimacy of the ridge below the Hilton, where you sat in the middle of a great sea of ebbing and flowing grizzlydom. My observation post below the Grizzly Hilton was the center of a great wave of bear activity. Animals rolled down one slope into the basins displacing the grizzlies already there, who, in turn, passed over my ridge and down into the opposite basin—causing another wave of bears to break.

I walked down the high ridge and crawled into the Hilton at

dark. I listened to the sounds of elk bugling until I fell asleep. At daybreak, I dressed and started down the ridge toward my observation post. I heard large rocks rolling down the mountain. The big brown bear I had seen yesterday was digging on the far slope under a fir tree. He tugged at roots and threw the dirt out in clouds. He seemed to be digging a den. I suspected that this bear denned around here, since I had often seen him in the area late into October feeding on mountain ash berries. Grizzlies may den repeatedly in a single small area, but they usually dig a new den each year.

The bear dug on until the sun hit him, then retreated to a clump of trees and bedded. I walked over the ridge and peered down into the deep basin to the north. A fan of avalanched snow still lingered in the shaded bottom. A sharp, high-pitched trumpeting broke the stillness: a bull elk, late in his rut. A few minutes later I heard brush breaking and an eight-hundred-pound bull elk with a magnificent rack of antlers stepped to the edge of the snow, where a small pond of water filled a sump. He strode into the water, lowered his head, and slashed the surface with his antlers and hooves. After five minutes of battle, he ceased warring on the tiny wallow and strutted down the basin.

Just as the elk reached the trees I saw the peculiar gait of a lanky, dark grizzly. It was Happy Bear, whom I first came to know in 1976 when he was a skinny four-year-old. Now he was about my age in bear years, one foot already in the grave. Happy Bear is the most playful solitary bear I know. Once I filmed him sitting in the tarn contemplatively blowing bubbles in the muddy water and biting them. Then he attacked the water, like the elk, beating it with his paws and slashing the surface with his jaws.

Happy Bear ambled across the basin, lumbering in the stiff, swinging gait that made him so easy to recognize. He walked up to the snow patch and sniffed at the scat of another grizzly. Suddenly he leaped into the air as if stung by a bee, careening and prancing up and down the anvil of whiteness like a baby buffalo. Leap for joy, grizzer bear! Happy Bear approached another caviared pile of berry scat with feigned seriousness only to repeat his magic dance. He shook his head like a shaggy ox and leaped in tight circles. I filmed him leaving the snow, prancing across the tiny sedge meadow into the brush.

I returned to the ridge and took off my shirt, basking in the last warm rays of the brief northern Montana Indian summer. I caught movement down the ridge. My stomach tightened—it was a man and I panicked for a moment. It turned out to be Lucas, visiting the Grizzly Hilton as I had thought he might. I ran down to meet him. He was breathing heavily.

"There's been another grizzly bear mauling," he gasped. "A biologist at Oldman Lake. They jumped a sow with cubs at close range in a berry patch."

"Did he get it bad?" I asked.

"Naw, he was lucky," said Lucas. "He tried to climb a tree and the bear pulled him down and just nipped him a couple of times. It just sorta played with him like a cat with a mouse."

"How the feds reacting?"

"Same old shit. They closed the area and sent in all kinds of rangers armed to the teeth. . . . Everybody's nervous as hell. Every night the game warden sets a trap at the dump and every night me and Whitebird spring it."

"Thanks," I said. "More grizzlies visit that dump than anyone knows. It's the drain plug on a quarter of the bears in the park. They ought to close the son of a bitch."

We walked up the ridge and Lucas glassed the slopes, finding the pair of subadults browsing in the berry bush high on the hillside. Lucas was best when it came to spotting bears. Even I could not keep up with his hunter's keen patience.

"Those two could be the last litter of Mom and the Kids," said Bud, referring to a family of grizzlies we had named two years ago.

"Yeah. I think she's back with two new cubs. Those four-year-olds seem to be hanging around her."

"Wish I could stay and watch, but I got to get back tonight. Gotta bartend at the Deerlick."

We whiled away the afternoon, alternately walking the ridge and glassing for bears. In addition to the pair of four-year-olds, we spotted the sow and two cubs I had seen from below the fire lookout. Far to the north were five more brown and silver shapes moving through the brush. Both Happy Bear and the big den bear had apparently bedded. The day was cooling off and high clouds blew over. Lucas wished me luck and started back down the mountain. It was important to get below the zone of ripe huckleberries before the late afternoon, when grizzlies are active. Nobody wants to run into a bear on a dark bushy trail. Bud disappeared into the trees. It was too bad he couldn't spend the night. I wouldn't have minded the company and Lucas loved this place.

I watched the grizzly family feed throughout the remainder of the afternoon, until shadows fell and the big brown grizzly came back out. Happy Bear failed to reappear. I saw a sow with a single light-colored cub in the north basin, feeding up the slope in my direction. Not wanting to disturb them, I climbed the steep ridge to the Grizzly Hilton, allowing the bears to use the ridge in peace. I sat just below my camp glassing the basins in the fading light. Just at dark, a big black grizzly appeared at the snow patch.

The wind whipped the tent fly. I could not hear a sound over its scream, and that made me nervous. The Black Grizzly had arrived, and the time of secure camping and sound sleeping was over. I pulled the wool cap off my ears and listened to the wind in the trees. Now and then I thought I heard something moving in the brush, but I was never sure. I was completely helpless, dependent upon the whim of the most unpredictable and powerful animal I knew. Drops of wind-driven rain exploded against the tent. The din of wind and rain lulled me to sleep. I dreamed of white bears until a change in the sounds outside woke me up. The wind died and the thud of rain on the tent softened: it was snowing. I burrowed deeper into my sleeping bag, only dimly remembering that the previous afternoon I was sitting shirtless in the sun. The snow meant the huckleberries would freeze and drop off their bushes in three or four days, and this congregation of grizzlies would begin to disperse, a process that would accelerate as the season advanced, markedly hastened by the badass presence of the Black Grizzly. I wondered where he was. That curiosity kept me awake until daybreak.

I shook the snow off the tent flap and peered out. A four-inch blanket of snow covered everything. The morning was gray but at least I was not in a cloud. I could get some spectacular movie footage today. Moving off the edge of the knoll, I glassed the basin below. The big brown grizzly dug at his den again. The day before, winter seemed a long way off. Obviously the brown grizzly knew something I didn't.

The Black Grizzly worried me. He was the one animal up here who regarded me as a subordinate. All the other grizzlies treated me much as they did other, more dominant bears and ran away most of the time. A few, including the den-digging griz, showed neither fear nor aggression and stood their ground. The Black Grizzly, on the other hand, charged and ran off other bears. He hadn't charged me because I hadn't given him a chance. The big brown griz and the Black Grizzly seemed to be the two top animals in this group of thirty or so bears, and they had a pact. I'd seen them feed within 150 yards of each other as peacefully as cattle, though the brown bear deferred slightly to the Black Grizzly in leaving him the prime berry areas.

The signaling between these two dominant animals was not obvious. More overt communication appears where hierarchies are formed for salmon or other foods. At salmon streams as well as in huckleberry patches and other places, the dominant bears will walk across a flat or clearing with no sign of wariness, showing utter disdain except for the constant but subtle visual monitoring of the area. The degree of nonchalance often indicates where a bear stands in a social order, though any rule about grizzly behavior has its exceptions.

Normally the pecking order is big males, sows with young, younger males and females without cubs, subadult pairs or groups, and solitary grizzlies including weaned yearlings. Most of the time you can't tell males from females in the wild, so the classes are: females with cubs, solitary adults, and younger or subadult grizzlies.

The only bear a mother with cubs will *never* tolerate close to her young is a big boar. Bears of equal status may challenge each other with threatening postures. The most extreme of these are straight-on nose-to-nose bite threats when bears square off with mouths open, ears back, and rear haunches lowered, sometimes roaring or salivating and tossing their heads up. The resolution comes when the weaker bear remains still but indicates that he or she would fight if attacked. The dominant grizzly often breaks off. Both bears avoid any sudden movements. The threat of mutual injuries makes actual combat a rarity and fights to the death even less common.

I carried my garbage bag–covered camera down the ridge, where I could look into the north basin for the Black Grizzly. The snow-covered slopes were deserted. He was probably bedded despite the chilly weather. It would warm up—this was not real winter yet. I settled in to shoot some film of the brown grizzly, who was feeding on berries near his den. The reds and yellows of the shrub fields contrasted sharply with the fresh snow. There was no sign of any of the grizzly families or Happy Bear, who might have left the range already. The arrival of the snow and the Black Grizzly were signs that this gathering of bears was mostly over. The berry crop would fail, and increased competition for the few remaining bushes would bring on more aggression from the big bears in defense of their diminishing food supply. I ought to get the hell out of here, I thought. There was enough risk in this job without pushing my luck.

I was brooding over leaving, when Happy Bear emerged from the timber in the north basin. I dragged the camera across the ridge and filmed him in the wallow below the snow patch. He picked up sheets of ice that had frozen on the meltwater during the night and played. Maybe he was looking at his reflection. He broke the thin ice with his nose and then rolled on his back in the muddy water, all four feet in the air.

Happy Bear romped and waddled back into the trees. Likewise, the den-digging grizzly disappeared. The temperature had risen and the snow was rapidly melting, so they were probably bedded for the day. I spent midafternoon walking the ridge looking for bears, but I did not find any. My original plan had been to use up all my movie film, which could take four or five days, but with the

Black Grizzly on the scene, the situation was more tense. Since he drove most of the other bears out of these mountains, there would not be many left to film. On the other hand this animal holds endless fascination for me: he is my Moby Dick of grizzly bears.

By late afternoon the snow melted and I had not seen a thing. I started breaking down my camera, getting ready to return to the Hilton, when I heard movement in the brush below me to the north. The sow with the dark patch on her hump, from the previous night, and her small, light-colored cub walked onto the false hellebore-studded meadow near the snow field. The cub leapt and nipped at its mother, who wanted no part of the play. She was clearly nervous. The cub paused to graze on the low sedges growing on the wet flats below the snow, then ran to catch up to the sow, who had started climbing the long ridge between me and the Grizzly Hilton. She would pass over the saddle just in front of me. I did not want to disturb the grizzly family, but I did not want to be stuck on the ridge after dark either. I decided to let the bears pass over the ridge first, then slip by them and climb the rest of the way to the Hilton. If I was careful, they would not get my scent.

Darkness was falling and the grizzlies had not hit the ridge top yet—they had stopped to feed on huckleberries. I was waiting in the shadows when my heart skipped a couple of beats: below, in the meadow, stood the Black Grizzly, nibbling sedge. I hoped he would stay down there. I already had two grizzlies between me and my camp, and it would be dark in forty-five minutes.

The Black Grizzly crossed the meadow with his usual disdain for scents and worlds beyond his immediate one and started browsing his way up the side of the ridge. He climbed rapidly and was halfway up the ridge when it dawned on me that he was going to catch up to the grizzly family feeding just below me. I was going to be stuck there in the dark with a sow, her cub, and the Black Grizzly between me and my sleeping bag. I edged off to the side of the steep-sided ridge to get a better view. The Black Grizzly browsed a hundred feet or so below the sow; neither bear seemed aware of the other. I considered dropping off the back side of the ridge and trying to circle around the three bears, but I would never make it; the steep brush was nearly impenetrable.

Suddenly there was a roar, and I heard a huffing and the sound of animals running through the brush. The sow broke into the open a hundred feet in front of me and raced across the saddle. The tiny cub struggled with the brush, running at her heels. I could hear the intake and exhalation of each breath with each stride. They contoured along the rock outcrop below the ridge, oblivious of my presence, running for their lives before the Black Grizzly, who tore up the slope and burst over the ridge top. He galloped like a racehorse and moved just as fast. The sow and cub flew below the small cliff. The cub fell a couple of yards behind and I could make out a high-pitched coughing, a panicky sound as if the little bear knew it had but seconds left to live. The Black Grizzly gained ground until his jaws were but a yard from the cub's hindquarters.

At the last second the sow spun on her heels, allowing the cub to slip under her as she braced for the crush of the huge grizzly with a chilling roar. The boar bellowed back, and they locked jaws. The Black Grizzly slashed with his teeth. The sow parried and warded off the attacking jaws of the bigger bear. The cub retreated to a rock thirty feet above and stood there bawling. The boar leapt forward and knocked the smaller sow off balance, forcing her to expose her vulnerable flank. The huge male lunged and seized the female by the neck. She yelped in pain, throwing her head against the bigger bear, and broke the grip of his jaws. The sow quickly recovered. She held her own.

I could see no blood, though both bears must have been wounded by then. They alternately slashed and parried, then stood nose to nose roaring amplified growls, the likes of which I had never heard in nature. The Black Grizzly slowed his attack. Abruptly he changed tactics and lunged once again for the throat of the sow. She leaned into the attack; they locked jaws and rose to their hind feet like circling wrestlers. They broke and dropped to all fours, roaring and bellowing into each other's snouts.

The face-off stabilized as the Black Grizzly gave up trying to kill the sow. The last roars rumbled throughout the valley. Though a little shaken by the proximity of this battle, I managed to run a few feet of film.

The smaller of the two huge carnivores backed slowly up the hill, still growling with the hair on her neck straight up. The Black Grizzly roared again, his head slightly lowered, his ears flattened back. She inched away from him a few feet at a time and turned her head to the side—a sign she was done fighting. He read it and turned away almost regretfully. The battle was over.

I was in a predicament. It was almost dark and I was perched on a knife-edged ridge with steep, impassable brush on either side and nowhere to go but up to the Grizzly Hilton. Between me and the Hilton, one hundred and fifty feet away, stood the baddest bear in the mountains, now at his ugliest after an inconclusive fight.

I let my instincts loose: I had no choice but to face down the great grizzly. Any failure of confidence could be fatal. I picked up two large brown bags that had been covering my camera and held them at arm's length. I was wearing a black sweater; both black and dark brown grizzlies were often big males. The Black Grizzly turned just off the crest of the ridge a hundred feet away and pretended to feed. He still had not seen me.

I made my move. Slowly I inched up the ridge and spoke. "Hey, grizzer bear, it's only me, good old Arapaho. Sure hate to bother you." The words were irrelevant, but tone and posture were everything. The grizzly reared and spun. He took a huge breath, exhaled like a sounding whale, then dropped to all fours facing me. I continued inching toward him, my arms outstretched holding the silly garbage bags, talking nonsense with my head cocked off to the side. The grizzly clicked and gnashed his teeth. I stopped at fifty feet and the bear advanced stiff-legged toward me. His ears were flat back against his head. I was finished. "I'll make it up to you, griz, honest." At fifteen feet away the great bear stopped, his head lowered. There was something in his eyes that I would never quite put my finger on. The Black Grizzly turned his head to the side, almost sadly, spun gracefully on his rear feet, and ambled off into the brush leaving me alone on the ridge top.

Only half believing my good fortune, I wasted no time. I slid by the spot where the bear disappeared and shot up the ridge to my hilltop camp. By the time I got there it was dark. I leaned into the darkness listening for sounds and caught myself shaking uncontrollably. The last time I had shaken like this was 1967 near Ba An, after my Montagnards and I had been strafed by gunships flying for the 101st Airborne.

Normally I build no fires at the Grizzly Hilton because I don't like to spook the bears, but that night a fire was my only defense against the roaming bear I had just escaped. I worked fast, kindling a tiny blaze a few feet from my hidden tent. The fire bolstered my shaky nerves, and I stepped to the edge of the hill. Somewhere, down in the darkness, was the unmistakable sound of a big animal moving through the brush. I listened breathlessly. The Black Grizzly was coming uphill. I stoked up the fire and gathered beargrass plumes. I made a torch of them, but the stalks burned poorly. I added branches and got the whole thing flaming. I heard the snapping of brush just over the edge of the knoll. Again, I had no choice but confrontation. Walking to the brink of the hill, I heard the grizzly moving not forty feet downslope. I spoke softly, telling the bear I was sorry that I had invaded his territory, thanking him, and assuring him I would move on. Waving the flaming plumes and branches in the air, I saw the small eyes shine red for a second. They blinked off and disappeared into the darkness. I heard the huge bear slowly move through the bushes back down the hill. I went back and huddled by the fire.

Half an hour passed, maybe more. I was beginning to think the bear would leave me in peace when I heard thrashing in the shrub field on the other side of the knoll. Again I gathered firebrands and walked to the edge of the steep drop-off. I stared into the darkness and heard the angry grizzly fight his way up the hill. When he got thirty feet away, I threw a burning branch down the slope. The bear stopped. I waved the brands in the air and said, "Hey, Black Grizzly, it's me again. Why don't you give me a break?"

Silence. I peered into the blackness, seeing nothing. The torch had almost burned down, leaving me unprotected. The big bear slowly withdrew down the mountain. An hour later I heard him probe the third side of the pyramid-shaped hill. The scene was repeated.

The wind rose, bringing dim sounds of dark shapes to my ears. The snapping of a twig carried to the fire, and my head jerked toward the black trees, finding nothing. It must have been midnight. I could not remember being so tired. I could not afford to fall asleep. I tried to keep my mind moving. My thoughts drifted, landing on the irony of meeting my end at the jaws of my favorite beast. For a moment I could imagine the flickering fire reflecting the hint of a smile on my face. It vanished as I heard another branch break.

By about two in the morning, peace returned to the mountains, broken only once by bugling elk in a distant basin. I dozed by my tiny fire, waking every half hour to rekindle a small blaze. Gray dawn broke in the southeastern sky. With each moment the daylight spread and my confidence returned. Still I had to get out of these hills, past the Black Grizzly.

I picked up my binoculars and walked to the edge of the knoll where I could see down onto the basin. A couple of hundred yards to my right the brown grizzly with her two lovely blond yearlings ate berries. She sniffed the air and trotted away from me. Shit, she got my scent. The bears ambled through the steep brush, then picked up a near-vertical bear trail leading to the bottom of the basin.

In the trees near the edge of the sedge meadow I saw a dark shape. The Black Grizzly stepped into the open and began grazing. The sow and her two yearlings continued dropping down the steep trail. Just as they hit the bottom, the big boar lifted his head and saw the family a hundred yards away across the flat. Without pausing, he charged full tilt over the log-filled meadow. The sow and her young turned, scrambled back up the steep game trail, and climbed above a rocky outcrop out on a low cliff. The Black Grizzly stopped at the foot of the hill and looked up, allowing the family to reach safety on the cliffs.

Another close one.

I was upset with myself. I had almost run those little bears into that black bastard and got them killed. That's it, I'm leaving as soon as he beds. I was angry at the Black Grizzly for being such a cantankerous son of a bitch, but he was just being a bear. I was a blundering nuisance who was not doing the bears a bit of good.

I returned to the Hilton and broke camp, deciding to take a walk in the opposite direction to give the bear time to bed down.

Overhead, a jet trail bisected the single patch of blue sky. It probably was an air force jet out of Great Falls carrying a full payload, ready for the Big One, finger on the switch.

I lay back on the grass and looked up. Those buttons, the wonders of technology, had safely removed us from the evolutionary realities that we had once faced along with the grizzlies. Future pathfinding would be in space—the last frontier, as they say. We were out there right now trying to discover what had already been lost here. Orbiting satellites were being used both to keep tabs on our commie terrestrial enemies and to radio-track collared grizzly bears who seem to be wandering.

Back on the ridge above the Grizzly Hilton, I held onto a fistful of beargrass, firmly tethered to earth. Fuck space. There was no way in hell I could imagine the Black Grizzly straying from home. There was no doubt in my mind who was really lost.

I hiked back to camp in the afternoon to finish packing up. The bears should have been bedded by now. I approached the Grizzly Hilton and stopped short. Something was wrong. Down stuffing covered everything. My cache of gear had been pulled down from the tree and the contents scattered. My sleeping bag was torn to shreds. I found my dirty brown T-shirt chewed to pieces. The bear had eaten everything that smelled of me.

I packed up the remains of my camp, threw it in the backpack, and started down the ridge. I glassed the timber just below the basin and caught a flash of the black bear on his day bed. He was so arrogant he did not even bother hiding in the timber like other bears. I could see half of his enormous body stretched out in the open.

I approached my observation post with apprehension. Two of my one-gallon water canteens lay on the ground crushed by the grizzly's jaws. The camera and the tripod were knocked over. The foam sound blimp had been chewed off Gage's old Bolex, which, outside of a few canine dents, was undamaged.

I stuffed my pack with damaged equipment, trembling slightly out of mixed rage and fear. I walked the ridge to the spot directly over the Black Grizzly's day bed. I pried loose the biggest boulder I could find and rolled it down the slope, crashing into the timber. The great bear lifted his head and looked up at me. A piercing cry shattered the silence as I roared at him. He yawned and his head disappeared again in the thick trees. I turned and slipped on down the ridge, leaving the bear and the mountains behind.

20
NOTES FROM THE SEA OF CORTÉS

In the calm of daybreak, the islands and headlands of the Sea of Cortés shift in the water—mirages, making the landscape impossible to discern even half a mile offshore. The colors of the Gulf run a wider spectrum than the Pacific; rose and mauve at dawn, then shades of gold and crimson at dusk.

South of Loreto, the Sierra de la Gigante dominates the coastline. There are desert bighorn sheep and deer and lions in these rugged mountains, and mysterious rock paintings of larger than life-size figures of men and animals in hematitic ocher, splashed by ancient Indians on an overhang of dacite fifteen to twenty feet above, as if slapped on with pole-size Matisse brushes by giants.

At midday, the early calm is replaced by a mild breeze and choppy water. We head for the island of Santa Catalina, best known for a species of restless rattlesnake found nowhere else. The truth is that everything living on each of these islands is a bit unique, having evolved on volcanic peaks sinking in the waters filling the San Andreas Fault, which slipped violently 4.5 million years ago and created the Sea of Cortés. On an island to the south, melanism has prevailed in a species of jackrabbit living among gray andesites and scabrous vegetation—also unique. On Catalina the barrel cactus reach ten feet and nothing is like anything else.

Everywhere are birds: gulls of three species, terns, and

boobies dive-bomb seamounts and dolphin-slashed schools of her-
ring. Along the coasts brown pelicans and cormorants perch on
rocks and headlands. Hammerheads check out the boat and manta
rays leap perhaps to dislodge parasites. Finback whales are resi-
dent, and, before the sea grows rough, dolphinfish cruise by.
Roosterfish, yellowtail, or bonito rip into schools of baitfish the
size of baseball diamonds, accompanied by the diving birds that
turn the ocean surface greasy.

Underwater the mass of critter life boggles the mind. The
upwellings teem with plankton, making the sea a bit cloudier than
the crystalline Caribbean. Swimming along any of these islands
are triggerfish, parrotfish, needlefish, groupers of several kinds;
close up are scorpionfish, puffer blowfish, blennies and gobies,
and rafts of smaller fishes. To eat there are cabrilla and black sea
bass. In the sandy bays off Santa Catalina, four-foot-wide eagle
rays crowd so closely in four feet of water you can barely find
standing room; deeper are brown electric rays with a spot on their
back, and smaller rays are closer to shore. Sea urchins with three-
inch spines cover the rocks below a sheer cliff. Garden eels wave
like grasses growing out of the sandy ocean bottom. Among the
rocks there are moray eels, some spotted, who look frightening
when caught in the open. Three miles south of the sea urchins is
some of the best shallow-water spiny lobster habitat in the world.

At night you burn driftwood, which often flames green and
red or orange from trace elemental materials, because the local
bursera and paloverde make poor firewood. During the long
nights of winter's new moons you learn all the visible northern
constellations. The unique species of rattlesnake is aggressive by
Arizona standards and shakes his rattleless tail under a huge native
fig tree.

Heading north, you find clams, snails, and mussels most
anywhere, especially in the mangroves, which are rich in shellfish
and red snapper (huachinango, al mojo de ajo, broiled over root of
saltbush). Green and black-crowned night herons, egrets, and
mangrove warblers fish the bayous.

This intertidal zone was once known for powderhorn-shaped
pinshells, whose hinge muscle eaten raw with a tomato picante
sauce is a treat. You might also notice the depletion of large sailfish,

marlin, and totoaba, though the Gulf still feels the way Nebraska did, maybe in 1870, a decade before the buffalo went away—there were still so many no one felt the threat.

The oasis town of Mulegé: the inmates at the prison, I am told, go home at night to sleep with their wives and girlfriends and return in the morning. The desert is the wall. The dominant plant here, as on the islands of the midriff, is the cardon, saguarolike though a hulking brute in comparison, the largest of the cactus. There are also organ pipes and a low-growing relative, agria (the sour pitaya), which crawls reptilelike over the ground.

The Midriff Islands lie ahead. A low island has osprey nests on the beach just above high tide mark; very unusual, perhaps no predators. La Raza is a third of a square mile and rocky, a rookery for royal and elegant terns and Heermann's gulls. Eggs were gathered here commercially until 1964, when it was made a sanctuary.

Grunion appear on the beaches of the northern Gulf from February to April after the big tides of the full moon. Some beaches are covered with pink murex shells. On calm March mornings a thin line of lobster krill might lie at the high tide mark. Larger relatives, six-inch Pacific-type shrimp, swim alongside the boat in deep water and hide under piers. At night you can always see dinoflagellates bioluminesce in the surf, seasonally blooming as red tides. On the rocky shores and islands the easiest way to travel is often at low tide on the wave-cut benches below the cliffs and headlands, as long as you don't get caught in rising tides.

To the east is Isla San Esteban. Beyond is the larger island of Tiburón, traditional homeland of the Seri Indians. The Seris spoke the language of lower California and made reed canoes, balsas of carrizo. It is theorized, though never proven, they paddled across the Gulf—an idea made unlikely by treacherous currents and sudden storms until one day when, standing at the hillside spring above Bahía los Angeles, you see the Sierra Seri and Cabo Tepoca on the mainland crystal-clear, and three routes across to Tiburón navigable by inner tube leap into the mind. Later that day the sounds of blowing finbacks and blues are audible from miles away, coming every few minutes and so distant you can only see every fifth whale on the still ocean.

On a rare crystalline day when the route across to Tiburón is indeed navigable, that quality of light and shape-shifting typical of Gulf mornings lasts all day. The limonites of the big island, Ángel de la Guardia, pour gold color into the water, and headlands seem to split off into islands and then float upward as a yellow cloud. You can't tell where anything stops or begins.

Guardian Angel, the second largest island in the Gulf, has never been inhabited. Blue whales and orcas have been sighted offshore, and every promontory has an osprey nest. Oyster-catchers nest on the cobbles above high tide. Brown pelicans have rookeries on isolated headlands, and at the northeast tip of Angel is a place known as Refugio.

If you have not traveled much outside the hemisphere and you prefer solitude, Refugio might be the most lovely stretch of beach and coastline you have ever seen. The sand beaches are white crescents connecting headlands and ridges of volcanic rubble.

In 1972 there was a guano-white arch in this seldom-used harbor. By 1977 it had collapsed. There were always cormorants there and the diversity of reef fishes found around vertical relief. Underwater this place is richer and cloudier with upwellings than the rest of the gulf; you can scarcely hold yourself to rocks during changing tides in the east-west channels. At the high tide line on one of the beaches are the five- to seven-inch shells of a white Pismo-like clam (*Dosinia ponderosa*). You can live on the hinge muscle, which tastes like a tough scallop, with a drop of Mexi-pep.

Life revolves around the flow of the tides, an empirical under-standing of cycles comprehensible in days; at low tide you explore, skirting the sea cliffs, then return twelve hours later to collect dinner. For a third of a month, I lived off the land there. On nights of the full moon, only the barking of sea lions troubled my sleep.

21

CLOSE-UPS:
THE BLOND GRIZZLY

I inched my way up the steep slope, climbing over red boulders and outcrops of argillite slick with morning dew. The crisp autumn air, still in shadow, was cool, though I was beginning to sweat under the straps of my pack heavy with film equipment. I stopped to peel off one of my wool sweaters, which I tied by its sleeves around my waist. Far below, the white ribbon of Beartail Creek bisected the timbered bottom of the huge glacial valley. Above me a series of steep ledges and eroded cliffs climbed up toward the Piegan Range of Glacier National Park. The tops of the peaks were immaculately white in the morning sun, still dusted with the previous day's freezing rain.

I paused to catch my breath and pull off strands of mountain goat hair caught up in a serviceberry bush. These ledges are winter range for goats, who sometimes get ambushed by grizzlies when they venture too low into the thick brush. Seven springs before, not a hundred yards from here, I kicked a grizzly off a wolverine-fouled carcass of a freshly killed mountain goat.

My route was a ladderlike series of subalpine ledges leading to a mile-wide flat where grizzlies sometimes concentrated to dig for the corms and tubers of the spring beauty, mariposa, glacier, and other lilies during the last days of September and on into October. The tiny bulbs of these plants provided a nugget of starch late in the year, when bears were trying to lay on the last layer of fat for the approaching winter hibernation.

I crossed an outcrop covered by a thick pad of moss and climbed up toward a brushy ravine of alder and tall cow parsnip. The visibility was poor, and I stopped to listen and scent the air. Something faint drifted down the gulch—a musky, almost sweet, doggy odor.

I froze. The wind rustled the last yellow leaves of vine maple. Fragments of rock clattered. An animal moved upslope. I contoured along the ledge to get a better look. A small brown grizzly bear moved out of the brush and up toward the cliff. The bear was young, perhaps only a yearling, which was unusual since grizzlies here normally wean cubs as two-year-olds. He was clearly a subordinate animal, cowering against the rock, probably driven to these near vertical slopes by larger bears.

Late September and early October is a tense period for bears in the high country. The killing frosts of the previous weeks have softened the huckleberries, knocking the fruit off the bushes. Bears now move from their berry patches to compete for limited fall forage areas. Aggression by dominant animals toward smaller bears is most common during this time, and sometimes it gets transferred to humans.

The little griz just sat at the top of the talus fan pretending to eat serviceberry, turning his head slowly away in an act of displacement behavior—a response inappropriate to its stimulus. He pretended to feed not because he was hungry, but because he was nervous or uncomfortable. I approached the little bear, and when I was only thirty feet away he crawled even farther up into the rocks. He squatted like a sitting puppy who has been scolded. I was ashamed of myself for testing him. He turned his head to the side. I broke off and returned to my backpack. Sorry, little bear, I lost my head.

Climbing another hundred yards upslope to leave the little grizzly alone, I sat down on the edge of a cliff looking out over the immense valley. The bear seemed used to human beings; he didn't run away when he scented me. His familiarity with man during the formative years made this small bear vulnerable. Since the area is surrounded by well-used hiking trails, he was a prime candidate for trouble. Pushing him into a corner did not help.

I would have preferred not being in this racket of taking pictures of bears, though I needed the money—there would be a new mouth to feed. I had to get the close-up grizzly shots I did not get at the Grizzly Hilton. Though my business appeared harmless enough, there was plenty about it that troubled me.

The unmistakable lesson of my war was not to confuse means and ends. All the lofty ideology boiled down to killing strangers. Crimes of passion were different—I could understand bashing in the skull of the drunk driver who had run over your favorite dog. I was filming bears, bothering them in the short run, hoping my long-term plans would alleviate their plight. When the bear most needed to be left alone, I had to get in even closer to make the grizzlies' predicament more clear. The best compromise seemed to be to choose only those grizzlies who were already accustomed to the presence of humans, not unlikely in this place where only a month ago three hundred people a day hiked by on the Ptarmigan Trail, which runs along the base of the divide. Bears who modify their natural wariness by getting used to something foreign are called habituated. So I would be looking for particular animals, the bears some people considered the most dangerous, the man-habituated bear.

The crankiness of the grizzlies added to the danger. Bear behavior changes during the last half of September in this part of northern Montana, as I found out from watching bears every year at the Grizzly Hilton. When the berry crop begins to fail, the number of agonistic incidents—those characterized by hostility and aggression—shoots way up. Grizzlies get ornery with one another, with black bears, and, I think, with humans. It's hard to know if this was true at the Grizzly Hilton, because I was about the only person who visited and I stayed well out of the bears' way. But here it's different. Lots of hikers pass through late in the visitor season, so the likelihood of someone running into a bear with an ugly disposition increases. Half of all the grizzly-caused human deaths in Glacier National Park since 1967 and a third of all killings by bears had occurred in the last week of September.

I seem to be the only one who holds this opinion. When I mentioned my late-September apprehension to a world-class biologist, he said that the opposite should be true. Metabolically grizzlies should be fat enough to get a cellular signal to wind down toward denning time, making them lethargic and tolerant. Maybe the cantankerous grizzlies I kept running into were the still-hungry animals who did not get enough grub in September. Or maybe it was just too early for bears to be slowing down.

I climbed upward, stepping on hummocks of beargrass, sweating freely in the morning sunlight. There were goat beds in the dirt along the tops of cliff faces. A network of trenches around a marmot colony showed where, years ago, a grizzly tried to dig out the fat rodents, who by October had already gone under for the winter. Above me, the talus and sparse vegetation tapered out and leveled off. A few more struggling steps and I was at the top; before me there was a great flat stretching out to the sheer wall of the Piegan Range.

I lay back against my pack among the tufts of beargrass and the patches of spruce and fir separated by open bedrock ledges. Beyond the subalpine meadows were the white cliffs of the Continental Divide, still capped with shimmering hoarfrost. It was a great day to be alive. I sat contentedly on a slab of glacially striated metamorphic rock left stranded after the first advance of the Ice Age.

A decade or more before, when I began this bear business, I was too unfocused and angry to be capable of feeling complete. That day, I felt only the pale warm sun, its unique quality of light—which is about as Zen-like as I get, though the wild is conducive to Zen behavior. But I wasn't in Santa Monica. There are bears out here who make it dangerous. Not that Santa Monica doesn't have its own dangers—automobiles, smog, crime, and more deaths from infected carbuncles than grizzly attacks everywhere else. But grizzlies are dangerous in a primal way that cannot be controlled.

Within fifteen miles of where I was, grizzlies had killed five people in the previous two decades. The high count reflects the number of people who swarm over these magnificent alpine slopes each summer. As long as we insist on packing hordes of people into every mountain basin, there will be conflict and occasional fatalities. Up here, there is a well-used and easy trail into every sizable pocket of wilderness. The grizzlies have nowhere else to go.

The first of these fatalities occurred in August of 1967, when a young woman and her friend camped near one of the backcountry chalets. These chalets were built in the first few decades of this century, when the National Park Service was trying to sell the idea of land preservation by attracting large numbers of tourists, and the railroad was trying to capitalize on it. Glacier Park ended up with two of these historic chalets, which provide a good bed and serve up three hearty meals a day in the middle of the wild.

One of the chalets dumped its garbage in a gully, deliberately attracting and feeding grizzlies. Three hundred yards away there was a backcountry camping area, where the young couple bedded down for the night. In the early hours of the morning they were awakened by a grizzly. The bear mauled the man and dragged the screaming woman off into the night. She was abandoned alive but mortally wounded a hundred yards away. The search and rescue operation, which might have saved her life, was put off until daylight, and she died shortly after being found.

The second fatality occurred on September 23, 1976, five miles east of the same chalet, at the Many Glacier campground. Five coeds from the University of Montana were tent camping at the head of the trail they had intended to hike but had found "closed" because of bears. Mary Pat, one of the women in the tent and the victim, was a friend of a Missoula writer, Bill Kittredge, who later became a good friend of mine. I was also out on that particular day.

At seven in the morning a grizzly ripped into one of the tents, retreated for a few seconds, returned and dragged off the nearest camper, Mary Pat, who was in her sleeping bag, and killed her. Although two young subadult grizzlies were killed by the Park Service later that morning, Dr. Charles Jonkel, one of the members of the board of inquiry that investigated the incident, thinks the real culprit was an older male who was captured sometime later. No blame could be cast. The young women were well informed and maintained a clean camp. "They did everything right," said Dr. Richard Knight, leader of the Yellowstone Interagency Grizzly Bear Study Team.

Fifteen miles to the east, on the border between Glacier Park and the Blackfeet Reservation, two young people were killed by a five-year-old male grizzly on July 24, 1980. This attack occurred at the edge of the townsite of St. Mary's, and the bear who was responsible was on his way back from the town dump, where he had been feeding on a dead horse. I checked out the site a week after the fatal mauling with Ed Abbey, who was visiting from Tucson. The couple were sleeping on top of their tent—it was hot—beside a tiny creek running through a willow thicket. The narrow defile was a natural animal trail. By the time the bear noticed the couple in the early morning along the noisy creek, the grizzly and the people must have been only a few feet apart. I've seen the spot. A small cottonwood grows just across the little creek. The wall of brush all around seemed claustrophobic; the thought of finding ourselves in there at night with a bear threw a chill up our spines and we quickly withdrew. Marks on the terrain of the kill site and the nature of the young man's wounds made it clear he had fought courageously and desperately for both their lives. As I told Ed, the dead man had been the brother of a friend of mine who was himself mauled by a grizzly bear in Glacier Park. My mind won't accept this totally improbable course of events.

The most recent grizzly fatality in the same area took place the last week of September 1980, although no one knows the exact date because only a skull fragment and pieces of chewed femur were found. The bear had eaten everything else. The victim's self-winding Seiko had run down at 1:30 P.M. on September 28. A friend of mine found his remains in a willow bottom at the lower end of Elizabeth Lake on October 3, after spotting his torn-up camp from a helicopter. A piece of clothing had been found there as well as a bloody T-shirt farther into the willow thicket near the bones.

The victim had been a man in his thirties, an ex-pilot from Texas, who traveled alone. He was said to have mailed his mother a picture postcard just before his last trip. The card had a print of bears on it, and there was an arrow pointing to one with the inscription: "This is the bear who is going to eat me." The Texan was something more than just a man who liked to hike alone—an activity discouraged by park authorities. He was a spiritual man. I always refer to him as "the Christian" because of his habit of carrying several Bibles and pieces of religious literature in his pack. A small camera was found near the wreckage of his tent. The authorities developed the film. In the last four pictures—which I was told about but never saw—was a shot of his camp in the afternoon. Another picture, taken later in the day, shows his camp destroyed. The next-to-last picture was of his tent resurrected on the carnage. The last shot shows a bit of the wrecked camp and a brown blur on the hillside beyond.

It took either tremendous nerve or stupidity to pitch a tent where only hours or minutes before a bear had destroyed a camp. I imagine him calling on his faith, waiting for the grizzly at his tent, perhaps trying to escape into the water on the logjam, only to be caught and dragged back into the willow thicket. We will never know. But it sounds as if this bear was out to kill and eat a human being. No one had ever seen that happen before. They killed a bear, of course. It probably was the grizzly who got the Christian. It had a tag in its ear and a short history of man troubles.

But what if the real killer escaped? I see myself about to enter a mountain valley alive with the Legend of a Killer Grizzly: you could never feel the same out there again, knowing a man-killer shares the drainage with you. The valley would not get as many visitors and I would not sleep as well at night. And there might not be another place left in the country that felt as wild or formidable.

I was there in 1976 and 1980, on those deadly September days, and can testify to the general irritability and aggressive dispositions of bears. But on the twenty-third of September, 1976, I noticed something else. I smelled a urinous odor on the wind and the unmistakable fetor of something dead and decaying. I never located the source of these smells, nor did I find a bear except for an instant when I caught sight of a striking blond grizzly who immediately, and mysteriously, vanished.

I had a feeling something was wrong—nothing logical, but a sense so compelling I trusted it. Lucas and Lisa were with me. At first I was only mildly alarmed, but when I caught that particular odor again I nearly panicked.

I ran at Bud and Lisa, pushing them down the trail, shouting, "Get the hell out of here." They stared at me unmoving.

"Get the fuck out of here quick!" I screamed, so there was no mistaking my meaning.

We got out. Never before or since have I had such an acute sense of impending danger in grizzly country. That was the day Mary Pat was killed.

Predation by bears on humans is exceedingly rare. Predation by grizzlies on anything is mostly opportunistic. They tend to feed on dead things. Most talk of bears killing and eating people is steeped in murky fact, though there have been the rare exceptions. Most documented cases have occurred at night, when people are in or on a sleeping bag, sometimes in a tent. These events are uncommon, and the grizzly involved usually has prior experience with human food or garbage. I know of only two instances of likely grizzly bear predation on humans during daylight, and one of them was the Christian. But beyond these few facts and this primal dread, little can be said. Such behavior cannot simply be dismissed as "unnatural." It is the stuff of nightmares.

Except for the absence of those strange odors, this October day in the mountains was similar to the one on which Mary Pat was killed. From about mid-September on, grizzlies are more visible during daylight hours because of cooler weather and the need to pile on fat for the winter—the hyperphagia, or hunger, and polyuria drive bears to put away some twenty thousand calories a day, with consequent gain in weight and increased output of urine. My guess was that grizzlies did not switch to that slower metabolic rate preceding denning until sometime later in October.

I needed to be patient, to sit and watch, for days if necessary, to see if I could locate and identify all of the individual grizzlies that use this huge flat. I would try to pick out one who would tolerate my presence.

I tucked my backpack and the unwieldy tripod back under a spruce tree and climbed up a little knob for a better view. High on a distant ridge I picked up white shapes running—yearling mountain goats chasing each other in play. I glassed the finger meadows, where most of the bear food is, for sign of grizzlies. Even at three to five hundred yards, I could see bear diggings in two of the finger-shaped meadows along ledges of mossy argillite—prime spots for the corms and tubers of lilies and other plants.

I decided to wait before checking out the meadows on foot, which would only spread my scent about and risk my stumbling onto a bedded bear. I would study this fall range carefully for a day or so, locate the feeding areas, the probable bedding sites, and the travel corridors, before I wandered in on foot. The wind blew smack in my face, making my rocky knob a perfect observation point.

Before I set up on the little hilltop, I checked out my camera gear. On the off-chance I spotted a bear, I needed the equipment ready. Reaching in the backpack, I dug out the old Bolex. I ran a few feet of film, checked the gate, removed and cleaned the pressure plate. I inspected the gelatin filter for scratches and dirt. I pulled out a long telephoto, a 300-mm, and carefully cleaned the lens.

This ritual represented a shaky marriage between technological necessity and some vaguely romantic notion of connecting with nature. I probably would have preferred living a hundred and fifty years ago. But I have achieved a peace with the times by maintaining my modern tools with the same care I lavish on my knives and snowshoes, having arrived at this point with a history of warfare against machines acquired in Southeast Asia.

The war I faced back home from the jungle was one I could not turn off, especially when machines were used by greedy scumsuckers who raped and desecrated the last refuge for sanity on the planet. So I did what I could. Little things mostly, like pulling up survey stakes in roadless areas. Using a little discretion, I put into practice in the American West the guerilla warfare experience I spent my life gathering. I imagined myself a full-time saboteur defending wilderness and dreamed of blowing up the dams that tamed my favorite rivers. But talk was cheap. Down deep I lacked any instinct for taking up causes, caring only about wild places and resurrecting a few of the dead.

I mounted the long telephoto on the camera, then screwed the lens securely on the tripod mount. The entire assembly weighed, I would guess, less than forty-five pounds, and I could easily throw it up onto my shoulder and stalk bears with it. The lens mount was fragile but it would hold up on quarter-mile stalks if I was careful.

Leaving the camera, I climbed back up the hill and sat, looking out at the gently rolling slopes and flats of open meadow. I leaned back against the rock out of the breeze. The grass was dry and the flowers gone; even the last harebell had faded. It must have been about midday. Glassing the hillsides near the cliffs, I saw the goats had bedded. The hoarfrost hung steady above seven thousand feet. Looking off to the southwest, I could see a few tiny hanging glaciers, steel blue in shadow. I drifted back to the time of the gigantic short-faced bears, dire wolves, and their extinct prey, imagining this land little changed through the millennia. Everywhere I looked I saw ice, tundra, goats. The entire landscape was Pleistocene, the age of both *Ursus arctos horribilis* and ourselves, my ancestors' only time and its animals our only companions for forty thousand years.

I dozed off in the sunlight and dreamed of oceans, waking to the caws of Clark's nutcrackers. Before me was the white face of the Continental Divide, fossilized algae and ripple-marked sediments thrust thousands of feet up into the sky, the result of the collision of tectonic plates some 150 million years ago in a forgotten sea. I shook myself awake and grabbed my binoculars, catching movement across a narrow opening three hundred yards away. Two fat young grizzlies loped across the meadow. The smaller, a light-colored subadult of maybe two hundred pounds, broke into a run to catch up with its litter mate. They were probably a pair of three-year-olds who were skittish about crossing open ground on their way to somewhere else. The bears disappeared into a grove of subalpine fir, then popped out and ambled into another finger meadow. They turned upslope, avoiding a clump of mature spruce. When they reached the crest they ran along the ridge top until they finally dropped off into the far valley. All this happened in two or three minutes.

For these young bears to be making a hurried move in the middle of the day was normal. But they must have veered around the patch of tall trees to avoid a bedded grizzly. Three years ago, I had cut through the edge of that same thicket of spruce and fir forgetting that six hours before a big grizzly bear had lumbered in there. He growled at me from his day bed as I stumbled by thirty feet away.

I was reckless and I got off easy. I am less rash these days. Still, you can know only so much about grizzlies, and getting along with them involves a lot of luck. What works with one bear could offend another. Sometimes you just get a feeling about an individual bear and play a hunch. Mostly you accept a set of circumstances beyond your control and just ride out the consequences. The notion of dominion over nature never comes up.

I watched the meadows around the patch of tall timber for an hour, then decided to look for a place to sleep that night. There was no secure place to camp on the flat—grizzlies could be bedded anywhere. It would be better to drop down and find a ledge on the goat cliffs, a safe though uncomfortable berth.

I stepped off the lip of the flat and slid down the steep talus. Off to my right, above a tangle of vertical alder and dwarf aspen, was a heap of Buick-sized blocks of dark rock with a hint of lichen growing on the surface. The plant growth meant that these rocks had not rolled for a while and indicated relative stability on this near-vertical habitat. I selected an eight-foot angle between two slabs and plucked out the smaller boulders from the crevice, leaving a shallow, gravelike depression in which to lay my sleeping bag. It was an altogether miserable place to sleep.

The shadows had settled over the cliffs as I made my way back to my observation knob. Before I got halfway up, I saw a dark brown shape moving over the tundra on the distant hillside. A large grizzly clawed and tugged heavily at the clumps of sod and thin sheets of moss in the tiny meadow near a cluster of tall trees. He pulled with all his weight at a cobweb of roots and soil. Then he walked carefully around his digging and nosed the underside of the clods for dime-size bulbs of starch from the lilies.

It was too late to go after the big grizzly with the camera. Besides, I needed another couple of days of observing. The sun's rays reached down from dark cumulus clouds lying just above the rugged peaks. I sat watching the far hillside where the big bear fed in the long shadows cast by subalpine fir. Reluctantly I left the little knob, dropped down to my camera, and tied all the gear to trees after wrapping plastic garbage bags around it. Then I scrambled down the scree to my rocky bed.

Although not the most uncomfortable bed I have ever tried to sleep on, that pallet of argillite ranked right up there. I picked some of the sharper rocks from the crack between the big slabs and wedged myself in. I nodded off listening to the breeze blowing down the gully rattling mountain ash leaves. At about two o'clock the moon rose over the cliff and I was awake for good. I sleep lightly enough in grizzly country to wake up when I hear animals. By this late in the season, my otherwise rusty senses can differentiate between the noise elk or deer make and those of bear while I sleep. But nothing, not even a mountain goat, moved that night.

Stiff and sore, I rose at first light. I hurried to the knob and glassed the slopes. The big dark brown grizzly dug and grazed on the rocky hillside. A pair of ravens flapped by croaking. I walked off to the east a couple of hundred feet from where I could see into a draw filled with berry brush and stunted fir trees. I stopped to listen. Somewhere in the bottom a branch broke. The bushes parted and a medium-size honey-colored grizzly stepped out into the open. The bear had dark ears, ink-dipped forelegs, and an oval of black over the hump of its back—one of the most beautiful grizzlies I had ever seen.

The bear moved rapidly and did not notice me standing motionless in the morning shadows. I couldn't remember seeing this bear before, but it was somehow familiar. I followed it with my binoculars until it disappeared into the timber.

I spent another day thinking about what the bear was up to, and the next watching other grizzlies to find one I might approach to film. Since so many of these bears accommodate humans, I watched their behavior around passing hikers. But the blond bear was an enigma that kept gnawing at me; I thought I had seen her before.

A magpie dropped off a dead snag and glided by when it hit me: I had seen the blond grizzly on the day Mary Pat was killed in 1976. It had crossed the trail to the chalet and disappeared into the brush just above a tree where I was watching—with Lucas and Lisa—a flock of Cooper's hawks harass five magpies sitting on a dead snag. Neither Cooper's hawks nor magpies lived up there. Magpies live on the east side in the plains and bottoms; Cooper's hawks are even rarer. The chicken hawks were attacking the scavenging birds, who hopped and twisted evasively. I took the belligerency of the birds as a portent. I did not know the role the blond grizzly may have played in those events, but nearly everything I encountered that day seemed ominous.

Two years ago I saw a blond grizzly here again. It was early June and mating season, another tense time in grizzly country. I was out to film bears mating among fields of yellow glacier lilies and had Lucas and Eric—who later became my brother-in-law—with me. It was first light on a clear morning less than a mile from where I now watched. We were flopped down in our sleeping bags at the lip of a subalpine mesa. From my warm bag I watched mule deer feed, then heard the sound of running over my shoulder. I looked up and saw a brown subadult grizzly racing full tilt downhill with a honey-colored blond bear in pursuit ten yards behind. They were heading directly toward the bottom of the ravine where Eric still slept. I could hear the animals huffing and snorting as they ran down the slope. My movie camera was all set up next to me. I had a choice between filming some spectacular movie footage or waking Eric, who was about to get run over by a pair of grizzly bears. I chose to remove Eric from his bag. The bears swept by forty feet away without breaking stride and disappeared over the next rise.

I had no way of knowing if the bear I had seen that morning was the same blond grizzly. It was unlikely, since so much time had passed. Also, there were enough people up this way in the summertime to notice a bear who stuck out as unusually aggressive; that kind of grizzly would draw attention. Just the same, the idea of being out there with the blond grizzly—the bear who visits my dreams—made me nervous.

The rest of the morning I watched the large brown grizzly go about his business. He dug on the hillside and grazed on bits of grass or sedge, sometimes exploring anthills and sniffing dried pearly everlasting flowers. He pounced on a clod of turf as though capturing an escaping ground squirrel. Other times he looked reflective, and I felt I could spend all of my days watching bears. If I had a handful of lives, this would be a perfectly good way to live at least one of them. Bears had become more than bears and I glimpsed a transcendence.

A faint but brash jingling interrupted my meditations. The obnoxious clanking of metal bells drifted down from the trail above—hikers wearing "bear bells" as the Park Service recommended. You'd think the feds had stock in the manufacturing firm. Bear bells are an obscenity. Every disturbance of animals takes vital energy away from them and, in exceptionally lean years, human harassment of wildlife can make the difference between life and death. Bears and wildlife are risky propositions, as they should be.

On any given day in grizzly country, it is necessary to make noise only in rare situations like rounding a sharp bend on a trail thick with ripe huckleberries during prime feeding hours—time periods that last only seconds. Then the human voice suffices. Bells disrupt the life of virtually every animal who lives in grizzly country. The endless tinkle of bells can be heard for miles. Bears either run from the sound or ignore it, and it's possible grizzlies learn to be attracted to the sound, associating it with food. Human clamor is unnecessary. There are plenty of other respectful but safe ways to survive in grizzly country.

Government pamphlets are often filled with a lot of nonsense about what to do in bear country. One agency handout suggests climbing trees, making noise, not fornicating, not menstruating, not running away. The next leaflet says the opposite. Some of this conflicting advice results from the agency's worrying about covering itself legally and assuming its clientele are hicks. But much of the confusion is the honest product of unpredictability—the individuality of bears and the uniqueness of each situation.

My advice is to travel down the trail—or bushwhack—like an animal. Stop and listen every five minutes or so, more often in brushy country. Your senses are generally better than you might think, especially smell and hearing. By listening keenly and smelling, you have a better chance of seeing the grizzly before the grizzly is aware of you. And it's easier than it sounds. I prefer to move into the wind, contrary to the advice in government brochures. My intent is to see bears, not avoid them. I move into the wind and stop to listen every other minute or so depending on the acoustics of the habitat. Bears make a lot of noise when they're not wary of intrusion. Once you see what a bear is doing, you can avoid it or get out of its way. If you have to pass one on a ridge top, you will have time to retreat to a safe cliff face—as female grizzlies with young often do—or climb a tree. This is the only time I recommend climbing a tree.

If you feel you need airhorns or bear bells in the wilderness, please stay home. We are visitors to ecosystems of animals with no place else to live. I talk when bears are active on brushy trails around blind corners. Not too loud, but I talk. Sometimes I sing quietly, but never country and western.

Similarly, do not disturb grizzlies with human scent. Be aware of air currents or wind directions. The bears do not like the way we smell, and it does not do a grizzly any good to become too familiar with human scent. There are times, of course, when I allow my scent to blow before me into willow thickets, riparian downfalls, Krummholz, and other potential bedding sites when I can't otherwise avoid going around them.

I glassed the upper slope, finding the line marking the hiking trail that had been blasted out of the face of the cliffs. Contrasting against the gray siltite were an antlike string of hikers, clothed in Day-Glo orange—one of the reasons I sneak around using earth-colored or camouflaged gear. I could hear the din and clamor of the bells and the voices from a mile away.

Meanwhile, the big brown grizzly had disappeared. I should have been watching the bear's reaction instead of worrying about the irreverence of intruders. Around noon the sun popped out and I watched the snow line retreat to above 7,500 feet in three hours. The noisy hiking party of four departed and silence returned. I was nearly out of drinking water, so I got up and crept over to an intermittent creek where snowmelt filled the deeper pockets. At one point the creek widened into a tarn partially covered by a long, reedy grass whose name I did not know. The tarn was at its lowest level, and the green grass curled and floated on its surface like tapestry. I filled my canteen in a knee-deep pocket and sat back against a small subalpine fir to admire the grass. I watched the long blades slowly undulate in the tiny waves generated by the afternoon breeze. In late spring this little pond swarmed with Western toads. A pebble flipped into the water close to shore draws a gang of male *Bufo borealis*, who try to copulate with the ripples in a frenzy of splashing.

Behind me, deep in the timber, I heard a gray jay scolding. A twig snapped. I looked up to see the little yearling grizzly dart through the brush and stunted trees fifty feet away. He ran nearly flat out, disappearing into thicker timber. He had probably stumbled into my scent. This spot was too close to major animal routes, and I was interfering with their movements—especially grizzlies who, within such a small forage range, tended to be creatures of habit. I should not have been there.

I retreated to my hilltop outcrop. Scanning the far hills, I saw the big brown grizzly digging again. Grizzlies seem to average about a three-day feeding period when they forage here in the late spring and about a five- or six-day cycle in the fall before moving on to another place. Anyway, I expected the dark bear to hang around for a couple more days in the same area.

The sun set behind lavender clouds. I watched from the rimrock above the goat ledges. A high-pitched trumpeting, followed by a glottal cough, drifted up from the valley bottom—a bull elk bugling. The actual run had ended weeks before; this bull was blowing an empty challenge.

Again the piercing call cut across the dark mountains, the quintessential sound of a Rocky Mountain autumn. I have always loved this time of year up here. I could wander aimlessly for weeks just watching the leaves fall and the snow line drop during these bittersweet days preceding winter.

The evening turned cool and I dropped down to the stony crypt I called a bed. The high clouds signaled a change in the weather. I would watch for a ring around the moon. You can disregard rings around the moon down in the desert, but up here it usually means your good weather is about to end.

The next morning I crawled out of my sleeping bag under a cloudy sky. I never did see the moon. It would not be the best day for filming—too dark for my longer telephoto lenses, which are optically slow and require a lot of light. The dark brown grizzly fed on in the dim morning haze. I decided to take a shot at him anyway. I threw my pack on my back and the camera and tripod over my shoulder and began a broad circle into the wind to bring me to the big bear. I took my time. The wind was gentle, but steady, out of the southwest, blowing my scent away from the bear.

I felt a trickle of sweat run down my face. Lowering the heavy tripod-camera assembly to the ground, I stopped to catch my breath. The bear was still a couple of hundred yards away. I stashed the pack and stuffed extra film and accessories into a multitude of pockets. There was no need to hurry; I would only make mistakes. The grizzly would continue digging in the same small area for hours. The important thing was for him not to smell, hear, or see me. I needed to watch him undetected for a while to see how close I could afford to get.

I started the climb up a series of low sedges to the level on the hill at which the bear fed. The gentle slope was a mosaic of tundra with clumps of small subalpine fir. I used the trees as cover and moved quietly in the bear's direction. Creeping forward, freezing every thirty seconds to listen and test the wind, I stalked toward the bear for half an hour. I circled around a little grove of trees and saw the dark brown hindquarters less than fifty feet ahead. I froze in a mid-step crouch for nearly five minutes. The bear kept on feeding and digging at the soil. Fifty feet was a hell of a lot closer than I had intended to get. The animal did not seem to be aware of me—or at least he pretended to ignore me.

I used a strong gust of wind to cover the sound of my footsteps and started backpedaling. I made it back to another clump of trees, which included several tall, climbable ones beyond the reach of a grizzly. A determined grizzly can sometimes climb fifteen or more feet up a tree if aided by a few lower boughs and a surge of predatory adrenaline.

I moved into an opening and set down the movie camera. A bit shaky, I leveled the tripod head and exchanged the zoom lens

for a 300-mm telephoto. I focused the lens and guessed the expo-
sure at wide open. I continued watching the bear through the lens
but delayed turning on the camera until I got a gust of wind
sufficient to cover up the sound of the noisy Bolex.

The waiting went on for nearly an hour. The wind never
surged nor did the grizzly show me anything other than his big
brown ass. The film world wants close-ups of grizzly heads, not
their furry backsides. When the big animal finally turned I was
surprised by the amount of silver-tipped hair in his fresh, dark
brown winter coat.

Every so often the bear walked a few steps to a new feeding
area. For the most part, however, he remained stationary. Hours
passed. About midday, he abruptly left off his digging and tugging
of the earth, walked into a half-acre timber patch, and disappeared.

He had bedded and I hadn't shot a foot of film. I backed off
another hundred feet, sat down on the grass, and got ready to wait.
If the grizzly maintained the same pattern he would only bed a
couple of hours. I wasn't sure if he had noticed me yet, although I
have known bears to pretend to be oblivious, or maybe disdainful,
by turning their backs. I didn't know if giving me his backside was
the grizzly's habit of heading into the wind, or some other sort of
displacement behavior.

Two hours later I was stiff and cramped and the bear had yet
to reappear. The sun was trying to poke through the thin clouds.
Although I am far from the patient type, I was used to waiting,
which is the largest part of the bear-watching game. Despite my
restlessness and aches, waiting was a piece of cake. I could have sat
there forever, never feeling quite so alive as in the presence of a
great bear.

A beam of sunshine sliced the afternoon haze. I squinted into
the wind. I blinked, scarcely believing my eyes, as a backlit shadow
moved across the nearest meadow only sixty feet away. I hadn't seen
the grizzly walk up on me. This could be a monumental screwup.

I did not move an eyelid. He seemed to look at me. I remained
kneeling next to my tripod like a statue. The bear turned and
began to pull at the tundra. The wind blew in my face. I bent to the
Bolex, thinking the wind would muffle the grinding of the camera.
The sun was behind the bear, illuminating a halo of silver-tipped

hairs circumscribing a powerful silhouette. I ran a few feet of film. The grizzly turned his head, curling his lower lip and gnashing his teeth. He lowered and extended his head but did not move. Saliva flecked his mouth.

I tried running the camera again. This time the big bear leaped a few yards up the slope. He exhaled in a loud rush of air. Alarmed, I tried talking to the bear. "Hey, griz, I'm just passing through. . . ." No dice. He woofed again and turned directly toward me. His neck was extended, the hair on his hump was up, and he was gnashing his jaws.

Somehow—but with no amount of grace—I managed to shoulder the tripod, ready to get the hell out. I slowly backed away down the hillside. I reached the bottom and turned away, walking rapidly through the brush. I looked back one more time and saw the big brown grizzly standing his ground. Such a clever asshole I was. Once again, the bear gave me a break. That was a close one.

I made my way back through the trees and sparse ash and berry brush toward my rocky observation post. By the time I climbed to the top and glassed back toward the rolling ledges, the big bear had disappeared. Obviously, I had picked the wrong animal.

The behavior of the big griz was altogether consistent with an irritable dominant animal who was not about to give up any of his newly acquired late seasonal forage range. Apparently he had not had enough berries to feel any of that metabolic docility fat bears were supposed to feel before hibernation. His head and body positions indicated aggression; the slobber, stress. This bear was probably well accustomed to humans and that was why he chose to ignore me until the end rather than charge or bluff. He let me off easy. It was difficult to say what might have happened if I had insisted on hanging around. At the least, it would not have been safe. That sort of behavior was the prerogative of a big, probably male, grizzly during a dominant stage of his life.

I squatted, leaning my back against a rock, trying to regain my composure. I still hadn't gotten any useful footage of grizzlies, and I had yet to locate a bear who would let me hang around for even a few minutes. Off to the west, young mountain goats played in the setting sun. I focused the binoculars on their pure white winter coats and watched them leap and gallop in circles. Clouds gathered though the rain was holding off. I had better find a spot to pitch a tent tonight.

I returned to the rise and glassed the slopes until dusk. Just before dusk, I saw the blond grizzly skirt a line of trees and disappear into the distant basin.

Despite my past experience, I threw up my tent among the trees and crawled inside. This was the best campsite of several poor choices in terms of bear danger, but I was expecting freezing rain and snow. On the goat cliffs I would get into trouble with cold. This was right at the altitude and time of year where the mere discomfort of wet and cold could quickly grow hazardous.

Sleeping in grizzly country is a hell of a lot more dangerous than just walking around in it. On rare occasions grizzlies regard a sleeping human less as a formidable equal than as a subordinate source of irritation or even food. The trick, if there is any, seems to be in not letting bears approach too closely, if you cannot avoid them altogether.

When I have to camp where I probably should not, I stay up most of the night listening. Whenever a bear or an animal I cannot identify approaches, I make noise; I hoot or bang on my canteen cup. For grizzlies who persist on coming in, I keep a carefully prepared fire in a garbage bag ready to torch. I have had to light one once, and the only paper I had at that time was a *Newsweek*, which did not burn worth a shit.

I was still awake when the wind picked up and the first drops of heavy sleet slammed into the tent fly. Within a half hour it turned to snow and I was surrounded by a thick silence. I dozed off and when I awoke it was quiet. I slept, trusting my unconscious instincts to bring me around at the first animal sound.

The morning was dark. I unzipped the tent fly and stared out into a dense and gloomy fog. The three inches of fresh snow was already beginning to melt. I was running out of time. I had to get Lisa to a midwife by October and then drop down into Yellowstone a week later. I could use a paycheck. Baby would need new shoes, and I had yet to get the close-ups I needed to turn in the kinds of grizzly footage networks in New York imagined as everyday. The job and the responsibility I had been ignoring were beginning to hang over my head.

The blond grizzly might be my only chance that year, although I was more than apprehensive about the animal. This bear was too unpredictable and my bundle of feelings about that day back in 1976 too unresolved.

The fog was too thick for anything besides waiting—visibility was only about fifty feet. The white morning lingered. I crawled back into the tiny tent.

By early afternoon the snow melted rapidly, dripping off the spruce and fir trees, a staccato beat upon the tent. I ventured out. Far off to the southeast, the clouds broke and I saw a piece of distant cliff. The fog would soon dissipate and this cloud lying on the divide would lift. I dug out several wool sweaters and prepared to wait out the day.

Afternoon arrived and the visibility had increased to about a mile. Somewhere in the timber a Steller's jay tried to mimic a golden eagle. The clouds broke, allowing a sliver of sunlight to roll across my knob. Six hundred yards to the south three brown animals moved against the tundra. A silver-tipped grizzly sow and her darker yearlings walked out into one of the narrow meadows and began to nose about the grass and faded flowers. I watched from my lookout, knowing there was no way I could approach a female with young. Either the family would run away, or, if I blundered too close, the mother would charge.

The sow appeared tense and wary today and I saw little playfulness. She raised her head and scented the air. I wondered if the big brown boar was still around. After less than an hour and a half of feeding, the mother suddenly broke off and ran into the far drainage with the yearlings close behind.

I waited on the knob until last light. The clouds parted and I was treated to a fine and chilly sunset. Just at dusk, the blond grizzly, which I was pretty sure was female, stepped out of the trees a third of a mile east and made her way across the flat, stopping only once or twice to sniff at things.

One of the problems with these sitting, waiting days was that

I did not get enough exercise to put me to sleep at night. Instead, I lay back wide awake, staring out at the dark sky. A distant sound drifted down: the wing whistles and honking of Canada geese heading south. I wondered if it meant an early winter.

I drifted off, then dreamed again of a fearful white bear. I work out my fears in my dreams, a luxury I do not have while awake, when any fear or less than coldly objective assessment of grizzlies could translate into immediate misfortune.

My dreams of white bears—the most frequent type, at least during that year—are benign; the animal never harms me. This time I was threatened. My first child would be born in less than a month. My investment in the future had risen considerably, and I planned on hanging around. I was clinging to life a bit more tenaciously than usual.

Crowding in on a wilderness animal like the grizzly is a paradoxical undertaking that carries a special onus. The relationships of ancient hunting peoples with animals were contractual; there were mutual obligations based on principles of reciprocity. Animals were seen as earthly relatives living in spiritual configurations, not as soulless creatures who activated no moral relationship. The blond grizzly worried me. Though I sometimes consider my relationship with bears a reciprocal arrangement— like the one a Paleolithic hunter might have had with his prey— the contract has its liabilities. It was quite conceivable I could be mauled or killed by a grizzly. A few years ago, I had neither these dreams nor these concerns.

Morning was clear and cold. I bundled up and headed up the hill. The dark divide cliffs sparkled brilliantly. A layer of frost covered each blade of grass, which crunched underfoot. In the center of the largest of the finger meadows on the distant hill, the blond grizzly dug in the grass. Without hesitation I ran back, unwrapped my camera, threw my pack and tripod over my shoulder, and moved out through the icy brush. I tested the wind, then circled into it. This could be my last chance and, despite my misgivings about the blond bear, I had to give it my best shot.

I stalked into the wind, watching the bear dig. It looked to be almost three hundred pounds. Its head, relative to the big brown bear's of two days ago, looked small. This elegant animal was probably female. I crept toward her each time she lowered her head or turned away. At about a hundred fifty yards, I set up to film. She should not be able to hear the camera running at this distance. The lovely creature looked almost white as it tugged behind a dead log left over from the 1967 fire. I ran a little film with my longest lens on the mount. The beautiful grizzly gave no sign of alarm. Still, this was no ordinary bear. I did not push it.

The hours dragged into early afternoon. I stretched my back, weary from having bent over a movie camera for five hours, although I had shot less than five minutes of actual film. The bear still had not given a hint that she was aware of me, and I had not pushed closer than about 250 feet. The wind picked up. The grizzly seemed content to feed on in the same small meadow. This medium-size grizzly did not act like the skittish, honey-colored bear I had caught a glimpse of a few days before.

I decided to try to get closer. The frost had melted and the grass no longer crunched. I waited until the blond animal had her face in the dirt, then darted forward carrying the heavy tripod, using the dwarf trees for cover. I was two hundred feet away. Wrapping my extra wool sweaters around the camera to dampen the sound, I ran off ten feet of film. The bear walked from the log to the center of the small meadow. Abruptly she stopped, looked up, and sniffed the air. I did not move a hair. After a minute she turned and walked away through the trees. I waited five minutes, then followed. I inched through thin rows of fir trees separating the tiny patches of tundra. I took advantage of the steady head wind.

I stopped dead. Not seventy feet in front of me, the blond grizzly tugged at the soil. Again, this was too close to a bear I was not sure of. After what seemed a long time, the animal lowered its head and I slowly backtracked. My blunders were being repeated with increasing monotony. Sneaking up on a grizzly bear and ending up closer than I had intended was a miscalculation I normally made only once a year, not three times in three days.

I retreated to the edge of the trees about a hundred yards away and tried to think. So far the lovely critter looked like any other wild grizzly who had lived part of its life around humans. It showed some discomfort at the foreign sounds of my noisy camera; the bear had walked off a short distance when it might have caught my movement, but it did not run. Habituated animals will generally show you when they have had enough of your company by their mouthings and teeth gnashing. I decided to take my chances and moved in for some closer shots.

Approaching to about a hundred fifty feet, I ran off my next-to-last hundred-foot roll of film. The bear looked up once but tolerated my presence. I would be relieved when I ran out of film. Two and three-quarters more minutes at sound speed and I would be done for the year.

I dropped behind a tree and changed film. The blond grizzly fed and dug on. Remounting the camera on the tripod, I looked into the viewfinder and prepared to run off the last roll of film. The wind blew cold on the back of my neck. Damn, the wind had shifted. I watched as the bear jumped up and bolted away from me, running across the tundra and into the trees.

I watched every move, following the bear, at first with regret for having spooked it, then with a bit of concern as the animal veered off two hundred yards away and turned without breaking stride. My concern grew into alarm as the grizzly turned again and headed back in my direction. The honey-colored bear slowed to a lope, then walked stiffly and directly at me. I looked for a suitable tree, even though I knew it was too late. The bear lumbered toward me, stopped at sixty feet away, then bedded behind a small tree.

I was in a world of shit. Why the blond grizzly had pretended to bed behind a skinny little tree a stone's throw away was beyond me. The wind blew my scent right into the bear's face and she pretended not to notice. I moved out into the clearing so the bear could see me.

After lying down for about three minutes, the grizzly got up and walked straight for me. I did not know what to do, so I ran the camera. The bear arched her neck and smacked her lips. She ambled toward me. Forty feet. With head down she closed to twenty feet. I kept the camera running. Her nose and mouth filled the entire frame. The grizzly was twelve feet away, so close that the telephoto lens would not even focus on her, and she kept coming. I stepped back from the camera with my arms outstretched and spoke to the animal for the first time. The blond bear stopped, her mouth still moving. She stood only a few feet away.

Abruptly the great animal, more white than blond at that distance, turned her head to the side. She reached up and nibbled at red mountain ash berries, then slowly lowered her head to the ground. She began to dig. I grabbed the tripod and moved back ten feet. The bear clawed at the soil. I had thirty-five feet of film left that year, less than a minute, and I wanted to use it up. I decided to shoot it. Not too bright, but what the hell. I ran off a few feet of the film. The bear pretended not to notice. I ran some more. The blond grizzly turned her back, tugging at the turf as if nothing else mattered. I could see the muscles of her shoulder ripple. I could have touched them if I wanted. I kept at the camera. Twenty seconds of film left. I had never been so close to a grizzly bear in all my life.

The blond bear redirected her irritation and tore hell out of the tundra instead. I did not know how long it would be before the bear really got pissed. She pretended to feed. She picked up grass in her mouth and dropped it.

The blond grizzly was quartered away from me. I saw the darker fur underneath her silver-tipped guard hairs. Her fur coat was almost ready for the winter. The wind ruffled her lovely white pelt. I watched the ripples run along her side from ten feet away. I recorded all this on film. Thanks, griz.

Slowly I backed off. On my way out I stopped and paused for a minute. I turned back toward the grizzly, who was a hundred feet across the slope. I saluted the bear, militarylike. I did an about-face and left. Not too fast, but I did not linger either.

I glanced back over my shoulder a few times but did not stop until I was two hundred yards below and beyond the tangles of ash and alder. I breathed heavily. The sun shone against the hoarfrost of the frozen white cliffs, and I smelled the sweet fetor of huckleberry leaves rotting under the wind-stripped bushes. The grass creaked. I was as high as I get.

The blond bear still poked about the small meadow four hundred yards away. She seemed less disturbed than I was. When she was fifteen feet away and still coming, I think she intended to come all the way. I think she planned to nail me. She changed her mind that last minute. Maybe because I moved and talked—but maybe not.

22

LEGEND OF A
KILLER GRIZZLY

SUMMER (1984)

When I heard the news, I was working as a fire lookout on Scalplock Mountain in the southern part of Glacier National Park. The news trickled in, a little bit at a time, beginning on the first of August. A young Swiss woman camping in the Yellowstone backcountry had been killed by a bear. Killed and mostly eaten, the radio said. A huge area surrounding the site of the mauling had been closed off and a massive trapping operation and search for the killer bear were in progress.

The camp where the girl had been killed was just off the arm of the lake where I had seen the tame loons, and only a couple of hundred yards from the abandoned eagle nest.

"My God," I thought, "that's him!"

But no one knew. At first, park officials were saying they were not sure whether the killer was a grizzly or a black bear. By the end of the week the park reported that the tracks and teeth marks of a small bear, probably an immature grizzly, had been found.

Although shocked, I was not surprised that a human had been attacked by a bear at tame-loon lake. I had always thought the site was dangerous, and doubted that this impression was entirely subjective. I just had not put my finger on the combination of factors yet that made it unsafe.

I could see another such place five miles due east from my

lookout. For some reason grizzlies over there were unusually aggressive toward humans. Bears tended to charge you there, or
stand in the middle of the trail without budging. One man was
mauled there, another killed. I knew it was a hazardous spot and so
did the subdistrict ranger who investigated the mauling. The
horse-packer for the trail-clearing crew noticed it too. A short
cutoff trail led out of the creek below Scalplock and back over a
low pass to Highway 2. Above the trail was a dangerous place. The
bad spot was only an instinct, but we all trusted it.

Down in Yellowstone, any bear trapped in the area around
tame-loon camp would be suspected and killed by the authorities. I
was worried that they might get my favorite Yellowstone bear, the
Bitter Creek Grizzly, although, from what I had seen of his wary
reaction to human sign I considered him an unlikely candidate to
fall for a human trap. For the same reason, I doubted he had killed
the girl. But of course I did not know.

On top of Scalplock Mountain I listened to the radio and held
my breath.

Two weeks later they still had not caught any bears. For
grizzlies in Yellowstone, 1984 had been a strange year. Bears were
showing up all over the place. It was another lousy year for whitebark pine nuts—grizzlies wandered more widely and ran into
more people.

In early August a bear had mauled a boy sleeping in a tent at
Grant Village, a campground twenty-some miles to the southwest
of the abandoned eagle nest. South of there, another marauding
grizzly was raiding the backcountry. One expert wondered if these
incidents and the killing of the Swiss girl were related: was it
possible a single bear could be responsible?

Probably not, though you never know. The weather at the
time had been unusually tempestuous; there had been lots of
lightning and rain, perhaps agitating the bears—as some people
think may have happened in Glacier Park back in 1967, when two
young women were killed by two different grizzlies on the same
stormy night.

By October 1984, an official inquiry into the fatal mauling
had been conducted, and I was back in Yellowstone talking to
friends who were close to the sources of the various official reports

and unofficial rumors. The facts were that no bears had been captured and the killer had never been identified. Based on available evidence, the board of inquiry thought the woman's wounds had been inflicted by a single subadult grizzly, an animal two or three years of age. The biologist on the scene felt that the killer grizzly was a male who was accustomed to some human contact. A sow grizzly with two young and accompanied by a single subadult bear had been observed numerous times near a main hiking trail just a couple of miles to the east. There was speculation that the subadult might be the culprit.

Everyone who had visited the scene of the mauling seemed to agree that the tracks and bite marks found in the area belonged to a young grizzly. The only other item of agreement was that the woman had done nothing wrong; her camp had been immaculate. Beyond that, facts blurred and opinions diverged. It had been raining and tracks were hard to find in the forest duff of the camp. One support ranger complained that all the stomping around had obliterated any prints or other evidence left outside the small staked-off area where the woman was killed. He felt that the investigation had been poorly conducted.

There was more. My oldest Yellowstone friend—the man whose tracks I followed at Cinnabar Mountain years ago—had talked about "some weird things out there; things that didn't make the newspapers."

For example, a day or two after the body was found, another park employee spent the night in a patrol cabin located a few miles north of the old eagle's nest. Throughout the night a bear terrorized the cabin. "The stuff of nightmares," my friend said. Judging from the reports of claw marks left on the door and window covers of the cabin, this bear was no puny subadult.

My concern was that park officials, in a frenzied hunt to capture a suspect bear, would trap and kill the Bitter Creek Grizzly. I wanted that bear to be free and alive. Would I have felt less protective if I was certain that he was the killer? And how would I feel if the victim had been someone I knew and cared for? I thought about the Swiss woman, a person knowledgeable about the wilderness, someone I probably would have liked, a loner who had insisted on her right to solitude in defiance of the conventional tame wisdom of park bureaucrats, who tell us crowds are safer.

To get my tangled feelings sorted out, I knew I would have to drag myself back out there again. Alone.

In late September, 1980, a thirty-three-year-old Texas man disappeared at the foot of Elizabeth Lake in Glacier National Park. About six days later, his skeletal remains were found by my boss. During the course of the subsequent search and eventual destruction of the grizzly who probably, though not certainly, did the killing and eating, the acting superintendent of Glacier Park had remarked: "The last thing we want out there is the legend of a killer grizzly."

✻ October 1985 ✻

The bitter cold of the Yellowstone dawn felt more like December than October. I shouldered my backpack and began walking east toward the head of Bitter Creek, thinking, for whatever it was worth, that a killer grizzly at large was indeed what we had out here.

The route to tame-loon lake led up another sour-tasting creek, then climbed up out onto the ridges when the creek bottom filled up with details. I followed game trails all the way. Though everything looked the same as it had years ago, I felt I was stepping into uncharted country, with the smell of discovery blowing off the pines the way it had when I was a boy in the woods of Michigan.

I was grateful Yellowstone Park had shown some restraint in not killing any bears. In the past, when a human was fatally mauled by a grizzly, the usual bureaucratic response was retribution and vengeance. But since the death of the Swiss woman policy had hardened again. Any bear tasting human blood would be destroyed. Despite flexible "Guidelines for Determining Nuisance Bears," agencies kill any animal they consider dangerous. These decisions are based on the entirely unproven and debatable theory that a grizzly who kills or injures a human—especially if the bear has consumed human flesh—is likely to do so again. If that was true, the park might be sued. So Yellowstone no longer tolerates this risk, even though this hazard includes a sizable spectrum of the natural behavior of the grizzlies. These hazy boundaries between what is natural and what is debatable could result in the loss of big money in court. Better to play it safe. It is an unwritten law of wildlife management that any bear who kills a human must die. No one wants the Legend of a Killer Grizzly alive out there.

I climbed up the steep game trail and topped out on a rocky bluff overlooking an old forest-fire burn. Beyond the burn lay the lake and the abandoned eagle nest. My heart raced. My fatigue surprised me: I thought I was in better shape. For a moment I rested my chin on my chest. I jerked upright at the alarm cry of a shafted flicker. I stared off over an indifferent forest toward the lake and remembered that I was not in control out here.

A mild breeze drifted over my right shoulder, but I could detect no scent on it above the ambient smell of lodgepole. I wanted to rest for a few minutes. A dry sump lay next to a toppled block of pitchstone. I lay down in the shallow, grave-shaped depression and put my head on my pack. The deep azure October sky beyond the gently swaying pine boughs mesmerized me. I was weary far beyond the excuse of a ten-mile bushwhack.

I fell into a deep slumber and dreamed. A white bear walked across a pale surface. My toddler daughter crawled on hands and knees, following the grizzly. I imagined them mother and child but was still afraid for my little girl. All bears are dangerous.

The chill day roused me from sleep. It was midday and I had dozed less than an hour. The dream still gripped me, and I shuddered with the bottomless fear of losing my daughter. I sat up and tried to shake off the terrible apprehension.

I had known the fear of losing this child—the most important person in my life—to bears before, back in July. My daughter and I had flown to Michigan to visit my parents. We traveled alone; my marriage was shaky. My parents' home was on a lake in the north woodlands of the lower peninsula. We had taken our daily walk in the woods. My daughter was riding on my shoulders. A dirt track led through an open forest of beech and maple and then into a denser plantation of white pine. We crossed a deer trail. I put my daughter down to play in the sandy loam and checked out the game trail, following it out into the pines for twenty or thirty feet.

When I turned back she was gone. I conducted a frenzied search for a couple of minutes, then screamed her name: no answer. Child-size bracken fern obscured my vision. I knew she was gone. I tried following her tracks. I thought I saw the rear pad of a bear superimposed over her tiny shoe print. A black bear had carried her off. Another three-year-old girl had been carried off by a bear north of here when I was a boy of five. The bear had killed and disemboweled the child.

I lost the trail and felt the paralysis of hopeless panic creep down my limbs. Ferns rustled behind me. I turned. My daughter was standing ten feet off the track, nose-high in ferns. She was holding a fistful of green toothed leaflets.

"Look, Bap, strawberries."

Among the Kootenai, a dream of bears was a sign to hold a ceremony asking for immunity from bear attacks. Protection was granted by the bear himself. On the bluff of pitchstone and rhyolite, still numbed by sleep and troubled by my dream, I noted that I had neglected to hold such a rite.

I stood up and shouldered my pack, dropping down into the broken country. By midafternoon I had reached the hill overlooking the arm of the lake. The first place I looked was where the old eagle nest used to be. Not a sign remained of the abandoned nest. I glassed the area and lakeshore: a single shoveler scooted out of sight. There was no sign of my loons.

Cautiously I dropped down the open slope to fill my empty canteen. I squatted by the shore and submerged the plastic water bottle. The bubbles rose and I watched the tiny waves push a single yellow willow leaf along the beach. Abruptly I stood and looked along the shore beyond the leaf. On the coarse mud was a set of huge bear tracks.

Only the rear pads showed clearly, but I could tell by the crooked pattern it was the old Bitter Creek Griz. I felt a tightening in my lungs and then one of those crushing chest pains you imagine to be a coronary but that goes away when you laugh. "I'm too old for this stuff," I thought. I sat down on the bank and stared at the tracks.

The bear print was not even fresh; it had frozen and thawed several times since the last snow six days ago. I wondered where the Bitter Creek Griz was heading. It was too early to move up to a denning site. He still could be around. I looked back up the slope and searched for a scent in the breeze blowing out of the timber. The old bear was, like me, in the autumn of his life. I looked again at the skewed tracks of the grizzly's rear feet and felt another chill that shook me free of any last anthropomorphic threads tying me to him.

I had tried to understand my favorite Yellowstone grizzly by putting myself in his place—which is not a bad way to learn about animals. There were those rare days when I succeeded in living the life of other creatures and gained a new insight into myself. But today I had failed; the larger animal escaped me. His world seemed older and more compelling than my own. I sat apart on the lakeshore, separated from the magic that once connected me to the Bitter Creek Grizzly.

Finally I packed up for the trip out. I trudged along the arm of the lake. At the tip of the arm the line of bear tracks turned east away from the muddy shore. I turned west. One last time, I looked back at the sign of the huge grizzly whose crooked print etched in crusted mud quietly refuted three thousand years of human dominion.

23

GRIZZLY
POLITICS

Saving grizzly bears is unlike any other animal preservation effort; it is not the same as saving baby harp seals. Grizzly bear agencies and experts seem to hate one another, and organizations dedicated to preserving the griz undercut one another.

In a way, these problems with grizzlies started on a hot and stormy night in August 1967. By tragic coincidence, two young women were killed by two different grizzlies in Glacier National Park. It was widely believed, though never proven, that one of the killer bears had been feeding on garbage thrown into a ravine near Granite Park Chalet, only a couple of hundred yards from the site of one of the fatal maulings. This dump had been attracting grizzlies for years. The killing made the press, and the National Park Service received considerable attention and criticism.

This was not the first time a bear had killed a human in a national park; Yellowstone had two deaths before 1967. The first occurred in 1907, when a man poked a young grizzly with an umbrella after chasing it up a tree. The mother bear tore his chest out.

But by the late sixties things were different. We had tort laws, governments could be sued, and litigation became the sport of kings. Bears were big liabilities. Since most of its grizzlies fed at open-pit garbage dumps, Yellowstone Park administrators were understandably nervous. Everyone agreed the dumps should be closed; the question was how rapidly.

Beginning in 1959, two brothers, Frank and John Craighead, studied grizzlies in Yellowstone, compiling the most complete data ever assembled on their age-sex structure and population dynamics. The Craigheads believed that the dumps served the function of separating people from grizzlies, since Yellowstone's principal open-pit dump was located far in the backcountry. A rapid closing of the dumps, they believed, would force bears to disperse widely and enter campgrounds and nearby communities in search of garbage. They recommended phasing out the dumps over a ten-year period.

The Park Service at Yellowstone, guided by a 1963 policy statement that called for allowing nature to run its course with a minimum of human interference, disagreed. Yellowstone was under an executive order and wanted the dumps cleaned up in time for its centennial celebration in 1972. The dumps were closed abruptly, and the Craigheads terminated their research when the Park Service demanded that they sign a memorandum that they felt violated their academic and personal freedom.

As the Craigheads had predicted, grizzlies wandered into campgrounds, where they were killed by rangers or captured and shipped to zoos. Many more were killed outside the park when they wandered into communities or ran into poachers, hunters, and sheepherders. No one knows how many died, but the more reliable figures suggest 150 to 200 were killed or removed from the Yellowstone ecosystem between 1968 and 1973. These grizzlies were taken from a population later estimated by the National Academy of Science committee at 229 animals. By 1971, the number of grizzlies removed in a single year approached 50. If these figures were even close, no fancy degrees in wildlife biology are necessary to compute the trend: deaths greatly exceeded births and Yellowstone's bear population declined sharply.

Of course, by 1973 there was disagreement about nearly everything, and scientific arguments degenerated into the realm of professional squabbles, personal malice, and agency politics. To this day the active players keep their own data sheets. Any interpretation of this pivotal decade in the history of Yellowstone's grizzlies is based less on historical reality than gut feeling. The resulting polarization into camps supporting either the National Park Service or the Craigheads became the decade's major wildlife controversy.

These pogroms of the late sixties and early seventies might have taught us that there are no inviolate sanctuaries for animals like grizzlies, and that we cannot depend upon state and federal agencies to take care of our wildlife for us. Squabbling over numbers was the basis for emotional infighting, upon which the careers of a large number of biologists and bureaucrats depended. To these ranks we should add bear preservationists and lobbyists: the same enthusiasm and energy that had generated our interest in the first place was closely akin to that which had pushed grizzlies toward extinction in most other regions. So much for objectivity. We all had axes to grind, grants to submit, funds to raise, and clientele to satisfy.

At the heart of these sometimes petty arguments lay assumptions—usually unstated and often poorly perceived—that bore on issues far beyond the war for the grizzly. In the seventies the grizzly controversy was seen as just another management problem, to be solved by agency tinkering and adjusting. Wildlife management is as much a business as a science. It is rooted in concepts of Christian dominion and is still in the process of sorting out "good" from "bad" animals. The grizzly could accommodate our notion of what a stroll in the woods ought to be or go the way of the passenger pigeon. In the end, we wanted the bear to submit to the domestication we had demanded of the rest of the animals and join the barnyard that had become our bestiary.

The effort that resulted in listing grizzlies as threatened under the Endangered Species Act in 1975 has not done a great deal to help the bear. In 1975, there were only a handful of grizzly bear advocates in the world. Now they are coming out of the woodwork. Studying, managing, and saving the griz is a big business. There are now more bear biologists, bureaucrats, photographers, preservationists, and cinematographers than there are grizzly bears in the lower forty-eight. All are elbowing for space, trying to get a front-row seat around the arenas we once called wilderness.

With preservation organizations fighting more over political turf than for the bears, few actually represent the interests of the animals. No one speaks for the female grizzly and her cubs whose small home range happens to be within sight of the Yellowstone National Park loop road over which a million humans travel annually. She knows that the nutrition of her family is best served by ignoring people. Moving her home range would be exceedingly stressful, perhaps fatal, to the cubs. This was her mother's home range before her.

And this bear is dangerous and will defend her cubs against anything. The government will move her anyway, although they will admit that her "neutral" behavior is only natural. They would prefer a bear who fears people and runs away. As it is, a tourist trying to take a picture might get too close and be mauled or killed. Then, the agencies say, there would be bad publicity. The sow would have to be killed and her cubs moved or abandoned. Either way, the little bears would probably die. The media would spread the story around and grizzlies would lose public support. Someone—a manager or biologist—might lose his or her job. The government could be sued and there would be lots of trouble all around. So the grizzly family will have to go.

If grizzlies are to survive in the modern world, the bedrock assumption must be that these animals, grizzlies, have the right to live a bearish life. To proceed from this assumption will be costly. Bears will always be in the way of commercial, industrial, and economic development. Grizzlies will always be dangerous. It is within the range of the "natural behavior" of any grizzly to kill a human during his or her average life span. The combination of a grizzly's disposition on a particular day and the nature of its confrontation with any particular human is also probably unique. It would probably never happen again. Nonetheless, it is the unwritten law of grizzly bear management that any bear who kills a human must die. Otherwise the agencies involved could be sued.

What grizzlies need most for survival is protection from humans who kill them and sufficient habitat for all their needs: den sites, food, beds, and cover or sufficient area for security.

Dens are usually located in the more remote regions of grizzly ranges. The dens themselves are invariably dug into steep hillsides and are not much bigger than the bear is. Sometimes there is an elevated chamber to trap body heat. Grizzlies normally don't use old dens, logs, or caves, although there are always exceptions. In Yellowstone grizzlies like the north-northeast sides of steep slopes between eight thousand and nine thousand feet. As in other regions where bears den, the distribution of denning sites depends on prevailing wind direction and depth of snow.

The most important nutritional item on the grizzly's diet is protein from plants. The omnivore bear evolved from meat-eaters who digested mostly protein. Bears have longer intestines than other carnivores, and this allows them to digest vegetable material, although in a limited capacity. What grizzlies require most from plants is soluble nutrients and protein, available mostly before the plants flower—a time span of perhaps a few weeks in the life of a plant.

In Glacier and elsewhere west of the Continental Divide, the sugars of these berries provide grizzlies with most of their food energy. On the drier east side of the mountains and around Yellowstone, berries are not as abundant and bears derive most of their energy from green vegetation, especially grass and sedge. Some years in Yellowstone and in the Scapegoat Wilderness of Montana, whitebark pine nuts are an important food item.

Small mammals, carrion, and sometimes large ungulates are taken throughout grizzly country. Among insects, ants top the list, although high in Glacier National Park and in the Mission Mountains, when the army cutworm moths proliferate, you find bears up there. Some grizzlies feed on these insects, *Chlorizagrotis auriliarius*, after the bugs have aestivated high up in the mountains. They may also eat ladybugs or ladybird beetles. The preferred food of this region during the month of August is the ripening huckleberry crop.

Carbohydrates in corms, fruit, and things like vetch roots are also important and have a seasonality of their own. Late in the year up here, sugar from berries for fat takes priority in the diet. Collectively, the phenology of these plant foods dictates most of the movements of grizzlies.

For beds bears prefer heavy vegetation; a cool microsite is important. At higher elevations they sometimes bed in Krummholz stands or under alder in avalanche slides. In valley bottoms they use the densest woods or willow thickets. In forested valleys, grizzlies find thick timber under downfalls, near trees and running water.

Studies of bears and timber relationships show instrumented grizzlies among trees 90 percent of the time. But even in the timber, grizzlies remain close to the edge of the meadow or open area, 99 percent of the time within a kilometer. When they do use the open areas, bears don't often venture more than a hundred feet from the timber line: three-quarters of all the times bears were seen in meadows, they stayed within a hundred yards of the tree line.

The overriding habitat requirement of the grizzly bear is security from human beings. Cover is a relative term; darkness and remoteness are as sheltering as a forest.

The current campaign among grizzly bear managers is to "delist" the bear, to remove the limited protection of "threatened" status and get the goddamned bear out from under the Endangered Species Act. The ESA's restrictions are seen as a pain in the ass to tourism and economic progress, since they require enormous piles of paperwork every time an agency wants to do something.

None of the management plans propose simply to leave the bear alone.

"Wilderness" is what keeps conventional wildlife management from speaking up for grizzlies. There is no paycheck in wilderness, nothing to manage. Yet human intolerance keeps anything less than true wilderness a deadly battleground where grizzlies always lose and die. The bears could probably adapt to us but we have not given them the chance. We don't maintain a culture that allows us to live with another clever and predatory species. So for now, grizzlies must have wilderness.

And that is fortunate because humans need it too, since, cribbing from Thoreau: In wildness is the preservation of the world. In practical terms, this means tearing up roads and parking lots and dismantling buildings, and saying no to capitalism or socialism of any size or variety. Grizzlies need big, uncompromised wilderness with no trails, scenic flights, human conveniences, human management, or "improvement" of any kind. The wilderness has to be there for its own sake, and for the grizzly.

It will also be there for us in another sense, because there is nothing new to be learned from animals who are products of our own selecting—that would be only another stroll down a museum hallway of mirrors. Grizzlies are wilderness incarnate. If we are to succeed in saving grizzlies with all their wildness, we will not do it by changing the bears to meet our needs. For the first time in our relatively short history on this planet, we will have to be the ones to bend.

24

CHRISTMAS ON THE PIEDRAS NEGRAS

DECEMBER (LATE 1980S)

I stepped into the thin shade of a saguaro cactus and wiped the sweat from my forehead. The creosote desert fanned out before me like a shimmering ocean. To my right, a low line of andesite hills drifted south toward the afternoon sun, squinting through the high-cirrus Arizona sky. Far beyond, almost two camps away, the mottled peaks of Piedras Negras Range broke the monotonous gray-green bajada. They held the closest water, a dark tank of rainwater which, with luck, I would reach a couple of days before Christmas, six weeks after the last grizzly has denned a thousand miles to the north.

I shouldered the awkward backpack with three eight-pound desert canteens hanging at odd angles from the aluminum frame, and stumbled through the greasewood toward the southern horizon. I ignored the sound of a truck gearing down on the freeway several miles north, where an incredulous Greyhound driver had left me on a dead-end off-ramp. It would be ten days' walk before I crossed another road or saw another human being.

I trudged off for Mexico, fifty miles distant, walking over shallow sand washes lined with paloverde trees, clumps of bur sage, and low thickets of spiny Christmas cholla, decked out in December with tiny red buds. A pair of huge red mule ears stuck up from a patch of dry winter grass. The ears of the jackrabbit were translucent, backlit by the afternoon sun, a road map of blue veins. I gave the hare my best coyote bark and it bounced away through the creosote.

A dozen grizzly seasons had passed since Gage and I had started taking trips out here. The early ones were by jeep and pickup, driving in on the Devil's Highway, into this stark expanse of desert, and even driving it took several days to penetrate the interior of the range. Years later, at a time when truck camping seemed tame and I needed adventure, I decided to try to walk across this area alone. Since then, I had taken the trek every year, usually at Christmas, covering about 140 miles, gracing myself with ten or eleven days of precious solitude, an indulgence, but one without whose perspective I would fear myself lost.

The Piedras Negras made Tucson look like a rain forest. Only three inches of rain fell there annually. Broad creosote playas stretched between northwest-trending granitic mountain ranges, great facets of naked rock thrusting two thousand feet out of the desert floor. I had to cross four of them on my eastward route. All the big ranges were single chains of mountains except the massive Piedras Negras, whose interior was sculpted into canyons and valleys emptying out on the bajada, themselves dotted with low volcanic hills—a harshly lit lunar landscape.

The problem out here is water: there is not much of it and you have to know where it is. Most of the water is in tenajas, water-holding rock basins drilled into shaded canyons by ancient torrential summer rains, whose location and spacing, sometimes thirty or more miles apart, would determine my route and the amount of water I would have to carry.

No one except a few prospectors and bands of Indians had ever lived here. Part of the region has the mixed blessing of having been a military bombing range—mixed because, despite the litter of 50 caliber linkage and the drone of aircraft on days when they fly, the military has precluded other human activity, such as mining or livestock grazing, from taking place here.

This desert has a bad reputation; summer temperatures have risen as high as 134 degrees. It is one of the most formidable regions on the continent and its sands have claimed more than a few lives. Yet people have traveled these arid mountains and playas for centuries. Ancient Yuman Indians wandered through, carrying their priceless water in fire-hardened clay ollas. A thousand years ago, the Hohokam trekked south from their Gila River homes along this route, down to the Gulf of California. They returned staggering under loads of glycymeris and cardium shells, which they carved into earrings, bracelets, and, beginning a couple of hundred years before the Hohokam disappeared forever, effigies of frogs.

Later, the Spanish came, the first of a long line of mostly wretched white visitors to the area. Melchior Dias crossed, going west to California in 1540, dying of an old wound in Caborca a few weeks after his return trip. Other Spaniards and Mexicans used his route, leaving their dead buried in shallow graves that still line the fearsome old trail from Sonoita to Yuma known as the Devil's Highway.

The Americans came, driven by dreams of California gold, beginning in 1849. Hurriedly organized and poorly equipped, they hadn't a clue as to what was waiting for them in the desert. They might have been on Mars. Nobody knows how many died here, but some put it in the thousands. Another surge of gold seekers, mostly from Mexico, swept through five years later, and again the loss of life was very high.

During all my walks out here I have never seen a soul, nothing but a few thin bootprints of illegal aliens heading north. There was nothing out here but rocks and plants, birds and rabbits, snakes and lizards, sheep and coyotes, and an occasional mountain lion living off a rare deer or javalina.

I waited in the darkness of early evening for an hour, then watched through the branches of an ironwood tree as the nearly full moon rose out of the eastern mountains. I dug into my pack and pulled out the plastic bag containing my food for the eleven-day walk: it was not much, a small bag of granola that would be eaten halfway across the Piedras Negras, protein powder mixed with powdered milk, and about five pieces of jerked venison stripped from a warm roadkilled Montana mule deer.

Straining under the heavy backpack, I continued southward, looking for a wash in which to camp. I avoided the occasional cholla cactus and trusted my feet to find the way.

The moon was high in the eastern sky as I reached the dark shadow of a large wash. Exhausted, I threw my sleeping bag under a huge ironwood tree and kindled a small fire into which I stared until I fell asleep.

I awoke with the sun shining on the top of the ironwood tree. Bushtits flitted in the parasitic mistletoe. I packed up and climbed out of the wash onto the alluvial bench. To the south, the jagged peaks loomed in the morning sky. The first water, a place called Stag Tank, lay near the northern edge of those mountains, about ten miles distant.

The sun passed its zenith and began its descent into the west. The heat of the midwinter day felt good on my aching muscles. I had reached a reef of rock apart from the mountains. Stag Tank was only a couple of miles away. I stashed my pack and walked up into the canyon to the tank. Overhead, a huge, dark bird disappeared beyond the ridge just as I brought my field glasses on it. I could have sworn it was a golden eagle, though I had never seen one here. My shoulders and back felt much better without the pack, but my feet were still sore. I took a handful of aspirin and walked on. The aches and pains were part of the trip.

Stag Tank was covered by a green algae slime coated with a carpet of dead moths, bees, and feathers. Still, the water was sweet. I swept the surface free of slime and bugs and filled my canteens with cool water and squirming larva, more protein for the trip. One should not complain about the quality of water out here. You take what you can get. A man called Pompelly, who traveled this country around the turn of the century, once griped about the water at Tule Well, which he had found offensive and brackish. Later, he ran into a friend who had been over the same route.

"How did you like the water at Tule Well?" the friend asked.

"Not much," Pompelly answered.

"Naturally," the friend said, "for we found and left a man in it two years ago."

I filled the last of my canteens with Stag Tank water and returned down the canyon to my pack. I wanted to keep moving; it was about twenty miles to the next water hole. My route across these basins and ranges follows no jeep trails but crosses valleys and passes on faint game trails no human has set foot on for centuries. Each year, I strike out on a different course. If I break a leg, I will be stuck. I have a signal mirror with which I might flash a passing aircraft, though it could be weeks before one flew by close enough to signal. I seldom tell anyone about my intended routes because I do not care to be rescued.

The day turned to evening. The crimson glow outlined another massive mountain range far to the west. I watched the shadows fade and waited for the moon. A cool breeze drifted across the playa, slightly chilling me. I dug a down jacket out of my backpack and put it on over my sweaty T-shirt. The down jacket emitted a trace odor of spruce and pine smoke, a campfire stoked during a snowstorm near a grizzly bear den in Yellowstone six weeks earlier. I sat back and listened to the wind blowing out of Mexico. I heard the background ringing of my own ears; outside, the silence was complete, broken finally by the cry of a distant coyote.

Five hours later, the moon had climbed up almost overhead, and I was looking for a place to make camp for the night. My body hurt in a dozen different spots; I was soaked with sweat and weary beyond caring. I was plodding along a shell trail followed by the Hohokam hundreds of years ago on their return from the Sea of Cortés; in the moonlight I could see white pieces of shell on the ground. There were also dark fragments of pottery the size of my hand, and I bent down, feeling potshards.

I arrived at a huge wash and found a spot to camp for the night. I threw down my pack in the middle of the wash, which, in the pale moon glow, looked like a beach on the ocean. I pulled off a handful of dried weeds and thorny twigs and started a small fire. The tiny flames crawled up the branches, illuminating the dark side of an ironwood tree from which dead branches hung. I went into the thicket of ironwood, gathering wood for the fire. A sting poked the back of my calf, and I moved away from what I imagined to be a cholla cactus. I dragged the wood over to the fire and stoked up the flames to see. I took the hemostats from the medical pocket of my pack and rolled up my pant leg, looking for cactus spines. I pulled a sliver from my calf, a curved, tapered thing less than an inch long. I took off the small flashlight I always string about my neck after dark and shone the light on my calf. There were two oozy red marks. I looked at the tapered sliver I was holding in my hand—it was a small fang. I had backed into a rattlesnake, probably a Sonoran sidewinder. Funny, I had not heard or seen a thing.

This could be serious. For the first time I did not have a snakebite kit with me. I had left it behind, figuring winter would be too cold for snakes. Now it was a dozen miles to the nearest water and maybe sixty to the nearest human. No one knew where I was. I had six quarts of water. In the flicker of a second my brain computed the odds: "You're going to die, idiot."

I lay on the sand next to the fire thinking about what I should do. Should I tie a constricting band around my leg? Should I try to cool the bite with a water-soaked rag?

Then it was dark. No moon. The fire had burned to white ash. I knew I was dead. Slowly I moved my arms and touched my face with my fingers. Everything seemed to be there. I grabbed the small flashlight and turned the light on the back of my calf, which I was sure would be black, bloated, and necrotic. The two puncture wounds were discolored and slightly swollen, but the leg was of normal size. So then I fell asleep—and survived. The next time I get nailed by a rattlesnake I will take two aspirin and a six-hour nap.

I threw wood on the fire and tried to reconstruct what happened. I must have backed into the rattlesnake in the pile of branches under the ironwood tree. Since it had been winter, although a mild winter, the snake would have been too sluggish to rattle a warning. My luck was that the rattler had not ejected venom. I know strikes without venom happen not infrequently, though I do not know why. Maybe the snake had just fed.

The sky lightened, and a band of sunrise hit the eastern ridges. I checked my calf one more time: a small but nasty-looking pair of puncture wounds, which should heal into a memorable scar. I heated a canteen cup of water on a bed of ironwood coals and dumped in a dirty-looking mixture of protein powder and dry milk, which, when warmed, was quite tasty. Thus fueled, I crammed my gear into the big pack, took a swig of water, and stepped out of the wash onto a bench of volcanic boulders and desert pavement, almost immediately picking up the ancient shell trail.

After a quarter of a mile, I came to a pile of dark potsherds. I picked up a couple of pieces of rim and fit them together; it appeared that the large part of a big olla was there in a heap. I was tempted to pick up the pot and stash it in my pack, carrying it out where I could have the fun of piecing it all back together. I did that once, and a year later carried the same pot back into these mountains and returned it. I never should have removed it. These artifacts are part of the landscape. Better to treat the dead and their leavings with reverence—to remind us that we are not the first, nor will we be the last, to pass that way. The shards rang like bells as I dropped them back onto the desert floor. I headed up the long canyon.

The wash pinched out between two fifteen-hundred-foot ridges, and I found it easier to continue walking on the canyon bottom. There was not much to see, but I would not have to struggle through all the side gullies. About midmorning, I climbed out onto the bedrock and crossed a small divide. At the pass was a boulder with the inscription, "John Moore 1909." I had run into the name John Moore more than once out here, etched on boulders in widely scattered areas of the Piedras Negras, usually where there was a pleasant view of the surrounding country. I wondered who John Moore was and what he was doing out here. One of my several grade schools was named John Moore. But whoever had run through these hills eighty years ago was crazy. This place not only gets up to 130 degrees in the summer but, I hear, is teeming with biting insects. The John Moore whose name I knew was a respected lumberjack who hacked down the last of the virgin white pines of Michigan.

I made my way up the ancient trail, which led toward the next water hole. On another large boulder, I came on it again; "John Moore 1912." At least he had made it a few more years. An air force jet screamed overhead. This was the day before Christmas, and I thought that the flyboys would take it off. I came to more markings on the rocks along the old Indian trail, this time petroglyphs—rock etchings of motifs and symbols, difficult to decipher, not the usual deer and circles.

A thin line of dampness marked a trickle of water seeping out of the lower tank. It flowed down a rock face and into a shallow basin, around which bees buzzed. I climbed up to the larger tanks, bigger rock basins that dry up only after six months of drought. Father Kino, the eighteenth-century Spanish missionary, had watered here. I filled my canteens and glassed along the shaded ledges for bedded sheep: nothing. Reading the ovoids of dung, I saw that desert bighorn must have frequented these tanks within the past week. Gage once saw a huge bighorn ram here. He had been sitting on a ridge top reading Kazantzakis when he heard rocks clattering on the slope above him. He looked up and saw a magnificent ram with a full curl swing down the ridge and pass down the slope below him. I lingered but a few minutes, then turned back down the trail lined with the petroglyphs.

The temperature rose into the seventies. I hiked across the soft sands of a small wash and saw the imprints of sandals leading to the shade of a palo verde tree. A broken plastic milk container lay on the sand, the leaving of an illegal refugee who wandered up from the border south of here. I hope he made it. A few summers before, the border patrol pulled five bodies off the playa I had just crossed, leaving six more they could not find. In 1980, just a few miles east of where I would end my walk, thirteen Salvadoran refugees were left to die by their Mexican guides in the heat of August with no water. The dead had been eating dirt. One man left tracks that looked as though he had died swimming in the sand. Another had the spines of a cactus in his mouth. Two were on their bellies, their faces flattened against open Bibles. Two women died on their backs, arms outstretched and hands touching, dry eyes staring at the sky.

I went on crossing the benches and flats just above the narrow, rocky wash of the valley. Tiny hoofprints dotted the desert floor, the blunted cloven tracks of javalina. A cottontail rabbit burst from a clump of brittlebush.

The short valley joined another and swept out eastward in a broad, sandy wash. I followed it out toward the playa, stumbling along on battered feet lugging a full load of water in the three gallon canteens. After twenty minutes of walking the soft sands, I rounded a corner and saw a number of scraggly bushes with dull gray leaves: smoke trees. This large unnamed wash, my favorite, rolled out of the Piedras Negras Mountains like a sand river. Large paloverde and ironwood trees stood like sentinels in this savanna-land of rock and sand. I found a spine of granite running out from a darker hill of diorite. In the wash, near a low pass in the ridge, I made my camp. It was Christmas Eve and I wanted to spend it in a good place.

The waning moon would not rise until two or three hours after dark, so I did not plan on doing any hiking. Instead, I would poke at a small fire. Christmas was never a very good time for me. Before Vietnam, countless little crises would peak at the holidays. The one Christmas I had seen in Nam was spent tying up Dinh Hun's shattered femur in a traction splint. The previous Christmas, Lucas's roommate had accidentally killed herself with an overdose of pills. To me it was a dangerous time. I was feeling low that day, probably from hunger. My lack of food was no accident. Grub was heavy and I did not come out here to eat.

I chewed my last piece of jerky for Christmas Eve dinner. I would begin my fast on Christmas. The fire warded off the chill of the winter night. I tossed another log of ironwood on the pile of orange casts. I tried to bring a little Christmas cheer to the fireside with a few bars of "White Christmas," which always reminded me of my dad's brother, who died toward the close of World War II. I left off the song. Off in the eastern playa a coyote barked. I returned his cry with my best wolf howl, which carried out into the desert. The silence crept back. "I wish you a fat jackrabbit for Christmas dinner, coyote." The exchange warmed me, and I huddled by the fire until I began to nod off.

I lay in the sleeping bag in the gray light of morning warming my fingers over the ash of the past night's fire. Somewhere on the ridge a rock clattered and rolled down toward my wash. The sound startled me. I reached for my field glasses and scanned the ridge for movement. The slope was open; only a few bursera trees dotted the hillside. Still, I saw nothing. Suddenly I heard more clattering and caught movement coming over the saddle. I saw what looked like a ghostly gray grizzly coming over the dusty granite toward me. I brought the binoculars up and looked at the animal's head. It had a curl of corrugated horn. The bear was a sheep, a ram with a full curl. The sheep did not see me until I dropped the glasses. The ram stopped and looked at me from sixty feet. As sunlight capped the tops of the highest peaks, the bighorn turned and ambled back across the crest of the ridge.

I scrambled up to the ridge for a look, but the ram had disappeared. My day was off to a good start. I packed up, anxious to get started while it was still cool. Far down the wash I could see a huge rock standing by itself, like an iceberg on a green sea, drowning in its own detritus. The rock was my landmark. I stumbled toward it down the wash, treading lightly on my bruised feet. I crossed a line of dimpled depressions and stopped to examine the tracks of Sonoran pronghorn antelope—thinner, more elongated and spread at the tip than either bighorn or deer. I followed the tracks out of the wash onto a patch of cryptogam, a primitive soil created by algae and lichen.

Entering another playa, I turned southward past an arc of basaltic mountains. Beyond, three small volcanic hills, pyramids of basalt, sat alone out on the playa. The center peak, a couple of miles away, was my destination. The afternoon sun was warm, and I headed for a wash at the foot of the curve of hills to find shade. No hurry, I had two full days. The closest shade lay in the shadow of a giant paloverde under which I dumped my pack. An Allen's hummingbird buzzed a knot of mistletoe. I lay back on the sand waiting for the bird to return. I fell asleep.

I dreamed of a wild valley, the swelter of the Rocky Mountain sun and the moon of ripe berries. My daughter and I are crawling along on all fours through the huckleberry brush. I nuzzle her side protectively because there are other grizzly bears around. My little girl reaches with her mouth and strips the blueberries from a branch overhead. I scent the air and snort, shaking my head at the smell of another bear on the mountain hillside.

The shadow of the paloverde tree drifted past my face, and I awoke to the glare of the late afternoon sun. The dream haunted me.

The sky faded crimson, then darkened, and a cool breeze blew from the southwest. A lizard that looked like a diminutive chuckwalla darted under an anvil of black rock near a dead mesquite where I was making camp. I started a fire with wood from the dead mesquite, a remnant of some earlier wetter period. From far out on the playa came the faint but rapid *chewk-chawk* of an elf owl leaving his hole in a saguaro cactus for an evening hunt. I wished him success, thinking that on such a winter night only a rare kangaroo rat would be out.

My stomach growled. The far-seeing lucidity sometimes achieved after a couple of days of fasting had not arrived yet. My mind reached, then fell back upon the mundane. I poked at the fire with a stick and fought off visions of venison. The fire flickered and snapped, throwing sparks into the night. Mesquite generates a hotter fire than ironwood, with less light because you cannot get as close to it. Of course, mesquite would be the best wood to cook over, if I had anything to cook. For a second, I thought of the fat lizard and my mouth watered. I once cooked one on a desert island in the Sea of Cortés, where I lived alone for ten days, mostly on a diet of clams and mussels. Actually it was a black chuckwalla, an ugly-looking critter whose tail meat was stringy and light and probably not all that bad in retrospect. The worst part was the cooking. Since I had no grill, I had laid the lizard uncleaned over the hot coals and, when he ripped open like a ruptured sausage, turned him on his back to finish.

A surge of loneliness ran up my middle, and I thought of Lisa and our little girl. Overhead, the distant roar of a jet swept west, the first aircraft on this perfectly silent Christmas day. They were always up there somewhere, even in the wildest pocket of desert or grizzly country, reminding me that we are all in this together.

The sounds of the military jet faded into the night, leaving me to stare into the tiny fire firmly rooted to earth, with no desire to travel supersonically or explore space. My needs were met here in the sands of the wash, drinking cool rainwater from the tenaja, warmed and comforted by a fire of fragrant mesquite. How I loved this place. Suddenly I was exhausted as the fullness of the Christmas day overwhelmed me. I crawled into the sleeping bag with not a thought left in my head.

The moon rose beyond the branches of the paloverde into the perfectly clear desert sky and I was awake. Winter had begun and I could not spend all of it camping out. The man living with grace in the wilderness was an utter fuckup at home. I once imagined that the acquired ease with which I lived my life in the deserts and

mountains might be transferred holistically to more domestic corners of my life. Apparently not. "He was all right before Vietnam
but came back a drinker," my mother once explained. Away from
grizzlies and wild places the Nam vet must tiptoe through life.
Winter is the most dangerous time. Last winter I almost blew it
again.

                                   ✝ ✝ ✝

She said she would plunk down the last two hundred bucks in the
bank account on a lawyer's desk tomorrow. I could see the kids on
the weekends. Then I was out of the house and running, down the
Baja Peninsula, pausing only once north of Loreto to pick a
chalcedony spearpoint out of the surf, nonstop to the ferry to
Puerto Vallarta. Mounted inside the ferry were seven Maskera el
Tigre carved long ago of balsam wood by Tarascan and Mixetec
Indians, each jaguar face so individual and powerful that the
carvers must have known the fierce tigers intimately. Their presence so affected me I had to step outside on the deck and stare at the
ocean for fifteen minutes, then go upstairs to the bar and slam
down four Herradura tequilas while I watched a fin whale sound
twice in the setting sun. The next day I saw ibis and crested herons
off the coast of Colima and trogons I had never seen before in the
Sierra Ixtlan del Rio. Still blasting south, now off the leatherback
turtle beaches of Michoacán, fleeing another poorly executed season of winter.

                                   ✝ ✝ ✝

I awoke to a cloudless desert sky, kicked myself free of the sleeping
bag, and stepped onto the cool sand. From down the wash, around
a corner of paloverde, the clucking of a covey of Gambel's quail
floated up into the morning stillness. I pulled on my boots, stashed
my sleeping gear in the wash, shouldered the pack, and started
toward the three volcanic peaks.
    Full of energy, I walked rapidly to the foot of the central peak.
Bucket-size blocks of carbonate-stained basalt teetered and rolled
as I inched my way up the jumble of rocks and stepped over a black
ledge onto the summit. In three directions, the land fell away to the
gray expanse of playa. To the west, the long arc of mixed volcanics

rose five hundred feet into the clear sky, then curved and tapered to the north and south like the black horns of an extinct bison.

Standing on the crest of the ridge, I faced the great crescent of stone. On the western end of the ridge was a pile of boulders about five feet tall, obviously man-constructed. I walked along the ridge to the cairn, feeling the morning sun on my back. At my feet, in the coarse ash of the ridge top, was an alignment of small rocks outlining two adjacent circles on a north-south axis like a figure eight.

I stood motionless, facing into the gentle wind for minutes, then lowered my pack, stepped over to the cairn, and dropped to my knees. I picked at several small angular pieces of basalt at the eastern base of the cairn and finally loosened a large keystone, which I pulled free from the tower of black rocks. Inside the pile of rock was a recess, a cavity I quickly checked for sleeping rattlesnakes. I reached into the chamber and pulled out a coyote skull, two pieces of green mineralized rock, a raven feather, two arrowheads, a wad of lizard-chewed paper, a candle, another skull (maybe a skunk), fragments of pottery, and pieces of white shell. I picked up and felt each object, then laid them out in the sun.

As far as the eye could see were chunks of empty land, great valleys, ranges, desert hills, fossilized sand dunes, and crumbled flows of black lava. Nothing moved save the faint wind. Far below, along the course of the wash, came the weak warble of a phainopepla. I sorted through the pack, finding two small bundles of coarse black hair, a handful of wilted desert marigolds, and the bleached, flat-nosed skull of a large bighorn sheep, the horny protuberances chewed down to short nubs, the horn sheaths missing. I laid everything out together and sat crosslegged next to the circles of stone.

The cairn was my memorial, a monument I had built to my dead, my fallen comrades, to those I had loved and lost, to Gage and others who did not make it.

One would think that war would have toughened me to loss, but it somehow exposed raw nerve ends. I handle death poorly. Each winter I have to walk out here and leave it behind in that pile of rocks.

I rested my hand on the weathered sheep skull and squinted

out across the playa. I talked to my old friends, and to Gage, who knew this place. What would have saved you? A phone call from an old friend that morning before all hope was lost, on that last day when you bought the shells? You conned me, but I will not forget I didn't make that call. Or a wife, a daughter, children who tie us to their needs? What about this empty desert you loved, or a chance of glimpsing a wild grizzly bear?

The sun climbed high in the southern sky and three ravens flapped and glided along the arc of rock. I kept my vigil over the pieces of rock and bone, mourning my dead. I blinked back a well of tears. The ravens croaked. I settled back into the present feeling exiled, as with Vietnam, from those who went before me. My list of bad men was long. I wanted to fill my pockets with those black rocks and never leave the earth.

I turned away from the pile of rocks and looked out across the valley to the distant ranges I had to cross to walk out. I charted a route across the playa through low passes and gaps in the mountains, thinking it might take me only three camps to get out. Winter passes quickly down here. Before we knew it, spring would be on the way. The grizzlies would be coming out.